The Baylors of Newmarket
The Decline and Fall of a Virginia Planter Family

The Baylors of Newmarket
The Decline and Fall of a Virginia Planter Family

by Thomas Katheder

iUniverse, Inc.
New York   Bloomington

The Baylors of Newmarket
The Decline and Fall of a Virginia Planter Family

Front and back cover illustrations courtesy of the Virginia Historical Society.

iUniverse books may be ordered through booksellers or by contacting:

iUniverse
1663 Liberty Drive
Bloomington, IN 47403
www.iuniverse.com
1-800-Authors (1-800-288-4677)

Because of the dynamic nature of the Internet, any Web addresses or links contained in this book may have changed since publication and may no longer be valid. The views expressed in this work are solely those of the author and do not necessarily reflect the views of the publisher, and the publisher hereby disclaims any responsibility for them.

ISBN: 978-1-4401-2990-2 (sc)
ISBN: 978-1-4401-2992-6 (hc)
ISBN: 978-1-4401-2991-9 (ebook)

Library of Congress Control Number: 2009926813

Printed in the United States of America

iUniverse rev. date: 06/01/2009

"By study and a few well-chosen books it is as easy to increase one's knowledge in Virginia as in Cambridge."

— William Bond, Cambridge University don, to his former student, John Baylor IV, Newmarket, Va., July 15, 1773

Contents

Illustrations

Preface & Acknowledgements

On February 5, 1808, John Baylor IV, a 57-year-old Virginia aristocrat, died in debtor's prison in Caroline County, Virginia. When Baylor was born, in 1750, he entered a highly privileged inner circle of the Virginia gentry, a network of fewer than fifty families—closely intertwined through overlapping ties of blood and marriage—that controlled Virginia. Like his father and grandfather, he was educated in England at Putney Grammar School and Gonville and Caius (pronounced *keys*) College, Cambridge. On the morning of September 29, 1770, as Baylor, in cap and gown, paraded through the college's ancient Gate of Humility, through which all matriculants formally entered the college and began their studies, his prospects could not have seemed brighter. Awaiting him in Virginia was a vast tobacco plantation and estate built upon a foundation of Croesian riches amassed by his grandfather, John Baylor II, the largest slave trader of his generation in Virginia, and expanded by his father, Col. John Baylor III, one of the colony's largest planters. As Baylor, no doubt jaunty, happy, and more than a little proud, sauntered through the college's hallowed entrance, he did not realize that the tobacco-centered culture that dominated Virginia for nearly a century and a half before him was no longer viable, or that the planter aristocracy into which he was born was doomed.

In the years following Baylor's return from Cambridge, he assembled one of the most remarkable private libraries in eighteenth-century Virginia. Though not as prodigious as the preeminent collections of Thomas Jefferson or William Byrd II, Baylor's library was larger than most others in Virginia and Maryland, and except for the enormous mélange of French titles that Jefferson and James Monroe brought back from Paris and those acquired by Byrd from London, it contained more books by French and European authors than any other known collection in Virginia. Baylor acquired his unusual books during nearly a year's stay in France, but when he decided to leave with his many trunks of gilt-leather tomes in January 1778, just weeks before France joined America in its War of Independence, he ran into serious trouble and was imprisoned in England. Following his release, he married his English cousin, a daughter of one of London's leading tobacco merchants, and circuitously made his way back to Virginia, where he continued to expand his library. Near the end of his life, in failing health and waning fortune, Baylor quixotically sought to erect a new mansion house, a structure so grand and elaborate that, had it been built, it would have been the largest and finest private residence in America. But the project soon stalled, and his personal estate, including his magnificent library, was sold off in a forced liquidation.

This study is really three books. It is a biography of John Baylor IV and of his father, Col. John Baylor III; it is also a bio-bibliography of these men in that it relates the story of their library in the context of a well-established book culture among the Virginia aristocracy that has largely been underappreciated by scholars. Finally, it is the tale of the decline and fall of an important Virginia gentry family after the Revolution.[1]

The first chapter discusses Baylor's family background and the founding of Newmarket, his Virginia estate, by his father, Col. Baylor III. I also briefly outline how Col. Baylor and his peers sought to live "genteely and hospitably" as an Anglo-Virginian elite. In Chapter 2, I summarize what is known about Virginia's largest and most important eighteenth-century libraries, and I make liberal use of the heavy lifting performed by Gunston Hall Plantation in transcribing and cataloguing 325 probate inventories of wealthy individuals in the Chesapeake. I also explain the importance of the *Virginia Gazette* to the dissemination of print culture in Virginia, among the elite and commoners alike.

Chapter 3 describes how Col. Baylor III began his library through his frequent book orders from London and in-store purchases in Williamsburg. I include an extended treatment of the importance of two popular British periodicals, *The Tatler* and *The Spectator*, in the spread of British culture and values in the

British Atlantic community, as well as a discussion of Col. Baylor's favorite periodical, *Gentleman's Magazine*, and its significance to him as a member of the Anglo-Virginian elite. In this chapter I also tell the story of Col. Baylor's passionate obsession with Arabian thoroughbreds—the way he followed the leading racehorses in Britain by perusing specialized imprints from London and how he ordered his *über*-elite horses, at ruinous expense, through his British tobacco merchants.

Chapter 4 discusses John Baylor IV's experience at Putney and Cambridge, followed by his deep discontent back in Virginia and his abortive attempt to be readmitted to Cambridge. Despite his failure to be readmitted at Cambridge, Baylor sailed back to England anyway in the late fall of 1775, beginning a European sojourn that lasted until June 1779. Chapter 5 recounts his return to England as well as his mysterious trip to France in 1777. Whether he traveled to Paris (and later Nantes) for the purpose of pursuing intrigue, acquiring books, or selling Virginia tobacco—or some combination of all of these—remains unclear, but whatever his initial motives may have been he became involved in each. In this chapter I draw largely upon mostly unpublished manuscript records from the British and French national archives in reconstructing the harrowing tale of Baylor's attempt to leave Nantes aboard a French vessel with a crew, cargo, and itinerary that were all—insofar as the British were concerned— highly suspect, followed by his capture in the Bay of Biscay by the determined crew of a British man-of-war. Baylor's humiliation and misery upon his seizure were just beginning: he spent weeks incarcerated in the clammy, putrid hold of the French ship and was subsequently detained at Portsmouth and formally interrogated by officials from the British prize court. Following the story of Baylor's eventual release, the chapter concludes with his November 1778 marriage to his British cousin in London and his return to Virginia the following year, where he was again investigated, this time by a committee of the House of Delegates that inquired into his American patriotism.

Chapters 6 and 7 discuss in detail the known content of Baylor's library. I begin with an explanation of the primary sources for the partial reconstruction of Baylor's book collection, namely: Col Baylor

III's business letterbook; the probate inventory of Col. Baylor III's estate; surviving ledgers for the bookstore operated by the *Virginia Gazette* newspaper and print shop in Williamsburg, Virginia; and a handwritten catalogue of French and European authors and titles found in the Baylor Papers at the University of Virginia.

In analyzing the Baylors' library, I compare and contrast their titles with what was typical for their gentry peers in the Chesapeake. I also puncture what I call a "countermyth," that is, a scholarly overcorrection of erroneous earlier historiography that, like the original myth it was intended to dispel, tends to become unquestioned orthodoxy even though it, too, is inaccurate. In this case, the "original myth" was the fervent but fallacious belief by a number of nineteenth-century New England historians, most notably Henry Cabot Lodge and Henry Adams, that Virginia planters had no book or literary culture. According to this viewpoint, the typical Virginia planter was an uncouth, unlettered, and unthinking boob, usually drunk and often violent, and utterly addicted to dice, cards, racehorses, or fighting cocks. Adams described his three Virginia classmates in Harvard's class of 1858, one of whom included a son of Robert E. Lee, as "little fitted" for the institution "as Sioux Indians to a treadmill." According to Adams, "the Southerner had no mind" and "no intellectual training."[2]

Beginning in the 1930s (a development that, in my view, was largely influenced by the restoration of Colonial Williamsburg), a few scholars, particularly Louis B. Wright (1899-1984), a South Carolinian and English Renaissance expert who later became director of the Folger Shakespeare Library in Washington, D.C., sharply challenged this conception of the Virginia planter. "Virginia," Wright wrote, "was surpassed by no other region in the number of leaders possessed of good breeding, intelligence, and wisdom" in the colonial era. "The Virginia gentry composed an aristocracy not only of wealth and position but of intelligence and learning."[3]

Through his many monographs and books Wright eloquently and convincingly demonstrated the intellectual attainments and literary interests of Virginia gentry families such as the Lees, Carters, Fitzhughs, Wormeleys, Beverleys, and Byrds. For instance, Richard Lee II, an accomplished classicist whom Wright called a "belated Elizabethan," wrote Greek, Latin, and Hebrew with great fluency and ease. William Byrd II (1674-1744), whose secret diary Wright co-edited in 1940, mastered ancient Greek at an early age and owned more Greek-language books than anyone else in colonial Virginia. Wright established that the dominant ethos of the colonial Virginia gentry was not, as the post-Puritan historians in Boston would have it, ignorance, but rather classical learning, intellectual refinement, and gentility. Concerned about his half brother Lewis's lackadaisical attitude toward his studies, Nathaniel Burwell (1680-1721), in a letter to his brother James, emphasized that a young member of the Virginia aristocracy without a sufficient classical education and ability to speak and write well would be "unfit for any Gentleman's conversation, & therefore a Scandalous person & a shame to his Relations." This is what the Virginia gentry believed, and it is what they expected from each other as much as one would expect a minimum of common courtesies from anyone today.[4]

Others followed Wright's lead, especially Richard Beale Davis (1907-81), a Virginian and literary scholar who wrote extensively on the intellectual history and culture of the colonial and antebellum South. Unlike colonial New England, which had a prodigious and steady output of mostly Puritanical tracts and writings, Davis understood that Virginia's literary achievement, supported by remarkable private libraries, lay in its secular compositions: epistolary exchanges, diaries, poems, speeches, pamphlets, and essays (many of which were intended for strictly private consumption, though some were published in the *Virginia Gazette* as what now would be called op-ed pieces). By its purpose, New England devotional literature was, like political propaganda, outward and widespread— it was intended to proselytize and frighten the masses into reverent submission. "To Puritans," one scholar noted, "the printed word was an essential ingredient in spreading their understanding of the true church."[5]

The literature of the Virginia gentry, on the other hand, was far more inward and private (at least until the run-up to the Revolution). The gentry wrote primarily for themselves and for each other—they had nothing to prove to anyone outside their own sphere, somewhat similar to a members-only Internet chat board today. The notion of actually publishing a work for general readership was considered by many among the gentry as unseemly. According to book historian Kevin J. Hayes, "[t]he tradition of circulating a written work in manuscript persisted much longer in the South than it did elsewhere in America." And unlike, for example, Cotton Mather or Jonathan Edwards, the Virginia gentry felt no need to produce any literature for the nongentry. The Virginia gentry understood they owed those whom they regarded as their socioeconomic inferiors the exercise of public virtue in their civic life and a duty of generosity and helpfulness in private life (i.e., the original, nonpejorative meaning of *noblesse oblige*), but they certainly did not believe they needed to publish voluminous books or tracts admonishing them on how they ought to think and behave. (The nongentry, in turn, owed the gentry a duty of deference.)[6]

Thomas Anburey, a British army officer captured during the Revolution and garrisoned in Virginia, found that, despite his enemy status, most of the gentry treated him with decency and respect. "Many gentlemen around Richmond," he wrote, "though strongly attached to the American cause, have shown the liberality and hospitality so peculiar to this province, in their particular attention and civilities to our officers, who are quartered here." These gentry, Anburey noted, ignored the accusations of the "illiberal part of their countrymen" that they were being "partial to Great-Britain" through their courtesy. "[T]hese are gentlemen of fixed principles, of affluence and authority, and therefore [they] despise all popular clamour." Modern American readers, nurtured on a culture of postmodern republicanism in which politicians communicate through incessant, carefully crafted media messages designed to appeal to the uninformed emotions and even the base instincts of their constituents, will have difficulty understanding this *mentalité*. But in approaching the Virginia gentry and their literature it is essential to appreciate that they had little inclination or desire to produce writing intended to kowtow to "popular clamour."[7]

The cumulative effect of Wright, Davis, and their intellectual progeny was to expose the myth of the Virginia planter as quasi-literate rube for the regionally biased falsehood that it was. But in their zeal to destroy the myth once and for all by highlighting the literary and intellectual accomplishments of Virginia planters, some of these scholars overstated their case. For example, in establishing that Virginia's Founders and planters widely read and owned books by Greco-Roman authors, some writers on the topic, well aware that Virginians such as William Byrd II, George Wythe, and Thomas Jefferson read classical authors in their original Greek or Latin lexicon, failed to realize or acknowledge the exceptionalism of these men and that the vast majority of the Virginia gentry who read works by ancient writers read them in translation (as did most of colonial America's educated elite). To be sure, most Virginia planters, including John Baylor IV, studied Latin and Greek texts in their youth, but relatively few retained any significant proficiency in either language as adults. Similarly, because of the presence of books by French authors and French dictionaries in eighteenth-century Chesapeake book inventories, some scholars concluded that French was widely understood among educated readers. Richard Beale Davis, for instance, asserted, "French appears to have been read with relative ease from Maryland to Georgia." In fact, as I demonstrate in Chapter 7, very few of the Chesapeake elite (or for that matter any of the elite in colonial America) had any appreciable French-language capability.[8]

In Chapter 8, I offer some thoughts about what we might make of the Baylors' library, and in Chapter 9, the final chapter, I relate the strange tale of "Baylor's Folly," Baylor's phantasmagorical plantation mansion that was never finished, and the sad and bitter end of John Baylor IV's empire, followed by the dispersal of his library and his death in debtor's prison.

In the Appendix, I provide a bibliography of the partially reconstructed library of John Baylor IV. Most of these titles listed in the Appendix are also mentioned in the text and discussed in context. Unfortunately, though I am able to list with reasonable certainty some of the books Baylor owned, I have located only one extant book, William Newton's *The Architecture of M. Vitruvius Pollio* (1771) (now held by the Virginia Historical Society), that is known to have been in his library. We are thus denied the ability to assess the particular edition, binding, condition, marginalia, ownership indicia (e.g., bookplates), and other physical characteristics of Baylor's books. Probably a number of Baylor's books still survive, in private collections and libraries, possibly even among the inventories of rare book dealers or within the catalogues of auction houses from time to time. Perhaps this book might lead to the discovery of some of them.

*　*　*

I have incurred many debts in the preparation of this work (though any errors or omissions are exclusively mine).

Two members of the Baylor family have been enormously helpful. Carter B. Filer graciously granted permission to reproduce the Baylor images in this book. Ms. Filer and her sister inherited Newmarket and were the last of the Baylors to own the storied property. I had the pleasure of her Virginia hospitality in her Richmond home, where she shared many Baylor stories and Newmarket lore.

Another Baylor descendant, Patricia Latford, has taken on the uncompensated (but not unrewarding) task of compiling and regularly updating "The Baylor Family in America," an informal, multivolume history and genealogy of the Baylors who migrated to Virginia in the seventeenth century and of their progeny. Ms. Latford unhesitatingly shared her wealth of Baylor-related information and materials.

Dr. Caroline F. Sloat, Director of Scholarly Publications at the American Antiquarian Association, Dr. Greg Stiverson, historian and former president of the Historic Annapolis Foundation, and Bennie Brown, an architectural historian and expert on colonial-era architectural books, reviewed early drafts of the manuscript and provided useful thoughts and commentary. Evelyn W. Pettit, a former copy editor who now runs an independent bookshop in Winter Park, Florida, provided helpful copy editing and suggestions.

I have acknowledged the assistance of many others in the footnotes. In addition, I am grateful for the resources and help I have received from the following institutions and their staff: Alexandria Library (Special Collections), Alexandria, Virginia; Thomas Balch Library, Leesburg, Virginia; Central Rappahannock Library, Fredericksburg, Virginia; Duke University Rare Book, Manuscript and Special Collections Library, Durham, North Carolina; Jesse B. duPont Library, Stratford, Virginia (especially Judy Hynson); Gunston Hall Plantation, Mason Neck, Virginia; LDS Family History Library (Southwest Orange County, Florida); Library of Congress, Washington, D.C.; Library of Virginia, Richmond; Maryland Historical Society, Baltimore; James Monroe Museum and Memorial Library, Fredericksburg, Virginia (especially John Pearce and Meghan C. Budinger); National Archives (UK), Kew, England; Olin Library, Rollins College, Winter Park, Florida; John D. Rockefeller Library, Williamsburg, Virginia; Albert and Shirley Small Special Collections Library, University of Virginia, Charlottesville; Earl Gregg Swem Library, College of William and Mary, Williamsburg, Virginia; and University of Central Florida Library, Orlando, Florida.

One

Newmarket and Col. John Baylor III

Colonel John Baylor III (1705-72), who owned nearly twenty thousand acres and more than 180 slaves, was one of the wealthiest Virginians in the pre-Revolutionary period.[1] Like his father, Col. Baylor was educated at Putney Grammar School and at Gonville and Caius College, Cambridge, founded in 1348. Robert "King" Carter (1663-1732), the undisputed richest grandee in the Chesapeake, remembered Baylor's father, John Baylor II (1650-1720), as the "great negro seller, and in all respects the greatest merchant we had among us." Contracting with slave-trading firms based in Bristol, England, John Baylor II imported thousands of African slaves into Virginia, and in the years just before his death, he was responsible for nearly half of all slaves shipped into Virginia for sale to planters and others eager to purchase them.[2]

Following his return to Virginia from Cambridge, Col. Baylor quickly established himself. In 1726 Virginia Lt. Gov. Hugh Drysdale (d. 1726) gave him two land grants totaling nearly twelve thousand acres along the Mattaponi River in what later became Caroline County. It was on this vast tract that he built Newmarket plantation, which he named after the famous horse racing course at the town of Newmarket, about ten miles east of Cambridge, England. Beginning with James I's first visit in 1605, Newmarket became Britain's most important venue for horse racing through royal patronage, which especially flourished under Charles II, who built the first racing stables there. An avid horseman, Charles II rode in a number of races and so loved the place that he perennially held court there for months at a time, a situation later satirized by poet Alexander Pope (1688-1744), who wrote, "Newmarket's glory rose, as Britain's fell."[3]

By the 1720s, when Col. Baylor attended Cambridge, Newmarket was, as a French visitor noted, the site of the "finest horse races" in Britain and the place where "all the noblemen and persons of distinction who take an interest in this amusement go ... with their horses." Newmarket was also a popular pastime—and often a vice—for Cambridge students, especially aristocrats with time and money on their hands. Until the nineteenth century, students from noble families attending Oxford or Cambridge universities were exempt from examinations and were not even required to attend lectures. These idle young men, who "enjoyed a degree of licence that certainly would not have been tolerated in a well-regulated home," frequented Newmarket, and "indulged in a lavish expenditure ill-suited to their years."[4]

Daniel Defoe (1660-1731), who had come to Newmarket in 1722 to witness the spectacle of "horse races and a great concourse of the nobility and gentry," was appalled that so many of the socially elite "were all so intent, so eager, so busy upon the sharping [gambling] part of the sport, their wagers and bets." So focused were they at "picking one another's pockets," Defoe fussed, "it might be said they acted without respect to faith, honour, or good manners." Defoe's point of view, however, was not shared by the British aristocracy or the gentry in Virginia, where wagering of all kinds was deeply entrenched among commoners and elite alike. (Archeological excavations at Jamestown in 2007 uncovered gaming dice dating back to the earliest years of the settlement.) Writing about the same time as Defoe encountered Newmarket, Rev. Hugh Jones (1692-1760), a mathematics professor at the College of William and Mary, observed: "The common [smaller] planters leading easy lives don't much admire labour, or any manly exercise, except horse-racing, nor diversion, except cock-fighting, in which some greatly delight." Invariably these fiercely competitive contests were the subject of high-stakes bets among the "gentlemen" in attendance.[5]

Though not noble, and a mere colonial to boot, Baylor must have made himself attractive and agreeable enough to have fallen in with the elite crowd at Newmarket. He undoubtedly spent many a leisurely day there, particularly during October, November, and December, when most of the horse races were run in the 1720s. It was in this cultural milieu that Baylor, while at Cambridge, sat for his portrait in a swank royal blue suit festooned with gold buttons (Fig. 1). In the painting, Baylor sports a fancy adult wig, and his left arm is cocked imperiously on his hip, just above a dress sword. Though a young man of only about seventeen or eighteen, he is portrayed as supremely but coolly confident, a budding master of his universe. Baylor left Cambridge before obtaining his baccalaureate degree, but a Virginia planter did not need a diploma. It was enough just to have been there. (At the time, actually taking a degree was something one usually did to become a cleric or scholar or to pursue a teaching career—possession of such a credential by a "gentleman" would have suggested overt ambition, which was not an admirable characteristic among the gentry of that period.) So it was that, in addition to his books that became the beginning of his library, Baylor brought back from England a lifelong passion for thoroughbred horses and racing that would make him one of the greatest horsemen in colonial Virginia and that would later threaten to bankrupt him.[6]

Fig. 1. A budding master of his universe: Col. John Baylor III (1705-1772) at about age 17. Courtesy Virginia Historical Society.

In December 1743, Baylor married Frances Lucy Walker (1728-83), daughter of Jacob Walker (d. 1757), a prosperous Yorktown merchant. Baylor served as a church warden and vestryman in Drysdale Parish, where he lived, from 1752 to 1761. He represented Caroline County in the Virginia House of Burgesses from 1742 to 1752, and then again from 1756 to 1765, only to be swept out of office for good the following year. Though Baylor was a dutiful member of the House of Burgesses, he did not wield great power or exert heavy influence within that body. His most significant political activity was as a justice of the peace of the Caroline County court.[7]

In colonial Virginia, the county courts, which were controlled by "gentlemen justices" like Baylor, governed the counties with an oligarchic, unchecked, and largely self-perpetuating rule utterly unthinkable in modern America. With legislative, executive, and judicial functions combined into a single governing body, the county courts impacted the day-to-day lives of Virginians more than any other civil authority. The county court adjudicated most civil matters, including debt and contract disputes, presided over nonfelony criminal cases (accused felons were bound over for trial at the General Court in Williamsburg), and determined whether wills were admitted to probate and whether deeds, mortgages, or other instruments were worthy of being recorded in the county records. The justices established the amount of the county levy each year and decided who was exempt from taxation and exactly how the money would be spent—no road, bridge, or public building could be built without their approval. They issued bonds, permits, and licenses, including permits for ferries and mills, as well as licenses for taverns and inns; they even set the prices that could be charged for alcoholic beverages. They appointed all county officers, including tax collectors, the county clerk, militia officers, the coroner, and the sheriff (some of these positions were subject to the royal governor's usually perfunctory assent). As historian Jack P. Greene points out, in colonial Virginia "[n]ot a single local civil or judicial officer was elected."[8]

The justices also apprenticed orphans to artisans or tradesmen; they fined the parents of illegitimate children or sometimes ordered they be publicly whipped; and they put able-bodied paupers to work or exiled them from the county if they were from somewhere else (under ancient English custom and law the poor were supposed to be dealt with in their home communities). The justices were most powerful when they sat as a "Court of Oyer and Terminer" under special commission from the governor. In that capacity the justices could—and did—try slaves for capital offenses and order their execution, without any right of appeal. In the summer of 1767 one of Col. Baylor's slaves, Tom, was tried and found guilty of breaking into a white planter's house and stealing items worth about five shillings. The Orange County Court, presided over by James Madison Sr. (father of the future president), noted that Tom was "precluded from the Benefit of Clergy" because he had already received it once before and ordered him executed.[9]

Virginia's "gentlemen justices," unpaid and—like Baylor— usually untrained in the law, were nominated by existing justices for approval by the governor, who, wishing to maintain good relations with the Virginia gentry, routinely rubber-stamped their suggestions. They were invariably men of wealth and influential family ties: according to historian Charles S. Sydnor, more than a quarter of the 1,600 justices of the peace who served on Virginia county courts during the two decades before the Revolution were from just fifty-five extended old Virginia families. Another historian, Thomas E. Campbell, studied all gubernatorial appointments to the county court in Caroline County in the fifty-year period preceding the Revolution and determined that the vast majority of them were what he called "great planters." Baylor was first appointed as a justice of the peace by Lt. Gov. William Gooch in 1740, and served intermittently on the court until his death thirty-two years later. Baylor, first among the "great planters" of Caroline as well as a vestryman, burgess, and justice, was, until about 1765, probably the most powerful man in Caroline County, and among the top elite in Virginia.[10]

Though by almost any standard colonial American culture, even among the rich, would come up risibly short when compared to the mother country, British America was blessed with one resource in staggering, indescribable, inexhaustible abundance—land, more land than anyone in England or America realized existed, more land than anyone at the time could accurately map or measure, or even imagine. Endless beaches, tidal coves, bays, rivers, hills, forests, plains, mountains, and valleys that extended to the horizons and seemingly forever beyond, land that could absorb without limit (if one ignored the Native Americans) all of England's Calvinists, Cavaliers, or criminals who wanted, or who were forced, to come and try to scratch out a living on it more than three thousand miles from where they and untold generations of their ancestors had been born and lived.

In Britain, land was the source of virtually all wealth, but most of it was held by the Crown and the aristocracy, who were not inclined to part with it. But in America land seemed as free and plentiful as the air (provided one could survive the disease-ridden environment of the early colonial Chesapeake to enjoy it). In his *Map of Virginia* (1612) Capt. John Smith described Virginia as "a Country in America that lyeth betweene the degrees of 34 and 44 of the north latitude," bounded on the east by the Atlantic Ocean, on the south by Florida, and on the north by "nova Francia." And "as for the West thereof," he wrote, "the limits are *unknowne*." William Strachey (1572-1621), secretary of the Virginia Company who arrived at Jamestown in 1610, declared that Virginia was "a suffycient space" with "grownd enough, to satisfye the most Covetous."[11]

And covet they did. In the seventeenth and eighteenth centuries the Virginia gentry, primarily through their use of political offices and reciprocal favors, granted themselves millions of acres of virgin land with titanic yet shameless rapacity. William Fitzhugh (1651-1701), a woolen draper's son who came from England around 1670 with legal training but no property to his name, took full advantage of his position as a member of the House of Burgesses from Stafford County and later as Thomas Culpeper's agent for the Northern Neck Proprietary to amass 52,260 acres by the end of his life. William Byrd II inherited 26,000 acres from his father, including Westover plantation, and was granted another 160,000 acres through his political appointments and connections. Robert "King" Carter exploited his position as property agent for Thomas, sixth Baron Fairfax of Cameron (1693-1781), the successor to the Northern Neck Proprietary, and acquired 300,000 acres of some of the best lands in the Northern Neck for himself and his family. According to George Washington biographer Douglas S. Freeman, "One verb told the story of the proprietorship for almost a century: it was grab, grab, grab."[12]

By 1700, in each of Virginia's twenty counties more than one-half of the land was owned by a quarter (or less) of all land owners, and in five tobacco-growing counties (James City, Henrico, Charles City, Middlesex, and King and Queen) the top quartile of land barons owned 70 percent of the land. During the period 1716-43, the Virginia governor and his twelve-member council granted an astonishing 2,350,000 acres to fewer than four hundred members of the interrelated gentry, an average of nearly six thousand acres per individual. In addition to Col. Baylor, the family names of the recipients are well known to students of colonial Virginia history, including Beverley, Bolling, Braxton, Carter, Cary, Harrison, Lewis, and Randolph. Lieutenant Governor Alexander Spotswood (1676-1740), who had been sent to Virginia in part to implement land grant reform, abandoned his initial resolve to counter the gentry's appetite for land and instead jumped into the feeding trough by granting himself (through nominal title holders) a total of 90,000 acres.[13]

In the second quarter of the eighteenth century the gentry, not sated with their gargantuan grants of eastern Virginia lands, turned a ravenous eye to land west of the Allegheny Mountains. The primary reasons were twofold: soil exhaustion and partible inheritance. "There is no plant in the world," wrote the anonymous author of *American Husbandry* (1775), "that requires richer land, or more manure than tobacco." Tobacco depletes soil of its fertility in as little as three years, after which it must lie fallow for twenty years (and even then it lacks its original fertility). "[T]his makes the tobacco planters more solicitous for new land than any other people in America," concluded the *American Husbandry* author. At the same time that the Virginia gentry worried about obtaining virgin tobacco fields, they mostly rejected the ancient British doctrine of primogeniture (probably due to the initial abundance of land), whereby the eldest son inherited the homestead and all real property. Though a Virginia planter typically gave a life estate to his wife in the family home with a remainder to his eldest son after her death, he was also expected to endow his younger sons with enough land to establish their own plantations (daughters usually received cash dowries). Robert "King" Carter, for example, divided his incredibly vast empire among his sons, John, Robert, Charles, Landon, and George, each of whom received tens of thousands of acres of land throughout Virginia. Although this approach, known as partible inheritance, certainly seemed more equitable (among sons, at least), its continuation through multiple generations would soon become infeasible without regular additions to a planter's landed estate.[14]

Colonel Baylor invested in several competing land companies that sought to acquire mammoth swaths of unmapped and largely unexplored western real estate from the British Crown. In 1749 he joined Peter Jefferson (Thomas Jefferson's father) and thirty-eight other prominent Virginians to form the Loyal Company of Virginia, which was organized by Dr. Thomas Walker (1715-94) of Albemarle County, Virginia, to speculate in western lands. The Loyal Company received a grant from the Virginia Council (the colony's supreme governing body) for 800,000 acres lying mostly in what is now southeastern Kentucky. In the same year Baylor also became a member of the Ohio Company, which was founded in 1747 by Thomas Lee, John Mercer, and others and which had already received a grant of 200,000 acres near present-day Pittsburgh. In addition to the 200,000-acre grant, Baylor and his fellow members of the Ohio Company unabashedly sought a further grant of 800,000 acres in an area west and north of the Virginia-North Carolina boundary line. But, like the majority of land speculators before the Revolution, Baylor ultimately received nothing for his time or investments.[15]

In June 1763, following the end of the French and Indian War (which the North American theater of the Seven Years War is usually called), four Lee brothers—Thomas Ludwell, Richard Henry, Francis Lightfoot, and William—established the Mississippi Company along with other speculators, including George Washington. The Mississippi Company audaciously planned to petition the British Crown for a twelve-year option on 2.5 million acres in the Ohio Valley in exchange for its promise to seat two hundred families on the incredibly vast and fertile expanse. Before the company's memorial arrived in London, however, George III declared, in what became known as the Proclamation of 1763, that all land west of the Allegheny Mountains was completely off limits for settlement. Undaunted, the Mississippi Company pressed on, its members firmly believing, as George Washington assured a Pennsylvania surveyor, that the proclamation was merely a "temporary expedient to quiet the Minds of the Indians." The company took on new members such as Col. Baylor, who joined in 1767, and later retained a fifth Lee brother, Arthur, as their agent in London for the purpose of seeking a reversal of the royal proclamation, or at least an exception for their enterprise.[16]

Like Washington, Baylor believed that America's eventual future lay westward. In the early part of the French and Indian War, years before the tide turned decidedly in Britain's favor, Baylor wrote Washington wistfully: "[C]ould we get a peacable or even Forcible Possession of that fine Country lying between the Mississippi & Ohio I had rather live there than any Part of America & more so after a late Confab. with Capt. Gist." Baylor and his fellow planter and magistrate Lunsford Lomax (1705-72) were the largest speculators in western lands from Caroline County, and when they caught word of the Proclamation of 1763 they became so agitated that they refused to perform their official judicial duties in protest.[17]

In addition to his Newmarket home, Baylor built an elegant summer retreat at Greenwood Farm, a 6,500-acre plantation he owned in the beautiful rolling hills of the Virginia Piedmont in Orange County. Greenwood Farm was adjacent to Mount Pleasant (later called Montpelier), the plantation inherited by James Madison Sr. after his father was fatally poisoned by his own slaves in 1732. Baylor was appointed an officer of the local militia, which is how he came to be called "Colonel," and served under George Washington at Winchester, Virginia, during the French and Indian War.[18]

*   *   *

To a very large degree, colonial Virginia's economy was "built wholly upon smoke," just as Charles I, who detested tobacco like his father, James I, had feared would happen. Sir William Berkeley (1605-77), who served as Virginia governor from 1641 to 1652 and again from 1660 to 1671, also strived to convince Virginians and

British officials of the importance of economic diversification for the colony. But by the end of Berkeley's first term it was already too late—Virginia and Britain were too addicted to the weed and its profits to seriously consider another path.[19]

Like most large-scale Virginia planters, Baylor grew tobacco and shipped it on consignment to his British agents in London and Liverpool in four-foot-high barrels called "hogsheads," each of which weighed more than a thousand pounds when fully packed. In a good year, Baylor might net £9 to £11 per hogshead after his agents deducted a colossal heap of charges, including shipping, insurance, storage, import duties, and, of course, the agents' commissions. Still, barring bad weather or crop failures at home or an unfavorable market in Britain, a planter could eventually become rich, at least in land and slaves, and many of Virginia's largest planters did so by the 1740s—Virginia's so-called golden age—including Baylor.[20]

Aside from the evils of slavery, there were two serious systemic problems with the Virginia plantation economy. The first was that planters could not be paid in cash, because the British Parliament prohibited the export of pounds sterling outside Britain. Instead, planters received an account credit that could be redeemed only through the purchase of British merchandise shipped back to Virginia or by means of a drawing a bill of exchange on their merchant. The second was that the planters, who always placed their orders before they knew what their tobacco crop would bring each year, often purchased far more than the net proceeds they later received.[21]

Typically, Virginia planters, including Col. Baylor, ordered large quantities of finished goods from their British agents. These included necessities, such as clothing, fabrics, farm implements, seed, nails, and household hardware. The same orders usually included, however, other items whose real purpose was conspicuous display of fashion and wealth or, as the Virginia gentry would have it, goods that were essential for one to live "genteely and hospitably" in imitation of the English squirearchy. Thus, in addition to what they truly needed, the planters also demanded of their agents silk ball gowns and fancy personal accoutrements, dress shoes with faux jewel buckles (for both men and women), china, silver tableware and service pieces (often with engraved heraldic arms), fine furniture, wine, carriages, and, of course, books. In a 1760 letter to his London tobacco agent, which was typical of planter-tobacco merchant correspondence in the mid-eighteenth century, Col. Baylor grumbled that he received a dozen knives with handles made from "common stagg" rather than the more genteel ivory and that the books and hosiery he ordered had not arrived. Virginia planter Robert Beverley (ca. 1740-1800) of Blandfield, who had been educated in Britain, also wanted to make his home as "commodious as the Place [will] admit of," and ordered his London merchant to send him a set of china "of the most fashionable sort ... sufficient for 2 Genteel Courses of Victuals."[22]

Superficially, at least, the Virginia gentry largely succeeded in their emulation of English gentlemen. Reverend Hugh Jones observed that the Virginia gentry "live in the same neat manner, dress after the same modes, and behave themselves exactly as the Gentry in London." A few years later Virginia Lt. Gov. William Gooch (1681-1751) boasted to his brother Thomas: "[T]he gentlemen and ladies here are perfectly well bred, not an ill dancer in my government." On the other hand, the austere founder and first president of the College of William and Mary, Rev. James Blair (1655-1743), was far less tolerant of the planters' extravagance and sermonized against their addiction to "all manner of Gratification of their Luxury, stately Houses, Furniture, and Equipage, plentiful Tables, Mirth, Musick, and Drinking."[23]

Eighteenth-century America was characterized by a staggering increase in the quantity and value of imported goods from Great Britain. British exports to the American colonies increased more than eightfold from the beginning of the century to just before the Revolution. From 1750 to 1772, which coincided with Col. Baylor's peak years of purchasing from his British agents, the value of British exports to America rose more than 120 percent. In 1770, for example, an astonishing 2.74 million pieces of glassware and earthenware were exported from Britain to America, an average of more than one piece for every man, woman, and child, including slaves.[24]

As Virginia planters were calling for imported consumer goods in ever-expanding volumes, they increasingly overdrew their accounts, making them debtors and their British agents creditors. "Virginians outrun their incomes," noted a British traveler in 1759, referring to planters, as they pursue "acts of extravagance, ostentation, and a disregard of economy." Six years later, a Frenchman traveling in Tidewater Virginia also noted the "Extravagant Disposition of the planters," adding that "many of them ... have very great Estates, but are mostly at loss for Cash." This state of affairs eventually lead to the financial ruin of many Virginia planters, including the Baylors. Because planters usually ordered their goods before their tobacco crop for the same year was harvested and sold, all too often the costs of their purchases exceeded the proceeds they finally realized a year or so later when the tobacco was shipped and sold. If the tobacco crop was less than anticipated, such as when a severe drought struck the Virginia Tidewater in 1758 or when harvests fell dramatically short in the mid-1760s, a planter could fall inextricably into a pit of indebtedness. In a 1762 letter to the Board of Trade, Virginia Lt. Gov. Francis Fauquier warned about the "Increase of Imports, to such a Height that the Crops of Tobacco will not pay for them." The planters, who were "greatly in Debt to the Mother Country," he wrote, "obstinately shut their Eyes" to "so disagreeable a truth." The Virginia grandees were, Fauquier feared, "not prudent enough to quit any one Article of Luxury."[25]

Two

Private Virginia Libraries

At its peak, the Baylor library held "twelve to thirteen hundred volumes," according to John Baylor IV's will. Much of this collection, likely more than half, was acquired by John Baylor IV during his adult life. This was significantly smaller than the library of William Byrd II, who owned approximately 2,345 titles, which Thomas Jefferson counted as 3,486 volumes following the suicide of Byrd's spendthrift, ne'er-do-well son, William Byrd III, in 1777. Jefferson, with a mercenary eye and insatiable appetite for fine books, was nosing around for interesting tomes to replace his first library, which had been lost in the fire that consumed Shadwell, his birthplace home, in 1770. By 1815, Jefferson had assembled at Monticello the largest private library in America, consisting of some sixty-seven hundred volumes, which he sold to the Library of Congress to replace its three-thousand-volume collection that had been destroyed by marauding British troops when they burned Washington, D.C., in August 1814.[1]

George K. Smart, the first serious scholar of private libraries in colonial Virginia, noted in 1938 that about half of the one hundred private libraries he analyzed contained fewer than twenty-five titles and, as he put it, "at the most, fifty volumes."[2] Smart's observations regarding the size of private libraries in pre-Revolutionary Virginia remain generally accurate today. In the 1990s, Gunston Hall Plantation, the organization that operates the eponymous historic mansion and grounds of George Mason IV (1725-92), surveyed surviving probate inventories from 1740 to 1810 primarily in Fairfax, Prince William, and Stafford counties in Virginia, and Charles and Prince Georges counties in Maryland, and selected from these inventories the personal estates of affluent decedents for further study (the selected estates comprised about 5 percent of all inventories for these counties during the period). Because no estate inventory of George Mason IV survives, Gunston Hall sought to conceptualize the likely furnishings and household contents of Mason's plantation home by drawing logical inferences from the inventories of Mason's socioeconomic peers in the Chesapeake.[3]

Of 325 probate inventories transcribed and catalogued by Gunston Hall Plantation in their Herculean effort, a third contained only that confounding and recurrent phrase, "a parcel of books," or the like. One hundred twenty-four of the inventories mention books by title or type (e.g., "divinity books," etc.), and another twenty indicate the presence of books without giving further information. Almost all of the 150 inventories in which books are itemized or quantified are under fifty volumes, and most contain far fewer. As intellectual historian Richard Beale Davis observed in his important study of private libraries in the colonial American South, planters, lawyers, clergymen, and physicians consistently owned the most books, and the Gunston Hall sample is consistent with Davis's finding. Twenty-six estates had more than a hundred volumes, but of these only three had a certain count of more than 200, which readily confirms the conclusion of an earlier study of colonial private libraries that any collection of "more than 200 books may safely be considered a very large library."[4]

While it is true that the average size of all private Virginia libraries was fewer than twenty-five volumes, most planters in Virginia owned at least fifty volumes, and many had between one hundred and two hundred books. George Smart, followed by historian Louis B. Wright and more recently by Richard Beale Davis, gave the lie to the supercilious myth propagated by Boston Brahmins Henry Cabot Lodge (1850-1924), Henry Adams (1838-1918), and others that the "Virginian planter thought little and read less." Some modern scholars have echoed the sentiments of Lodge and Adams. In 1952, for example, historian Carl Bridenbaugh made the following blunderbuss declaration: "[D]enizens of the Chesapeake country were not a reading people."[5]

But the reality was quite otherwise. The Virginia gentry loved their books. During the eighteenth century the proportion of all British books exported to America that were purchased by New Englanders declined relative to the Chesapeake and the Carolinas; *by 1770, Virginia imported more than 40 percent of all English imprints shipped to North America.* When Virginians, at the instance of George Mason and George Washington, resolved to "discourage all Manner of Luxury and Extravagance" in 1769-70 by boycotting a long list of British goods, including wine, liquor, carriages, furniture, silk, jewelry, shoes, and saddles, they consciously declined to ban imported books and periodicals. If they could afford it, and oftentimes even when they could not, the gentry insisted on the best folio editions in gilt-leather bindings. At the end of the nineteenth century, a leading bookplate expert counted more than fifty colonial-era Virginians who used custom-engraved bookplates featuring their name and, typically, their coat of arms. (He also noted there were undoubtedly many more he had not found.) Duc de La Rochefoucauld-Liancourt, a French aristocrat who toured Virginia in the mid-1790s, concluded that a "taste for reading" was "more prevalent among gentlemen of the first class [in Virginia] than in any other part of America."[6]

The most significant impediment to book ownership was not intellectual indolence but cost. According to historians Cynthia and Gregory Stiverson, "books clearly cost a great deal in eighteenth-century Virginia, many times more than they do at the present time." A bound fifteen-volume set of Tobias Smollett's *Complete History of England* and the first four volumes of his *Continuation* could be purchased at the bookstore operated by the *Virginia Gazette* in Williamsburg for £9, an amount that would have covered the cost of about one hundred eighty basic leather shoes for slaves, six head of cattle, or thirty hogs. It represented nearly a half-year's wages for a common laborer in mid-eighteenth-century Virginia. During the periods 1750-52 and 1764-66, only 565 people, less than one-half of 1 percent of Virginia's total population (black and white), purchased books at the *Virginia Gazette* office, which was the colony's largest and most important book retailer. Of those who bought books from the *Gazette*, only 182 purchased four or more titles, and three-fourths of this group was composed of planters (80), merchants (26), lawyers (23), and doctors (9). Clearly, the acquisition of anything more than the Bible and the *Virginia Almanack* and perhaps a few other volumes was an indulgence exclusively for the rich.[7]

For the nonelite, another major challenge to widespread book ownership in Virginia prior to the early national period was geography. Before the Revolution, the majority of book purchasers at the *Virginia Gazette* bookstore lived in counties relatively close to Williamsburg, though some planters or lawyers who lived farther away were able to pick up books at the *Gazette* if they had legislative or other business in the town. (For example, in April 1765 Robert Munford, a newly elected burgess from Mecklenburg County, Virginia, bought three books from the *Gazette* shortly before he took office.) Although the *Gazette's* newspaper and its annual *Virginia Almanack* were widely distributed throughout Virginia by means of the *Gazette's* post riders, its books, most of which were imported from London already bound, were not. Thus many larger planters who lived far from Williamsburg but near navigable rivers accessible to British merchant ships found it easier to order their books directly from London. "To a Piedmont tobacco planter," one of James Madison's biographers noted, "London was nearer than the Dixon and Hunter bookshop in Williamsburg." William Cabell (1730-98), a planter and statesman who lived in Amherst (now Nelson) County in Virginia's western hinterlands, regularly ordered books directly from his British merchants, usually "fifty or more" at a time.[8]

Smaller planters in the Piedmont, or backcountry, did not usually trade directly with merchants in London or Liverpool, but instead had accounts with Scottish merchants resident in the Chesapeake. These merchants carried a few titles, particularly devotional literature, but their selection was nothing like the broad variety of titles available at the *Gazette* bookstore. After the Revolution, by which time most Scottish merchants were long gone and the *Virginia Gazette* had closed, the availability of book titles for purchase in the backcountry was even less. As Virginia planter and lawyer John Breckinridge (1760-1806) prepared to uproot his family from their rural Albemarle County homestead to the Kentucky backwoods in 1791, he ordered from London merchants Donald and Burton about one hundred fifty volumes, consisting mostly of history, biography, and literature, including works by Gibbon, Hume, Rollin, Shakespeare, Swift, Milton, and Rousseau. Breckinridge knew that if books by these authors were difficult to obtain in the Virginia Piedmont, they would be practically impossible to find in the pioneer wilds of Kentucky.[9]

Reverend Devereux Jarratt (1732-1801), who was raised in rural New Kent County, Virginia, about twenty-five miles south of Richmond, regretted that his early education consisted of only basic reading and rudimentary arithmetic, and that no one in his neighborhood had any books on "Philosophy, Rhetoric, Logic" or other worthy subjects. At age nineteen, he took a job—for which he was singularly unqualified—as a schoolmaster in Albemarle County. Though painfully aware of his academic shortcomings, he realized there were no books available to purchase even if he had money for them. Hearing that a local "gentleman" owned a copy of William Burkitt's *Expository Notes, with Practical Observations, on the New Testament* (1700), he overcame his intense feelings of inferiority (which he called his "clownish rusticity") and easily persuaded the planter to lend him the "treasure." He also discovered that even backcountry clergymen usually owned books—more books than he had ever seen in one place—and so he borrowed and hungrily devoured them whenever the opportunity arose. At the ripe age of twenty-five, he swallowed his pride and entered a Virginia school run by Alexander Martin (1740-1807), who was scarcely eight years older but was a graduate of the College of New Jersey (later Princeton). At Martin's school, Jarratt quickly soaked up Latin, Greek, and other subjects in which he was lacking. Jarratt was later ordained in England as an Anglican cleric, a great accomplishment for an American colonial, especially one without a university education.[10]

After the Revolution, when booksellers began to appear in other cities such as Alexandria and Fredericksburg, the majority of books continued to be purchased by those who lived in or near towns. In their careful study of book ownership indicated by nearly 2,400 probate inventories in five Virginia counties (Fairfax, Lunenburg, Charles City, Botetourt, and Alleghany) and two towns (Fredericksburg and Petersburg), Joseph F. Kett and Patricia A. McClung concluded that during the period 1790-1840 the incidence of book ownership—beyond a family Bible and, say, a couple of religion tracts—was significantly higher in urban settings than in rural areas. For example, they found that 32.3 percent of probate inventories for Fredericksburg and Petersburg indicated books valued at $20 or more, while only 12.4 percent of the inventories for the five counties showed the same level of book ownership. Virginia, they point out, had far fewer towns than New England, along with a much smaller percentage of the state's residents living in them, which accounts for much of the difference in average individual book ownership between the two areas in the antebellum era. "Even among wealthy planters," Kett and McClung further observed, "there was no consistent development of book culture during the late eighteenth and early nineteenth centuries." Nor was there any in Virginia before the Revolution, they suggested, "unless we assume that a thriving book culture existed during the mid-eighteenth and then disappeared by the end of the century."[11]

In fact, there *was* such a thriving book culture among the pre-Revolutionary Virginia gentry, almost all of whom lived in the country and not in towns (other than temporary residence in Williamsburg during legislative sessions). From Virginia's founding period, its elite relied on books as a bulwark against boredom and isolation. Desperate to overcome the "solitary uncouthness" of Jamestown in 1619, Cambridge-educated John Pory (1572-1636), colonial secretary and later the first speaker of the House of Burgesses, "resolved wholly … to have some good book always in store, being in solitude the best and choicest company." Nearly a half century later, Virginia lawyer and planter William Fitzhugh complained to his London correspondent: "Society that is good & ingenious is very scarce, & seldom to be come at except in books." By the end of the seventeenth century, books were being exported from London to Virginia in vast quantities that scholars have for the most part not acknowledged. During the twelve-month period ended March 25, 1698, for example, Perry, Lane & Co., a leading London tobacco merchant, sent books weighing a total of 3,129 pounds to the Chesapeake.[12]

As the Virginia elite consolidated their wealth and power by the close of the seventeenth century, books and libraries took on deeper cultural significance. A well-stocked library became essential to the Horatian ideal that the eighteenth-century Virginia gentry strived for. Former Cambridge University student Robert Beverley, who kept a large library at Blandfield, his Georgian mansion, informed his London tobacco agent that his "Books & Family Pleasures" made his pastoral life in Virginia "very agreeable." William Byrd II, commenting on the "rural entertainments" of isolated Virginia planters, remarked: "A library, a garden, a grove and a purling stream are the innocent scenes that divert our leizure." Moreover, Byrd, whose voracious sexual appetite was exceeded only by his insatiable rapacity for fine books, knew well that in Virginia, as in London, size mattered, and that the most admired gentlemen owned the largest plantations, houses, coaches, and libraries.[13]

As Beverley's and Byrd's observations suggest, the personal library as private space was as least as important as its function as a book repository. Beginning in the first quarter of the eighteenth century, the houses of the Virginia gentry evolved from two-room hall-parlor structures into Virginia great houses that often included rooms or areas dedicated for books and reading. As one scholar has noted, these *sancta sanctorum* were men-only spaces that offered an opportunity to enjoy what Hannah Arendt (drawing upon Greek philosophers) called the *vita contemplativa*, "the only truly free way of life," a place where the "necessities of earthly life" could be temporarily put aside. Thomas Lewis (1718-90), for example, a lawyer, surveyor and Shenandoah Valley pioneer who owned about 300 volumes, "was generally to be found in his library" when not dining or entertaining company.[14]

Aside from the most obvious source—probate inventories— further evidence of a strong book culture among the pre-Revolutionary Virginia gentry can be found in their incessant borrowing of books from one another. "The practice of lending books," wrote distinguished American historian Charles McLean Andrews (1863-1943), "was bound to be common in a country where they were rare and expensive and where neighborliness was a virtue." In the absence of public libraries or other convenient book repositories, the Virginia gentry maintained their own important book-lending relationships within the larger context of their social and kinship networks, thus making books a critical component of social capital. Despite the planters' rustic isolation, private dinners, balls, hunts, horse races, tavern gatherings, church events, court days, county meetings, elections, and legislative sessions all offered plentiful and ripe opportunities to discuss and swap books. A 1716 library catalogue of Godfrey Pole (d. 1730), a lawyer and legislative clerk for the House of Burgesses, lists 115 volumes and reveals that he loaned out nearly a quarter of his volumes to major planters such as Mann Page, Lewis Burwell, and others. Moreover, surviving correspondence from the eighteenth century among the planter elite frequently mentions a borrowed book, and the *Virginia Gazette* is replete with formal pleas for the return of lent books following the deaths of their owners.[15]

In surmising that the pre-Revolutionary gentry lacked a strong book culture, Professors Kett and McClung, who focused their study on the federal and early national periods, did not realize that book ownership was prevalent among the Virginia gentry prior to the Revolution but that by the 1790s and early 1800s the majority of them had been financially ruined by their extravagant living, excessive debt, poor agricultural practices, and the severe economic depression and disruptions that followed in the years after the war. The fate of most libraries of the eighteenth-century Virginia gentry (including the Baylor library) was ignoble dispersal amid insolvent estates, hungry creditors, and opportunistic book buyers, such as lawyers, doctors, merchants, or teachers looking to acquire good, formerly expensive books on the cheap. As socioeconomic and political power in Virginia began to shift from a rural oligarchy to urban professionals, the concentration of book ownership in the Old Dominion followed accordingly. It is hardly coincidence, for example, that after the Revolution, men such as William Wirt (1772-1834), a prominent lawyer who rose from a Swiss-German immigrant family of modest means to become the ninth U.S. Attorney General, became the prototypical owners of the largest private libraries in Virginia. In 1805 Wirt correctly observed, "Men of talents in this country ... have been, generally, bred to the profession of the law." Wirt understood that in a republican America, "the bar ... is the road to honour." (Alexis de Tocqueville, a French aristocrat and lawyer, likewise concluded in the 1830s that in America, lawyers largely composed the new aristocracy.)[16]

*   *   *

At nine hundred volumes or thereabouts, George Washington's library was the second-largest book collection in the Gunston Hall probate survey. (Dr. Nicholas Flood, who owned more than twelve hundred volumes, held the largest.) The size of his library notwithstanding, traditionally Washington's biographers and historians have held that Washington, as the consummate man of action, was not a deep thinker or particularly concerned with the world of ideas. The sour and squat John Adams, who possessed one of America's greatest political minds but who was also profoundly envious of Washington's towering fame, said Washington was "too illiterate, unlearned, unread for his station." To be sure, Washington was no intellectual like Adams or Jefferson. Compared to the libraries of Adams and Jefferson, Washington owned relatively fewer works of literature and philosophy; instead, his library was largely dedicated to more "useful" titles, such as farming, horticulture, husbandry, horses and horsemanship, and military strategy and tactics. But, as historian Paul Longmore has argued, "a thorough examination of his [Washington's] papers and libraries discloses that he gave more thought to reading, learning, and ideas than historians have credited." Having had little formal schooling, Washington harbored, as Longmore put it, "a consciousness of a defective education." He was, no doubt, as insecure about openly communicating on learned topics with most people as he was about smiling and showing his bad teeth. Yet, as part of his life-long commitment to self-improvement, Washington read and, to selected correspondents, quoted from Shakespeare and contemporary British literature, such as Henry Fielding's *Tom Jones* and Tobias Smollett's *Peregrine Pickle*, as well as works by Swift and Milton. He also read widely in world history and geography, and after the Revolution added a number of non-utilitarian books to his reading table. Washington was also innately curious; he never stopped experimenting with agricultural improvements and he advocated both a national university and a museum of natural history.[17]

John Parke ("Jacky") Custis (1754-81), Washington's adopted son, owned the third-largest library in the Gunston Hall sample, consisting of 327 titles and about 565 volumes. Custis inherited at least half of his library from his father, Daniel Parke Custis, and he also wound up with one hundred or so volumes from Washington, who ordered his London tobacco agents to purchase a number of books for Jacky when he was a student. Dr. John Stewart of Prince Georges County, Maryland, whose probate inventory mentioned 581 books and 393 pamphlets and magazines, had a library rivaling or perhaps exceeding Custis's collection, but unfortunately the two appraisers who conducted the inventory neglected to identify a single book or pamphlet.[18]

Washington's close friend Landon Carter (1710-78) of Sabine Hall owned about five hundred volumes, most of which survive intact at the University of Virginia. As a young boy, Carter had been sent to England for his education by his powerful father, Robert "King" Carter, the richest man of his generation in colonial America and himself the owner of more than 260 titles. King Carter's grandson, the cultivated and eccentric Robert "Councilor" Carter (1728-1804) of Nomini Hall, accumulated an extremely large personal library of perhaps as many as three thousand volumes, including what probably constituted the largest collection of music books and pamphlets in the eighteenth-century Chesapeake. Wilson Cary (1703-72), the father of Sally Cary Fairfax (1730-1811), with whom George Washington had a platonic affair prior to his marriage to Martha Custis, owned a fine library that probably equaled Landon Carter's in size and scope, but much of it was lost in an 1826 fire. Finally, George Washington's attorney, the irascible Irish immigrant John Mercer (1704-68), owned a magnificent library of somewhere between 1,500 and 1,800 volumes, but he left behind a heavily indebted estate and his son was forced to auction them off on a by-the-title basis and in small lots.[19]

Richard Henry Lee (1732-94), a lawyer, statesman, and signer of the Declaration of Independence, owned Chantilly, a large estate along the Potomac River not far from his birthplace, Stratford Hall. An estate appraisal shortly after his death recorded nearly nine hundred volumes of books, plus some 473 journals and pamphlets. Lee's literary tastes encompassed a wide gamut of Greco-Roman classics, history, geography, literature, and medicine. Not surprisingly, he also owned a large number of law books and tracts on political discourse. He bequeathed Abbé Millot's five-volume *Elements of General History* (1778-79) and the ten-volume second edition of the *Encyclopædia Britannica* (1774-84) to his son Cassius. His son Francis Lightfoot, a lawyer, received all of his law books. The bulk of the library, however, likely remained with Chantilly when it was sold around 1800 to Alexandria lawyer Thomas Swann. If Lee's books remained at Chantilly, they were almost certainly ruined when British gunboats, in an act of gratuitous barbarism, shelled the house and destroyed it during the War of 1812.[20]

Since (as previously noted) more than 40 percent of all books shipped from England to North America were sent to Virginia in the decade before the Revolution, there must have been numerous other important libraries in colonial Virginia, but unfortunately no inventories or catalogues survive. The primary reason is record loss. Unlike most of New England and many of the pre-Revolutionary communities of the Mid-Atlantic states, where probate, deed, chancery, and other official records are generally available in more or less unbroken sequence back to the seventeenth century, in Virginia more than two dozen counties have suffered complete or substantial theft or destruction of their public records. For instance, James City County, one of Virginia's eight original shires created in 1634, and the town of Williamsburg, Virginia's capital founded in 1699, shared a common courthouse and transferred their official records to Richmond for safekeeping during the Civil War. But the records, along with those of other Virginia counties that had likewise sent their records to Richmond, were destroyed in the conflagration that broke out on April 3, 1865, when Confederate forces evacuated the city. Another of Virginia's original shires, Elizabeth City County, also founded in 1634, was overrun by record-destroying troops during three separate wars: by the British in the Revolution and again in the War of 1812 and subsequently by Union forces during the Civil War. In Caroline County, home of the Baylors, Union soldiers ransacked the courthouse in May 1864 and stole, mutilated, and destroyed most of the public records.[21]

In addition to the heavy loss of documents at the county level, nearly all the state's official records, including those of the General Court, were consumed in the 1865 fire. The General Court, Virginia's oldest judicial body, held untold thousands of important and irreplaceable government files dating back to 1619, including, in many instances, the only official probate records regarding the estates of the Virginia gentry (whose executors often bypassed their local county courts, preferring the efficiency and prestige of the more senior judicial authority). So profound was the destruction of Virginia's official documents that when the state began publication of the *Calendar of Virginia State Papers* in 1875 there were not enough government papers remaining from the colonial period to fill one volume. For Virginia historians, the devastation wrought by the Civil War upon Virginia's official records was akin to the destruction of the ancient library of Alexandria.[22]

In a number of other cases, official records or newspaper accounts survive but provide only spectral evidence of large private libraries. Reverend William Dunlap (d. 1779), who owned a Philadelphia print shop and bookstore before he accepted a position as an Anglican rector in King William County, Virginia, was "possessed of a library of several thousand volumes in most arts and sciences." Colonel Philip Ludwell III (1716-1767), whose namesake father and grandfather served on the Virginia Council, moved to London to seek a better education for his two daughters and his orphaned niece, but left behind at Green Spring, his ancient Virginia plantation, "a large collection of the most valuable books now extant, neatly bound, gilt, and lettered" in four large bookcases. Eton graduate and master of Stratford Hall, Philip Ludwell Lee (1727-75), owned what must have been an enormous library valued after his death at £334. When Stratford Hall was sold out of the Lee family in 1822, it contained three or four thousand volumes, "generally of the best London and Paris Editions." Peyton Randolph (1721-75), who had studied law at the Inns of Court in London and later became the first president of the Continental Congress, owned a massive "Library of Books" crammed in six mahogany book presses. Thomas Jefferson, with his usual covetousness for scarce books, acquired Randolph's library, "book-cases and all as they stood," along with priceless manuscript records of the Virginia Company that Jefferson included in the 1815 sale of his library to the Library of Congress.[23]

Statesman and planter William Fitzhugh (1741-1809) built a magnificent Georgian mansion in 1768-69 on the banks of the Rappahannock across from Fredericksburg, which he named Chatham in honor of William Pitt the Elder, first Earl of Chatham, who advocated repeal of the Stamp Act. Like Col. Baylor, Fitzhugh was an accomplished turfman with a stable of thoroughbreds and a private race track at Chatham. He presided over one of the most genteel households in colonial Virginia and entertained lavishly. George Washington, a friend and frequent guest, reportedly informed Fitzhugh that he put his "legs oftener under your mahogany at Chatham than anywhere else in the world, and have enjoyed your good dinners, good wine and good company more than any other." Fitzhugh maintained a very large, quite possibly extraordinary library at Chatham, but, mired in debt, he left the bulk of it behind when he put his mansion up for sale and moved to Alexandria in 1796. (Chatham was finally sold a decade later, including its furnishings and books, but no inventory survives.)[24]

Colonial Maryland had fewer large private libraries than Virginia. Of some four thousand estate inventories from the colonial period examined by Joseph T. Wheeler, fewer than 3 percent had more than twenty books, and only four had more than one hundred titles. The largest library in eighteenth-century Maryland was owned by Edward Lloyd IV (1744-96), a wealthy planter and patriot who amassed 701 titles comprising 2,550 volumes of books and pamphlets. For a brief period, however, Annapolis offered something Virginia lacked: a large circulating library. In July 1773, William Aikman, a Scotsman who had opened a bookstore and stationery, advertised a "circulating library consisting of about 12 hundred volumes on the most useful sciences, history, poetry, agriculture, voyages, travels, miscellanies, plays, with all the most approved of novels, magazines and other books of entertainment." And to assure that his library would "be of real utility to the publick," Aikman promised to "have it supplied with all the new publications of merit from Britain so soon as published."[25]

Outside of the Chesapeake, the largest private libraries in eighteenth-century colonial America were owned by Cotton Mather (1663-1728) of Boston, James Logan (1674-1751) of Philadelphia, and Benjamin Franklin. Mather, a Puritan minister with a profound stutter but a prolific and powerful pen, was graduated from Harvard at age fifteen. He is most remembered today for his dubious theological contributions toward the hysteria that culminated in the Salem witch trials, but he also amassed somewhere between three thousand and four thousand volumes by the time he died. It was with considerable justification that Mather boasted to his diary that he was blessed with a "Library, exceeding any man's, in all this Land." In another passage, he claimed: "Seldom any new Book of Consequence finds the way from beyond-Sea, to these parts of America, but I bestow the Perusal upon it." James Logan, born in Ireland to a minister and scholar who converted to Quakerism, served in a number of important governmental positions in William Penn's provincial Pennsylvania, including mayor of Philadelphia, while writing scientific papers for European learned societies and berating his book agents in London, Amsterdam, and other Old World capitals to send him rare and arcane tomes in the best possible bindings and condition. Logan acquired 2,185 titles (in 2,651 volumes) that now mostly reside in the Library Company of Philadelphia, which was founded by Benjamin Franklin in 1731. Though Franklin is generally acknowledged as founder of the Library Company, it is not commonly known that he, too, possessed one of the largest colonial-era libraries in North America, consisting of some four thousand volumes, and quite possibly many more. Building on the work of Edwin Wolf 2nd, Kevin J. Hayes has compiled a remarkable reconstruction of much of Dr. Franklin's library prior to his death in 1790.[26]

Three

Books from London and Williamsburg

Colonel Baylor ordered the majority of his books through his British tobacco agents, Floweredewe and Norton. In a January 1759 letter, in which he admitted that his growing debt to the London firm "frightens me," Baylor ordered, among other publications: Lily's *Grammar*; two "plain common prayer books"; eight volumes of Thomas Salmon's *Modern History* (various dates and subsequent reprints); John Mears's *Forms of Devotion for the Use of Families* (1758); John Reeves's *The Art of Farriery* (1758); and *A New System of Agriculture; or, A Plain, Easy, and Demonstrative Method of Speedily Growing Rich* (1755) (anonymous). A few months later, Baylor's friend and former commander George Washington also ordered a copy of *A New System of Agriculture*.[1]

Baylor and Washington admired more than just the same books. Later the same year, Washington ordered a half-dozen pair of "Men's neatest Shoes and Pumps" from John Didsbury, a renowned cobbler of fancy shoes and boots at Pall Mall in London. One of Washington's "Rules of Civility" that he copied down as a boy in his school exercise book was, "keep to the fashion of your equals," and his footwear was no exception. Washington directed that his shoes be based on the same last (i.e., wooden foot model used in shoe making) on which Baylor's shoes were crafted, except that Washington wanted his made a "little larger" than Baylor's and he wanted "high Heels." Washington liked the shoes so much he ordered more, but finding Didsbury's effort "rather too short" for his elongated frame, he requested the cobbler to make them longer. (Washington towered over most of his peers at about six feet, two inches, and frequently complained that his clothes from Britain were undersized.)[2]

Baylor also eventually needed bigger—and softer—shoes. Along with William Byrd II, Robert "King" Carter, Mann Page I, George Mason IV, and a number of his Virginia elite contemporaries, Baylor suffered from severe gout, which Lord Chesterfield, who also was afflicted with the extremely painful condition, pronounced as the "distemper of a gentleman." In addition to causing excruciating pain, a fit of the gout was often debilitating for weeks at a time. Robert "King" Carter, in one of his many written complaints about the condition, grumbled to his London agent: "I have now bin confind to my house for above a month by that cruel companion the Gout." In 1761 Baylor ordered "a pair of large cork soles for the gout" from one of his London agents, and two years later he groaned to Didsbury that he had "a terrible fit of the gout" and needed more accommodating footwear.[3]

Baylor kept current on the latest publications from Britain by reading London periodicals, especially the *Monthly Review; or Literary Journal*. As Richard Beale Davis noted, this was how "[s]cores of books found their way into southern libraries within a few months, or at most a year or two, of their first printing in Britain." Several of the titles Baylor requested in his 1759 letter to Flowerdewe and Norton had been reviewed in the *Monthly Review* during the prior year (and two of them had been reviewed just a month before his letter). Founded in 1749 by its Whiggish editor and publisher, Ralph Griffiths (1720-1803), the *Monthly Review* was the first British journal devoted exclusively to reviews of books and other works of prose or poetry. Initially, Griffiths intended to review every book or pamphlet published in Great Britain, but this task soon proved so daunting that many reviews, especially of "technical" works such as medical books, were placed in an appendix at the end of the periodical with the briefest possible descriptions. Charles Martin's *Treatise on the Gout* (1759), for example, was dismissed with a one-word review: "Quackery." One cannot but wonder what Baylor, reclined in his easy chair with his throbbing, painfully swollen, gouty feet parked on a worn footstool, thought of this abrupt assessment as he perused his *Monthly Review* in the flickering candlelit glow of his library.[4]

British tobacco merchants regularly supplied books to the Virginia gentry. Books were among the items most frequently requested from John Norton, a major London merchant and Col Baylor III's brother-in-law. William Nelson (1711-72), a wealthy planter and merchant who served as acting governor of Virginia following Lord Botetourt's death in 1770, frequently directed Norton to procure books that he had read or heard about. In September 1766, for example, Nelson ordered: *A Collection of Poems in Six Volumes* (1758), edited by Robert Dodsley; William Gordon's *Every Young Man's Companion* (1755); and Samuel Boyse's *The New Pantheon* (1760). A year later he sent Norton a long (but now lost) list of "Books & Globes" that he needed for his son Hugh's education. In one of his many book orders, Robert Carter Nicholas (1728-80), a lawyer and treasurer of Virginia, instructed Norton to rush him a copy of Sir James Steuart's *An Inquiry into the Principles of Political Economy* (1767), "a Book much celebrated by the Reviewers," he noted. William Nelson also wanted a copy of Steuart's economic treatise, along with Lord Lyttelton's second volume of the *Life of King Henry the Second* (1767-71), Boswell's *Account of Corsica* (1768), and Bernard Lens's guidebook for armchair artists, *For the Curious Young Gentlemen and Ladies, That Study and Practise the Noble and Commendable Art of Drawing...* (1766) (the full title has 245 words, which Nelson simply called the *Art of Drawing Without a Master*).[5]

Robert Carter of Nomini Hall, described by his children's tutor Philip V. Fithian as "sensible judicious, much given to retirement & Study," requested that Edward Hunt and Sons of London send him a number of law treatises, historical works, and dictionaries, including the latest folio edition of Samuel Johnson's *Dictionary of the English Language* (1755), unless "there hath been published a work on the same Plan by another Person, which is higher in estimation, than S. J.'s Dictionary." Carter, an avid amateur musician who was deeply interested in science and philosophy, also asked Hunt to send him Dr. Robert Smith's *Harmonics, or the Philosophy of Musical Sounds* (1749) and an English translation of Sir Isaac Newton's Latin masterpiece, *Philosophiae naturalis principia mathematica* (*Mathematical Principles of Natural Philosophy*) (1687).[6]

John Page (1744-1808), a major tobacco planter and master of Rosewell, the largest private residence in colonial America, asked

Norton to obtain a French ephemeris, *Connaissance des temps ou des mouvements célestes à l'usage des astronomes et des navigateurs*, for his use in studying the planets. Page, an accomplished astronomer and one of colonial America's underrated intellectuals and statesmen, set up an observatory, including a telescope and other equipment that he designed or built, in one of the cupolas at Rosewell, where he invited like-minded intellectuals, such as his close friend Thomas Jefferson, to come and gaze in wonder at the heavens. Page and Jefferson had studied astronomy, along with a host of other subjects, at the College of William and Mary under William Small (1734-75), a brilliant Scottish professor of mathematics and science whom both revered in their writings. Guided by the "illustrious" and "great" Professor Small, Page read "natural and experimental Philosophy, Mechanics, and, in short, every branch of the Mathematics ... till they led me on to Astronomy, to which after I had left College, till some time after I was married, I devoted my time." A decade after they began their studies together at William and Mary, Jefferson teased Page about the latter's all-consuming interest in astronomy: "Why the devil don't you write? But I suppose you are always in the moon, or some of the planetary region.... If your spirit is too elevated to advert to sublunary subjects, depute my friend Mrs. Page to support your correspondences." Page's large library included works by Sir Isaac Newton and Edmund Halley, but unfortunately no inventory survives.[7]

Henry Fitzhugh (1723-83), grandson of emigrant and Fitzhugh dynasty founder William Fitzhugh, regularly asked his London merchants to send books to Bedford, his 2,000-acre estate in Stafford County. As the father of thirteen children, he placed orders primarily for Bibles, prayer books, catechisms, Greek and Latin primers, lesson plans, and music books. Like Robert Carter of Nomini Hall, Fitzhugh possessed a highly cultivated interest in the arts and music. In 1770, for example, he asked for "musick books for the harpsichord," including Robert Bremner's work, *The Harpsichord or Spinnet Miscellany* (1765), which was also sold in Williamsburg.[8]

Robert Beverley inherited Blandfield, a splendid Georgian mansion situated on 3,500 acres near the Rappahannock River, including the massive library assembled by his father, William Beverley (1696-1756), and his grandfather, Robert Beverley (ca. 1673-1722), author of *The History and Present State of Virginia* (1705). Like his father and grandfather, Robert Beverley regularly ordered books from his British tobacco agents. In 1771, for example, he asked Samuel Athawes of London to send him a set of Voltaire's works, Plutarch's *Lives*, and Sully's *Memoirs*.[9]

The direct connections between Virginia planters and their London merchants gave the planters a distinct advantage in obtaining current book releases compared to other readers in colonial America who lacked such a relationship. Even in pre-Revolutionary Boston and Philadelphia booksellers tended to order tried and true titles first published in Britain a decade or more earlier. Unlike Baylor and his peers, who regularly perused the *Monthly Review* and other British periodicals for discussion of the latest publications, most readers in colonial America did not have ready access to the *Monthly Review* or similar magazines. "Few Philadelphians," one scholar noted, "ever saw a book review" in the colonial period. In addition to titles they read about in recent issues of the *Monthly Review*, Virginia planters with account relationships in Britain regularly asked their merchants to suggest or add the newest titles they thought might be of interest. In 1765, for example, Col. Baylor asked John Norton to add "any thing new & in taste" to Baylor's order of books and periodicals. Contrary to the New England stereotype of the Virginia planter as bucolic bumpkin, Baylor and his Virginia peers were more current, more "hip," as one might call it today, than has been generally supposed.[10]

*   *   *

In addition to his book purchases through his London agents, Baylor also heavily patronized the bookstore operated by the publishers of the *Virginia Gazette* in Williamsburg. (As mentioned earlier, planters composed the largest occupational group of the *Gazette*'s book buyers.) Most of the books the *Gazette* proprietors sold were imported from London. The *Gazette* published some titles on its own, but these consisted almost exclusively of Virginia legislative and executive journals, pamphlets, almanacs, and broadsides. The store's customer account books, called "daybooks," survive only for the years 1750-52 and 1764-66. During just the latter two-year period, Baylor purchased no fewer than forty-two titles there, along with writing paper, copy books, and dozens of "best Dutch pens." The *Gazette* store offered about a thousand titles for sale in the mid-eighteenth century and was the most important retail book outlet south of Philadelphia. Whether it was cheaper for retail buyers like Baylor to purchase books in Williamsburg than to import them from London remains an open question, but clearly it was more convenient to pick up the latest novel in Williamsburg than to wait months on end for it to be shipped from London. The *Virginia Gazette* office also performed critically important economic and sociocultural functions that drew Baylor and his Virginia gentry peers to it regularly. It was, for example, a place where private lottery tickets could be bought or sold, bills of exchange accepted or cashed, and news, opinions, and information discussed and disseminated.[11]

Due to the limited chronological scope of the *Gazette's* extant daybooks and because Col. Baylor's surviving letterbooks are not a complete record of his correspondence with his British tobacco agents, we have only a partial glimpse of all the books he purchased from Williamsburg or London. However, a number of the books that were itemized in his estate not long after his death were prominently reviewed in the *Monthly Review* during the mid-eighteenth century when he was actively reading the periodical and dashing off letters to London or stopping by the *Gazette* office for titles that struck his fancy. For example, *A Natural and Civil History of California* (1759), by the Jesuit Miguel Venegas, received a five-page review in the June 1759 *Monthly Review*, and turned up in Baylor's inventory. Similarly, *Remarks on the Tenets and Principles of the Quakers* (1758), published anonymously by Rev. Daniel Gittins, was reviewed in the December 1758 *Monthly Review* and also appeared on the inventory list.[12]

Baylor was equally fond of another important London periodical, *Gentleman's Magazine*. Founded in 1731 by Edward Cave (1691-1754), *Gentleman's Magazine* was a monthly digest of news, politics, commentary, and brief literary works by prominent writers such as

Samuel Johnson, Daniel Defoe, Joseph Addison, and Jonathan Swift. *Gentleman's Magazine* had a connection of sorts to the *Monthly Review*—Cave had actually conceived the idea and even the name for the *Monthly Review*, but he was beaten to the punch in launching it by his upstart rival Griffiths. Still, despite the importance of the *Monthly Review*, of the more than seventy periodicals published in greater London in the mid-eighteenth century, *Gentleman's Magazine* was, in the words of one scholar, "without question the most distinguished and influential periodical publication in English in the eighteenth century."[13]

In addition to *Gentleman's Magazine*, Baylor also regularly ordered and read a competing periodical, *London Magazine*, which was founded a year after *Gentleman's Magazine* and which closely resembled it in form and content. However, no record indicates that Baylor ever ordered colonial America's two most popular periodicals, *The Spectator* and *The Tatler*. Founded and edited by Richard Steele (1672-1729), *The Tatler* had a two-year run ending in 1711, the same year Steele began publishing *The Spectator* along with co-founder and contributor Joseph Addison (1672-1719). Like its predecessor, *The Spectator* was published for only two years, but was by far the more successful of the two, both during its original publication and afterwards. Remarkably, reprints and bound copies of both *The Tatler* and *The Spectator* remained very popular in Britain and in America throughout the eighteenth century. In 1731, in its first order of some fifty titles from Britain, the Library Company of Philadelphia, whose founding members where "chiefly artificers" rather than the elite or wealthy, asked for copies of both *The Tatler* and *The Spectator*. By mid-century, the *Virginia Gazette* printing office in Williamsburg offered reprinted versions of both magazines, and by 1778, British cleric and essayist Vicesimus Knox (1752-1821) could declare with little exaggeration: "There is scarcely an individual, not only of those who profess learning, but of those who devote any of their time to reading, who has not perused the papers of the *Spectator*." "The *Spectators*," he further noted, "have been everywhere read throughout the British empire."[14]

"In southern collections," noted Richard Beale Davis with some overstatement, "the *Spectator* is almost as likely to be present as the Bible." Of some 2,200 South Carolina probate inventories examined by Walter Edgar, *The Spectator* was the most common title identified other than the Bible. In Maryland, too, during the first half of the eighteenth century *The Spectator* was by far the most common periodical mentioned in estate inventories. In the Gunston Hall collection of probate inventories, at least twenty decedents owned copies of *The Tatler*, and no fewer than forty-five owned *The Spectator*. Many had both publications, such as Maj. William Walker (d. 1763) of Stafford County, Virginia, whose estate included about sixty volumes of books, along with eight volumes of *The Spectator* and four volumes of *The Tatler*, or Traverse Cooke (d. 1759), from the same county, who owned "1 set" of each. Even those who owned only a handful of books often held one or both of these periodicals. Nathaniel Chapman (d. 1761) of Charles County, Maryland, for instance, owned fewer than a dozen books, yet he died with an additional nine volumes of *The Spectator* in his possession. A number of Scottish merchants were known to have carried copies of *The Spectator* for sale, even in the more remote Virginia Piedmont. In 1772, for instance, at his store in New London, on the far western edge of the Virginia settlement, Scotsman John Hook offered a four-volume set of *The Tatler* and an eight-volume set of *The Spectator*. By marked contrast, only two of the 325 inventories analyzed by Gunston Hall Plantation specifically mention *Gentleman's Magazine*, and one of those was the one for George Washington's estate. William Byrd II, the prototypical eighteenth-century Virginia aristocrat, was a regular subscriber to *Gentleman's Magazine*, as were Robert Carter of Nomini Hall and Richard Henry Lee of Chantilly.[15]

The Tatler and *The Spectator* were probably the most popular British periodicals in the Chesapeake because they were more middlebrow in their content than *Gentleman's Magazine*. Both *The Tatler* and *The Spectator* spoke to a literate, rising middle class that sought greater sensibility, taste, and refinement, that aspired to a society of "politeness," as recent scholarship has called it. James Boswell (1740-1795), whose household governor encouraged him to read *The Spectator* in his preteen years, later recalled that "it was then that I acquired my first notions of taste for the fine arts and of the pleasure there is in considering the variety of human nature."

Samuel Johnson placed *The Tatler* and *The Spectator* in the genre of courtesy literature that traced its modern beginnings to Castiglione's *Book of the Courtier* (1528). Johnson wrote that the magazines were the first in Britain to "teach the minuter decencies and inferior [common] duties, to regulate the practice of daily conversation, to correct those depravities which are rather ridiculous than criminal, and remove those grievances which, if they produce no lasting calamities, impress hourly vexation." In his *Autobiography* (1793), Benjamin Franklin acknowledged a heavy debt to *The Spectator*. As a boy, he consciously mimicked its writing style, and the magazine later informed his journalistic judgments as a printer and publisher. In a letter to his eleven-year-old nephew written more than a century after *The Spectator* first appeared, former President James Madison praised the periodical as "the best that had been written for cherishing in young minds a desire of improvement, a taste for learning, and a lively sense of the proprieties of life."[16]

In colonial America, *Gentleman's Magazine*, moderately conservative in its disposition, appealed to readers who were more elite (or at least those who perceived themselves as socioeconomic superiors) than readers of *The Tatler* or *The Spectator*. Thomas Jefferson, in a letter to his future brother-in-law Robert Skipwith, who had requested book recommendations for "a common reader who understands but little of the classicks and who has not leisure for any intricate or tedious study," suggested *The Tatler*, *The Spectator*, and the *Guardian*, but did not mention *Gentleman's Magazine*. (Interestingly, none of the four periodicals is recorded as having been present in Jefferson's personal libraries.) In a study of Northumberland County, Virginia, probate inventories, both *The Tatler* and *The Spectator* were common, but not one inventory mentioned *Gentleman's Magazine*.[17]

The situation in New York and Philadelphia appears to have been similar. British-born bookseller Garrat Noel, who for many years operated a New York bookstore where he sold titles published primarily in London, offered *The Tatler* and *The Spectator*, along with a half-dozen other British periodicals, but not *Gentleman's Magazine*. In his 1773 catalogue listing more than nine hundred titles,

Philadelphia printer and bookseller Robert Bell offered *The Tatler*, *The Spectator*, and *Guardian*, but not *Gentleman's Magazine*.[18]

In mid-1755 Benjamin Franklin's close friend William Strahan (1715-1785), the London printer who published Samuel Johnson's *Dictionary of the English Language* only a few months earlier, proposed a scheme to distribute *Gentleman's Magazine* to prepaid subscribers in America. Franklin eagerly replied and suggested distribution of the periodical in Philadelphia, New York, and New England, but "[a]s to Virginia," Franklin sighed, "I believe it will scarce be worth while to propose it there, the Gentlemen being generally furnisht with them by their Correspondents in London." Franklin added, "[t]hat Magazine has always been in my Opinion by far the best."[19]

For Col. Baylor and the Virginia gentry, British periodicals provided a vital connection with their "home," as Baylor and most of the gentry viewed England before the Revolution. The *Virginia Gazette*, published in Williamsburg, reprinted some news reports and brief literary items from London (including excerpts from *Gentleman's Magazine* and other periodicals), and a few tidbits of information and gossip could be gleaned from visitors, such as Scottish tutors or garrulous ship captains who arrived in Virginia to collect tobacco or deliver merchandise. ("No captain need dine alone once he reached Virginia," one scholar noted.) Correspondence from tobacco merchants in London or Bristol was mostly confined to business, and though letters from sons (and, much less frequently, daughters) attending school abroad were certainly warmer and more welcome, these, too, were often limited as sources of information about what was going on in Britain. But, particularly for men like Baylor who lived far from urban port cities such as Philadelphia, New York, or even Alexandria or Norfolk, no other communication channel was more informative about the mother country than *Gentleman's Magazine* and its rival periodicals. Lawyer and surveyor Thomas Lewis, who lived on the outermost periphery of white settlement in the upper Shenandoah Valley where Indian raids were still a serious threat, owned no less than seventeen volumes of *Gentleman's Magazine*.[20]

Where else except *Gentleman's Magazine* could the Virginia

gentry read in a single publication, during the mid-1750s for example, a compelling narrative of the Lisbon earthquake, a long, laudatory review of Johnson's *Dictionary*, political spiels regarding the resignation of the British chancellor of the exchequer or the dismissal of William Pitt the Elder from his official post, a richly illustrated feature on indigo production in South Carolina, a tragic tale of Gen. Braddock's defeat and mortal wounds at the first battle of the French and Indian War (not to mention a report about a young Virginia militia colonel named George Washington), and an announcement of the birth of the third Duke of Montrose? In addition to being repositories of important information, eighteenth-century British magazines, because of their content, their wide readership among the Anglo-American *cognoscenti*, and the esteem in which they were held, helped create and reinforce a shared culture and set of values within the British Atlantic world. *Gentleman's Magazine*, in particular, sought to define the way an eighteenth-century British gentleman should act and live, what he should read, think, wear, and eat, how he should converse, and what type of character he ought to have. For Baylor, it was the *vade mecum* of his gentility.[21]

*   *   *

Baylor followed Anglo-American political matters closely. In his 1759 letter to Flowerdewe and Norton mentioned at the beginning of this chapter, he ordered a copy of *A Discourse on the Conduct of the Government of Great-Britain, in Respect to Neutral Nations, During the Present War* (1758), which had received a favorable eight-page review in the *Monthly Review* only a month before Baylor's letter. Ralph Griffiths, the *Review*'s wily publisher, had also published *A Discourse* and composed the laudatory book review himself. Written anonymously by Charles Jenkinson (1727-1808), who was subsequently elected to the House of Commons and was later ennobled as the first Earl of Liverpool, *A Discourse* lamely sought to justify British incursions upon neutral shipping (especially Dutch vessels) during the Seven Years War in violation of principles of international navigation that had been laid down by Hugo Grotius more than a century earlier and that had been generally accepted throughout western Europe. Ironically, the same aggressiveness on the part of the British navy regarding neutral ships would entangle Baylor's son John IV almost two decades later (see Chapter 5).[22]

In 1762 Baylor asked one of his London agents, Robert Cary, who was George Washington's primary tobacco merchant, to send him "every thing that is lately come out of taste for and against Mr. Pitt." William Pitt the Elder (1708-78), nominally British secretary of state for the Southern Department and then leader of the House of Commons, had prosecuted the Seven Years War as de facto prime minister with ruthless efficiency and success, leading to the consolidation of British sea power and culminating in the defeat of the French. Pitt, just three years younger than Baylor, had been forced to resign his post in October 1761 amid bitter political wrangling, and like Baylor, he was badly afflicted with gout. A year later, Baylor directed Robert Cary to send him "all new political pieces of taste."[23]

During this period, *Gentleman's Magazine*, along with most other British periodicals, significantly expanded coverage of American political matters, which often consumed a third or more of each issue. Petitions to the Crown or Parliament from America were printed in whole or in part, along with Parliamentary speeches and proceedings bearing on the colonies. Debates in American legislative assemblies were regularly reported, and correspondence to and from colonial governors was frequently published. Letters reflecting a wide spectrum of opinion from both American and British readers were also printed each month. By 1768, new features of the magazine with titles such as "Interesting Advices from America" and "Papers Relative to the Troubles in America" appeared at the beginning of each issue.[24]

Baylor also closely followed the growing political crises at home. Prior to the Stamp Act crisis in 1765, the most heated political controversy in Virginia at mid-century was the Parson's Cause. In colonial Virginia, where hard money was chronically unavailable, public and private debts, including salaries of the Anglican clergy, were typically paid in tobacco. The clergy's annual stipend, fixed by law at 16,000 pounds of tobacco, was paid from a public levy in each parish. A severe drought in 1758 left tobacco in short supply, and prices skyrocketed. To provide relief to debtors generally, and following a precedent established after another crop failure three years earlier, the House of Burgesses enacted a one-year remedial measure, popularly called the "Two-Penny Act." The act allowed anyone who owed a debt in tobacco to discharge the obligation in local currency at the rate of two pence per pound. This amount was the approximate value of tobacco leaf in a normal year, but it was less than half of the commodity's selling price in that period's frenzied market.[25]

The clergy vehemently protested the legislation, which they perceived as but the latest in a protracted series of attacks and usurpations by the Virginia gentry. They appointed the Rev. John Camm, minister of the York-Hampton parish, to file a formal grievance with Thomas Sherlock (1677-1761), the Bishop of London, who had ecclesiastical jurisdiction over the Anglican Church in colonial America, and with the Board of Trade. On the advice of the Board of Trade, George III's Privy Council disallowed the Two-Penny Act in 1759 (by which time it had expired). In the meantime, several of the clerics sued the tax collectors in their parish in an effort to recover the full market value of their tobacco-based compensation. The litigation, which dragged on for years, and the broader political conflict surrounding it are collectively known as the "Parson's Cause."[26]

The dispute over the Two-Penny Act ignited a bitter pamphlet war that Thomas Jefferson later described as the "great paper-controversy." Lest anyone believe that the invariable degeneration of opinion threads posted on the Internet into vitriolic ad hominem attacks is a phenomenon unique to the present, a reading of the seven fusillades lobbed by the three principal combatants in this bitter public squabble will demonstrate otherwise. Each is fascinating in its blend of reason and rancor. Landon Carter, a wealthy planter and long-winded literary pugilist who once vowed he would "clip the wings" of the entire Virginia clergy, fired the first salvo in December 1759 when he published, anonymously through the *Virginia Gazette*, *A Letter to the Right Reverend Father in God, the Lord B[isho]p of L[ondo]n*. Carter's fifty-five-page pamphlet was a point-by-point refutation of the Bishop of London's letter of June 1759 to the Board of Trade regarding the Two-Penny Act. In a cleverly manipulative maneuver, Bishop Sherlock presented the issue to the Board as a power grab by a dissenting gentry who once "lived in submission to the power set over them," but who now were bent on challenging the authority of both church and state. The passage of the Act without the usual suspending clause (i.e., a provision that held the law in abeyance until it received the royal assent) was, Sherlock histrionically asserted, treason. Because the ultimate effect of the law was an intentional "diminution of the Prerogative and influence of the Crown," the right of the Virginia clergy to their full remuneration "must stand or fall with the authority of the Crown," Sherlock concluded. Carter found this conclusion so "twisted" that he suggested it was the work of a Grub Street hack—"a Hireling-Packer of Memorials, Remonstrances, &c."[27]

Before Camm could reply, Richard Bland weighed in with his own Williamsburg-published pamphlet, *A Letter to the Clergy of Virginia* (1760). Bland (1710-76), a planter from Prince George County, Virginia, whom John Adams described as a "learned, bookish man," had served for decades in the House of Burgesses and was likely its most productive and hardest-working member. Though only a handful of Bland's writings survive, historian Bernard Bailyn has deemed Bland "one of the ablest belletrists of eighteenth-century America." Far from the "Force and Conviction" of argument that Bland said he expected from the Bishop of London's memorial to the Board of Trade, Bland saw it as "only an Evidence of the Imbecility of the human Mind" and "a Demonstration that ... the most learned and pious Men are subject to the Impositions of the Crafty and Malevolent." Bland firmly rejected the Bishop of London's suggestion that the Burgesses had "any traitorous intent to lessen the Prerogatives of the Crown" or wished to become "absolute masters" of the clergy. Having arisen out of a "most pressing Necessity," the Two-Penny Act was entirely motivated, he said, by the "very laudable and Christian Principle" of "a Desire to relieve these People from the unhappy Circumstances they were under." In view of Baylor's interest in political matters and his purchase of later pamphlets in the fray, he likely bought Carter's and Bland's pamphlets, but the *Gazette's* surviving daybooks do not cover this period.[28]

Camm's reply, *A Single and Distinct View of the ... Two-Penny Act* (1763), was three years in coming because he could not find anyone in Virginia willing to print it. Joseph Royle, publisher of the *Virginia Gazette* as well as the official printer for all legislative materials in the Old Dominion, bluntly told Rev. Camm that it would "be very imprudent in me" to print "any Animadversions" against the Burgesses and that it was his duty "studiously to avoid giving Offence to the Legislature." Though Carter and Bland were prominent members of the Burgesses, Royle suggested that if Camm could manage to respond to their writings without assailing the legislature—his most important client and the very body that had enacted the Two-Penny Act—he would print Camm's rejoinder. Royle's requirement was probably insurmountable in any case, but Camm's pamphlet, which combined intelligent, withering arguments with snide, gratuitous insults (as did Carter's and Bland's), put the question beyond any doubt. "On looking over your Pamphlet," Royle sighed, "I find it not only a Reply to those of Colonels Bland and Carter but also intermixed with Satyrical Touches upon the late Assembly." Camm wound up having his pamphlet printed in Annapolis.[29]

Camm's strongest argument was economic. He accused Carter and Bland of "confound[ing] Poverty with Riches." The purpose of the Two-Penny Act, according to Carter and Bland, was to relieve suffering in a bad crop year. On the contrary, Camm argued, the poorest of the parish, the landless indentured servants and slaves, received nothing from the legislation while the already-rich planters derived the entire benefit. Since the parsons' salaries were paid from tithes levied in each parish upon personal property (i.e., mostly slaves and livestock), the act effected a "dividend," as Camm called it, to the planters in direct proportion to their wealth. "One would think," Camm huffed, "that in a Project for the Benefit of the Poor, the Poorer any Man was, the greater Share he should have in the Benefit of the Project." To drive his point home, Camm inserted into his pamphlet the entire tithe list of some 184 taxpayers in his parish, with the richest planters at the top of the list, including a column with Camm's calculation of their "dividend" from the Two-Penny Act. Camm published the tithe list with full names and the amount of each person's tithable estate, an act of shocking belligerence that today would be roughly akin to publishing the personal net worth statements of his parishioners.[30]

Landon Carter's turn was next, and in his *The Rector Detected* (1764) he did not disappoint. Carter's pamphlet, "thirty-nine pages of sheer verbal savagery," as Bernard Bailyn aptly put it, was the most vicious and personal of the whole series of pamphlets. Carter focused less on the various arguments at issue and did his best to attack Camm personally; he even questioned Camm's sanity. Camm quickly fired back a few months later with his *A Review of the Rector Detected: or the Colonel Reconnoitred* (1764), which Baylor purchased for two and a half shillings. Though neither Carter's nor Camm's pamphlets had anything substantive to add to the fight, they were both best sellers in Williamsburg: Royle sold on credit sixty-one copies of Carter's work and seventy-seven of Camm's.[31]

The sixth and penultimate pamphlet was Richard Bland's *The Colonel Dismounted: or, the Rector Vindicated* (1764), which Baylor also purchased from Royle. Putting aside the first twenty pages of Bland's pamphlet, in which he satirically reprises the arguments and posturing of all three parties in the war of words, the most important part of his work is his insightful discussion of what he saw as the constitutional issues at stake in the matter. Virginians, Bland asserted, were no less Englishmen than those living in Britain, who could only be governed with their consent. But Virginia had a representative government, and unless Virginia and the other colonies were to be independent, what was the proper constitutional role of Britain in Virginia? Answering his own question, Bland posited that matters of internal government, such as the Two-Penny Act, were the prerogative of Virginians to decide for themselves. On the other hand, external matters, such as the French and Indian War, were the province of the King and Parliament. Taking his analysis further, Bland presaged the core constitutional issue in the battle over the Stamp Act and concluded: "[A]ny tax, respecting out [our] INTERNAL polity, which may hereafter be imposed on us by Act of Parliament is arbitrary, as depriving us of our Rights, and may be opposed." The following year Camm fired his final shot in *Critical Remarks on a Letter Ascribed to Common Sense* (1765), but by then the Parson's Cause had been superseded by the Stamp Act imbroglio.[32]

Although Baylor temporarily refused to perform his judicial duties in protest over the Proclamation of 1763 (a matter in which he had a large personal interest), he was no revolutionary. At age sixty, he still regularly attended sessions at the House of Burgesses in Williamsburg, and he was present in the House chamber on May 30, 1765, when a twenty-nine-year-old firebrand named Patrick Henry, who had been sworn in as a new burgess only nine days earlier, gave his famous "treason" speech against the Stamp Act. Henry (1736-1799) proposed five resolutions that asserted the "inestimable" right of Virginians under the British constitution to tax themselves rather than being subject to taxes imposed by Parliament, in which Virginia had no representation.[33]

Only thirty-nine of 116 burgesses were present when Henry launched his tirade, most having retreated to their plantations prior to the conclusion of the legislative session. Baylor, along with sixteen other burgesses mostly from Tidewater counties, voted against the first four of Henry's resolves; twenty-two members, who were closer to Henry in age and geography, voted in favor of them. Lieutenant Governor Francis Fauquier, in recounting the episode to the Board of Trade, observed that Henry "carried all the young Members with him" and that during the heated debate over the resolves, the more mature burgesses were "overpowered by the Young, hot, and Giddy Members." A fifth resolution, which was somewhat more assertive than the others (it claimed the Virginia General Assembly had the "sole [and] exclusive Right and Power to lay Taxes and Impositions" upon Virginians), was approved by a 20-19 vote, but it was expunged from the House journal, probably extralegally, on the following day when Henry was absent. Baylor's vote would cost him his career as a Virginia burgess.[34]

Ironically, the difference between the legislators over Henry's resolutions was one of form over substance. The text of Henry's proposals was taken largely verbatim from petitions to George III and Parliament that had been drafted by a special committee of the

House of Burgesses and sent to London six months earlier (where it was set aside and completely ignored). Henry's version, which was entirely shorn of the careful obsequies heaped on the burgesses' petitions (e.g., "we entreat that your Majesty will be graciously pleased..."), was far more succinct and direct. But the real problem, as described by historian Edmund S. Morgan, was that "Henry and his friends were upstarts in Virginia politics, and their introduction of the resolves constituted a challenge to the established leaders of the House of Burgesses."[35]

Because Baylor died four years before America declared its independence from Britain, we cannot know what he would have thought about severing a 170-year political unity with the "home" of the Virginia gentry. Although Baylor opposed the Stamp Act (i.e., the House of Burgesses' deferential form of protest, not Patrick Henry's impetuous resolves), had he lived he likely would have had serious reservations about violent separation from Britain, as did a number of other Chesapeake gentry who were educated in Britain, such as Daniel Dulany II (1722-97), Robert Beverley, and Ralph Wormeley Jr. (1745-1806). Landon Carter, who had been schooled in London as a young child and who, like Baylor, had close business connections with British tobacco merchants, eventually supported American independence, but bitterly opposed the nation's growing republicanism. (He dismissed, for example, Thomas Paine's *Common Sense* [1776] as the "most nonsensical of all Pamphlets.") But Baylor's ongoing social, cultural, and familial ties to England ran much deeper than Carter's, and it is doubtful that he would have actively supported war with Great Britain.[36]

*   *   *

As the parents of eight children, Baylor and his wife, Frances, were much taxed with their general maintenance, particularly their education. (The Baylors had produced eleven children, but only eight survived.) "You know well the number of my children which the dictates of Nature loudly call upon me to provide for," Baylor groaned to John Norton in a letter explaining why Baylor was behind in reducing his ever-expanding debt. Donald Robertson

(1717-83), a Scotsman educated at Aberdeen and the University of Edinburgh, lived with the Baylors at Newmarket and tutored their children for five years—perhaps under an indenture—beginning in 1753. In 1758, Robertson established a school near the Mattaponi River in King and Queen County, Virginia, and over the next ten years many children of the Virginia gentry, including John Taylor of Caroline and James Madison, the future U.S. president, attended his highly regarded center of learning. Madison's curriculum, and therefore presumably the Baylors' also, included Latin, especially, Horace, Justinian, Terrence, and Ovid, along with arithmetic, algebra, geometry, geography, and French (pronounced with a "Scotch burr," Madison later recalled). The Father of the Constitution revered his first schoolmaster. "All that I have been in life," he fondly remembered of Robertson, "I owe largely to that great man." Robertson maintained a one hundred-volume library at his school for the use of his students, including Locke's *Essay Concerning Human Understanding* (1690), Montesquieu's *Spirit of the Laws* (1748), Smollett's *History of England* (1757-1758), as well as works by Hume, Montaigne, Dryden, Pope, and Milton.[37]

In addition to providing his daughters, Courtney, Lucy, Frances, and Elizabeth, home schooling under Robertson, Baylor subsequently sent each of them to boarding school at Croyden in Kent, England, a highly unusual act among the pre-Revolutionary Virginia gentry and no doubt an exceedingly expensive one. Typically, elite females in colonial Virginia received only an "ornamental" education consisting of reading, literature, music, dancing, and sometimes French. As the Baylor brood expanded, Col. Baylor acquired more books for his children. From one of his London agents he ordered, in addition to Lily's *Grammar* and Gordon's *Tacitus*, two copies each of Caesar's *Commentaries*, Ovid's *Metamorphoses*, Virgil's *Aeneid*, and an unspecified work by Erasmus, which was probably his *Colloquia* or *Adagia*. In 1764, the same year in which he complained to John Norton about providing for his expanding family, the *Virginia Gazette* sold Baylor a number of school and reference titles, including: John Clarke's *Introduction to the Making of Latin* (1721) and *Corderii colloquiorum centuria selecta* (*A Select Century of Cordery's Colloquies*) (1718); Anthony Brice's *Geographical*

Dictionary (1759); James Buchanan's *British Grammar* (1762); John Champion's *The Penman's Employment* (1762); and Elisha Coles's *Dictionary* (1676).[38]

Like Robert Carter of Nomini Hall, Peter Presley Thornton (d. 1780) of Northumberland County, and many others of the Virginia gentry, Baylor purchased a copy of Samuel Johnson's monumental *Dictionary of the English Language*. The educated elite in colonial Virginia anticipated Johnson's *Dictionary* even before it appeared. On April 11, 1755, four days before the *Dictionary* was released by its publisher in London, the *Virginia Gazette* reprinted the first of two letters by Lord Chesterfield praising Johnson's work. The second installment followed a week later, and on April 25, the *Gazette* reported that Oxford University had conferred an honorary master of arts degree upon Johnson, "Author of the new English Dictionary," a few months earlier. Shortly after its publication, British periodicals read by Baylor and many of his peers, including the *Monthly Review*, *Gentleman's Magazine*, and the *London Magazine*, gave the work high praise. In 1764 alone the *Gazette* sold ten sets of Johnson's *Dictionary*, four in a two-volume octavo edition published in London in 1760, and six (including Baylor's) in a two-volume folio set, which was probably the second edition published in London in 1755-56. Even remote backcountry gentry such as William Cabell of Amherst County owned a set of *Johnson's Dictionary*.[39]

*   *   *

Along with John Tayloe II (1721-79) of Mount Airy, near Warsaw, Virginia, and Benjamin Tasker Jr. (1720-60) of Annapolis, Maryland, Col. Baylor was one of the most accomplished importers and breeders of thoroughbred racehorses in colonial America. In 1757 he provided stud services for one of George Washington's mares—apparently without the usual fee—and invited Washington to "send a couple of Mares yearly to my Horses." Though Baylor was old enough to be Washington's father and Washington was then many years away from his fame and major accomplishments, Baylor gushed: "When we come to recounting Favours I find myself so largely your Debtor that I shall always insist on your Commanding with Freedom any & every thing wherein I can be serviceable." (Aside from his well-known virtues and abilities, one of Washington's least-known but most remarkable characteristics was his studied flair for making himself so attractive to his socioeconomic superiors in Virginia that they could not resist wanting to help him in any way they could).[40]

Of all the many books and periodicals shipped to him from London, Baylor most looked forward to the annual compendia of all official horse races in Great Britain. Each year Baylor ordered a copy of John Cheny's *Historical List of all Horse-Matches Run ... in England and Wales*, which Cheny published from 1728 until his death in 1751. Reginald Heber continued Cheny's publication until he died in 1769, and Baylor also ordered all of Heber's editions. When Baylor arrived on the scene at the Newmarket race course near Cambridge, England, in the 1720s, elite British horse breeding and racing was undergoing radical transformation due to the introduction of Arabian-pedigreed horses in Britain, a phenomenon that had begun during the reign of Charles II. An anonymous wag bitterly denounced the new order in *Gentleman's Magazine*: "Our noble Breed of Horses is now enervated by an Intermixture with Turks, Barbs, and Arabians, just as our modern Nobility and Gentry are debauch'd with the effeminate Manners of France and Italy." By the time this reactionary rant appeared in 1739, it was already too late: three important "foundational" Arabian stallions—from whom all modern thoroughbreds descend—had already been imported into England and had sired dozens of offspring.[41]

One of these sires, *Bulle Rock*, the first known Arabian thoroughbred in America, had been imported into Virginia a few years earlier by Samuel Gist of Hanover County. Many others soon followed; indeed, between 1730 and 1770 the Virginia gentry imported ninety-four thoroughbreds from Britain, which was more than half of all thoroughbreds (176) imported into colonial America during the same period. Aside from the horrendous expense of buying English racehorses, it must have been unspeakably difficult, for man and horse, to ship them on a four- to six-week journey across the Atlantic. A personal attendant was essential, as were hundreds of pounds of hay and oats. The care and feeding of a common horse during such a crossing would have been challenge enough, but as anyone who has been around thoroughbreds knows, they are by nature high strung, fidgety, and prickly. The complete lack of exercise while on board ship no doubt exacerbated these characteristics. These concerns were evidently top of mind when George Braxton Jr. (ca. 1703-61) of King and Queen County (father of Carter Braxton, a Declaration of Independence signer) informed his London merchant that he—like Baylor—had "selected out of the race Books (which are very authentick) a List of Horses very well bred." Braxton wanted his merchant to send him a "large [and] handsome ... fine Bay" stallion, and cautioned him to "let him [the horse] want for nothing to bring him over safe; insure fully [and] get a careful Servant to come over with him."[42]

A number of foreign visitors commented on the "excessive" fondness Virginians had for horseflesh. In 1759 Rev. Andrew Burnaby, an Anglican cleric, described Virginia horses as "fleet and beautiful," and observed that the "gentlemen of Virginia, who are exceedingly fond of horse-racing, have spared no expense to improve the breed of them by importing great numbers from England." Horses "are a prime object with the Virginians," noted a German surgeon, especially "racers and hunters, of which indubitably they have the finest in America." An English military officer marveled that in Virginia "even the carriage horses" were "products of thoroughbred studs and country mares, [and] are strong and fast."[43]

Ironically, despite having named his homestead after Britain's most famous racecourse, Baylor had largely abandoned horse racing by the late 1750s, having lost most of the races in which his horses competed. Instead, as he informed his Liverpool tobacco merchant, John Backhouse, he had "chosen the wiser Part of selling Colts & Filleys, Raceing being attended with too great an Expence." Baylor imported several thoroughbreds from England and had notable breeding successes. He even ordered up a British groom (a trainer) for his horses, whom his London tobacco agent boasted was "one of the best in England" and who commanded a salary of £40 per year— more than what most planters paid their children's tutors. In 1754 he imported a chestnut, six-year-old thoroughbred stallion, *Sober John.* "I assure you," his agent Samuel Lyde declared, "I found it a very difficult matter to get one according to your Instructions, as Blooded ones are very much advanced [expensive], nothing less than from 300 to 1400 guineas." Lyde added, "even untried colts, if they have any likeliness for running will sell from 4 to 600 pounds."[44]

Lyde's admonitions about the fantastically rising costs of thoroughbreds did nothing to deter Baylor. In fact, Baylor craved still more, and he was not afraid to spend whatever it took in pursuit of his passion. He scoured the racing results in every issue of Heber's *List*—he wanted a proven Newmarket winner—but that was just the beginning. From his boyhood days at the Newmarket races, his extensive reading and long breeding experience, and his contact with other horsemen in Virginia, Baylor had formed an idealized vision of what he longed for. In addition to impressive race results, he equally desired other, less quantifiable equine characteristics, such as appearance, poise, character, and racing heart. In short, Baylor wanted the *perfect thoroughbred*, and he was willing to give up much—too much as it turned out—of his kingdom for it.

In 1762 he wrote to John Backhouse, enclosing a list of horses he deemed suitable candidates for purchase and whose race results he culled from the 1761 edition of Heber's *Historical List*. One of these—*Fearnought*—had won three King's Plate races that year in England, and had been sired by *Regulus*, who had won an astonishing seven King's Plate races in one year and was unbeaten. (*Regulus* was the sire of the *Godolphin Arabian*, one of three foundational stallions imported into England in the early eighteenth century.) Although Heber's book provided Baylor "an opportunity of discovering their performance," as he put it, it did not provide other details regarding the horses, so Baylor gave Backhouse clear specifications. He wanted a "most beautiful strong bay" horse at least fourteen hands, three inches in height or "as much higher as possible, provided he has beauty[,] strength and spi[ri]t with it, and one that has won some Kings plates with a pedigree at full length and cert[ification] of age under a nobleman's hand." And, "as to his cost," Baylor added, almost as an afterthought, "I can say nothing more than [to go] as far as you think you can venture ... not exceeding 5 or 6 hu[ndre]d Guineas." By the spring of 1764, Backhouse came through, exceeding even Baylor's extraordinary expectations.[45]

Backhouse had procured *Fearnought*, a large, strikingly beautiful bay stallion of elite Arabian pedigree that stood nary an inch under sixteen hands and cost 1,000 guineas (£1,050). This was twice the amount Baylor had authorized—a jaw-dropping sum that was more than Baylor could expect to receive from his entire annual crop of tobacco (about one hundred hogsheads) in a good year on the London and Liverpool markets. In fact, it was more than anyone else in colonial America had ever paid for a horse.[46]

Despite his stellar cost, when *Fearnought* finally arrived in the third week of June 1764 on Capt. William Quinney's ship, the *Marlborough*, Baylor was hardly displeased. Indeed, as soon as he laid eyes on *Fearnought*, he was ecstatic, and he informed Backhouse soon afterwards that the horse was "a very great Bargain" and boasted that he was "much admired by every gentleman." According to the leading nineteenth-century chronicler of race horses, *Fearnought* "was one of the most distinguished stallions ever in America" and did "more to improve the breed of thoroughbred race horses than any other stallion in the United States, of his day." Thomas Jefferson proudly noted in his farm journal that favorite mount, *Caractacus*, was the grand sire of *Fearnought*. (While Virginia governor, Jefferson famously fled a contingent of British soldiers sent to capture him at Monticello astride *Caractacus*). *Fearnought*'s genes were so highly prized that by 1900 it was "virtually impossible" to find a pedigree of any "significant" American-bred thoroughbred that didn't have multiple strains of *Fearnought* ancestry, according to renowned thoroughbred pedigree expert, Anne Peters of Three Chimneys Farm in Midway, Kentucky. Due to intensive inbreeding from a select group of horses, today's American thoroughbreds are descended from *Fearnought* hundreds or even thousands of times over. *Big Brown*, for example, who won the Kentucky Derby and Preakness races in 2008 but failed in his Triple Crown bid at Belmont, is descended from *Fearnought* an astonishing 5,734 times.[47]

Baylor's purchase of *Fearnought* marked the apex of his extravagance as well as his irredeemable slide into indebtedness. Economic difficulties in London caused by the Seven Years War were accompanied by falling tobacco prices and a significant credit crunch in Britain. Impositions in Virginia, especially taxes on land

and an ever-increasing poll tax, pinched planters' profits even more. Beginning in 1760, a series of repeated droughts and dry spells that plagued the Tidewater and eastern Piedmont through 1768 dramatically reduced the quantity and quality of the planters' crops of tobacco and corn. In 1764 a severe epidemic of smallpox killed hundreds, both black and white, in Caroline County, leaving many tobacco fields unattended and crops in ruin. Baylor, along with the majority of his fellow tobacco planters, was in serious financial trouble.[48]

Though a debtor to his merchants in England, Baylor was a large creditor to his countrymen in Caroline. (Amid the complete absence of banks and an extreme scarcity of specie, many Virginia planters, including George Washington, served as de facto bankers for their neighbors and associates.) While Caroline County was being ravaged by smallpox, Baylor wrote to John Backhouse requesting an advance of £140 because he was unable to collect £3,000 owed to him by planters and farmers in Virginia. "Poor Virginia," Baylor cried, "what art thou come to sued and held in derision by the Merchants of Great Britain particularly those of the Metropolis [London] and the Factors of Glasgow[?]" Baylor informed Backhouse that he planned to sell many of his "Horses, Mares, & Colts" in order to raise money. The Caroline County jail could not begin to hold the otherwise law-abiding citizens who were seized for unpaid debts, and Baylor, along with two other magistrates, was appointed to a committee to supervise the construction of a separate debtor's prison. Ironically, one of the committee members, William Parker, was himself locked up in the new prison upon his failure to pay one of his Glasgow tobacco merchants. And Baylor's son, John IV, would also be detained there in his final years, as discussed in the final chapter.[49]

Two years later, in 1766, Baylor was sued by one of his tobacco merchants, the flinty sharp James Ritchie of Glasgow. Baylor owed Ritchie £152—about 15 percent of the cost of *Fearnought*—more than a trifling sum but certainly not an amount that should have caused a major Virginia planter to go into default and end up in court. Noting that Baylor "saith he cannot deny he doth owe" Ritchie the money, the court entered judgment for Ritchie.[50]

The same year in which James Ritchie obtained his judgment against Baylor witnessed the unfolding of Virginia's biggest public scandal of the 1760s, in which many of the Virginia gentry, including Baylor, were financially involved. The scandal erupted following the death of John Robinson (1705-66), who served as speaker of the House of Burgesses and treasurer of the Virginia colony for nearly three decades. In the face of a growing cash and credit crisis and shrinking tobacco profits, Robinson, the most powerful potentate of his generation in Virginia, secretly loaned about £100,000 from the colonial treasury to his fellow burgesses and other patricians. The borrowers' names read like a "Who's Who" of the Virginia aristocracy: Armistead, Baylor, Bolling, Braxton, Byrd, Burwell, Carter, Fitzhugh, Lomax, Moore, Page, Randolph, and Wormeley. Baylor borrowed £335, not a huge amount compared to the largest debtors on the list, who owed thousands of pounds each, but Baylor's debt to Robinson, like most of his other obligations, remained unpaid until the 1790s.[51]

In addition to his debts to John Backhouse, James Ritchie, and John Robinson's estate, Baylor owed large sums to other creditors. By 1770, for example, Baylor's indebtedness to John Norton had swelled to £1,495. According to Norton's list of 203 Chesapeake debtors in that year, only two Virginia planters owed more, Mann Page II (£2,027) and Philip W. Claiborne (£2,155), both of whom had also borrowed money from Speaker John Robinson. The sums owed by Baylor, Page, and Claiborne stood in stark contrast to the average amount owed by all the Norton debtors—£91.25.[52]

In a letter to John Backhouse, Baylor declared that he was "determined to strictly adhere" to a Virginia boycott of imported British goods, not for the political reasons behind the nonimportation accord, but because he needed to be far more frugal. As proof of his resolve, Baylor pointed out that his want list, which he enclosed, was much shorter than in prior years. Indeed it was, but Baylor's sudden thriftiness was too little, too late, and by the time he died at Newmarket in April 1772 he was very deeply in debt and probably insolvent.[53]

Baylor left a vast estate, despite his substantial liabilities, including tens of thousands of acres of land, more than a hundred slaves, and several hundred books. Cognizant of his large library, he bequeathed "all my books" to his eldest son John Baylor IV, but only on condition that he pay to each of his brothers, Walker, George, and Robert, £25 sterling "to assist in a library which I highly recommend to be yearly added to." John Baylor IV, who would also inherit Newmarket following his mother's death, was conscious of his legacy of books. He published a notice in the *Virginia Gazette* requesting that "[a]ny Gentlemen who may have borrowed Books of any Kind from John Baylor, Esquire [his father] ... are particularly desired to return them, by the first and most convenient Opportunities."[54]

Four

A Son Inherits a Troubled Estate

Contrary to Lodge-Adams mythology about colonial Virginia, the gentry revered learning, so much so that young men of humble origins could work their way into the upper social strata through education. Philip V. Fithian, College of New Jersey graduate and tutor at Robert Carter's Nomini Hall, informed a friend who was planning his first trip to Virginia that, due to his friend's college education, he "would be rated, without any more questions asked, either about your family, your Estate, your business, or your intention, at 10,000£; and you might come, & go, & converse, & keep company, according to this value." In Robert Munford's play *The Candidates* (1770), the electors esteem—and vote for—a candidate for the House of Burgesses in large part because he was a "learned" man, even though his social rank was lower than another candidate who had been knighted in Britain. According to the modern editors of Munford's play, in colonial Virginia education was "cherished by the aristocrats" and "respected by their inferiors."[1]

At age fifteen or sixteen, John Baylor IV was sent to Putney Grammar School in Middlesex, England, as his father had been at about the same age. Before attending Putney, John IV was, as previously noted, taught by Donald Robertson and subsequently by Rev. Jonathan Boucher at his school in Caroline County, Virginia. Reverend Boucher (1738-1804), an Anglican cleric, operated his highly esteemed school there from 1762 to 1768, until he was persuaded by Daniel Dulany II and others to relocate to Annapolis, Maryland, where he taught Jacky Custis, George Washington's adopted son, Dulany's sons, and a number of other elite children.[2]

At Putney, Baylor came under the instruction of another Scotsman, the red-bearded John Chalmers. No record survives of

Baylor's impressions of his two-year stay at Putney, but one of his fellow students, William Wilberforce (1759-1833), had very vivid but less than pleasant memories of it, which he shared with his sons many years later. Wilberforce, who later became a prominent member of Parliament and is most remembered for his successful campaign to abolish the British slave trade in 1807, was eight years old when he was sent to Putney, the same year Baylor arrived. "They taught writing, French, arithmetic, and Latin," Wilberforce recalled, but "with Greek we did not much meddle." The school "was frequented chiefly by the sons of merchants," Wilberforce explained, and "they taught therefore every thing and nothing." And, like boarding school students everywhere, he could not forget the frightfully bad food: "I can remember even now the nauseous food … which I could not eat without sickness."[3]

Baylor was admitted, in 1770, to Gonville and Caius College, Cambridge, where his father and grandfather had also matriculated. Baylor was one of only about one hundred twenty elite young men in colonial America who attended Oxford or Cambridge from the founding of Jamestown in 1607 to the beginning of the American Revolution. The Virginia gentry sent more of their sons, along with a few daughters, to Britain for their education than any other colony in pre-Revolutionary America. The gentry's purpose in sending their sons to England for their education was to make each of them a "Scholar and a Gentleman," as Robert "King" Carter reminded his grandson, Lewis Burwell III (1712-56), a student at Eton. Burwell later became president of the Virginia Council.[4]

In the early spring of 1772, John Baylor IV received word that his father was gravely ill and he left for Virginia, but his father died before he arrived at Newmarket. Shortly after his homecoming, Baylor quickly dispatched a letter to John Backhouse, who was by then Newmarket's largest creditor. "I am happy to reflect with myself," Baylor wrote with blithe but unwarranted optimism, "that we have few instances of a Man in this Country bringing up the Family that my father has done, with so much Credit, and at the same time leaving such genteel fortunes … to his Children." He acknowledged the £3,836 debt owed to Backhouse, but "you may be assured," he promised breezily, "that I will have the debt paid as soon as possible." But the American Revolution and subsequent events intervened, and the bulk of the obligation was never paid until a quarter century later, when Backhouse's heirs sued Baylor over it in federal court in Virginia.[5]

John Baylor IV was not as physically robust as his forbears. An early childhood fall left him with a withered hand and palsied on his right side, a condition that became worse as he grew older. Surprisingly, given his excellent instructors in Virginia and in view of the very large library he would later assemble, Baylor does not seem to have excelled as a student before he entered Cambridge, at least in the withering assessments of some of his British relatives. When he was seventeen and still attending Putney, his British cousin John Frere claimed Baylor "was so totally deficient in reading, writing[,] French & Arithmetic, that we all thought an Academy much the proper place for him." Frere, patronizingly noting that Baylor "seems very modest and tractable" and "thoroughly sensible [aware] of the Time he has lost," hoped Baylor "would take all imaginable Pains to redeem" his academic shortcomings. Two years later, Baylor's mother, Frances, wrote him at Putney informing him how pleased his father was "at what an improvement you made in y[ou]r studies." As for Baylor's apparent wish to attend Cambridge, she replied, "If you are to be away I highly approve of y[ou]r going *to Cambridge, the most renowned Seminary of learning in all of England.*"[6]

Baylor's uncle, John Norton (1719-77), who was married to Courtenay Walker (d. 1780), the sister of Baylor's mother, held a very different opinion. Norton was the wealthy principal of John Norton & Sons, one of the major London-based tobacco consignment agents. John Norton & Sons had held on and remained successful despite heavy competition from tobacco merchants in Glasgow, whose control of the Chesapeake tobacco market became dominant by the mid-eighteenth century through their aggressive use of easy credit and their widespread network of affiliates and subagents, called factors, resident within Virginia and Maryland. On learning of his nephew's decision to attend university at Cambridge, he remarked to his son John Hatley Norton (Baylor's cousin): "I hope it [Cambridge] may answer tho' I think he has not capacity to make a scholar & had better contented himself with learning the grammar in Mother tongue properly, & reading history instead of attempting Greek Authors." Norton did not think highly of Baylor's personal finance acumen either. In another letter to John Hatley Norton, who was a partner in his father's firm, the elder Norton discussed, in his usually detailed and astringent manner, current matters with their customers, including one client who was a "perfect Quixotte" because of his spendthrift habits and for being "above taking advice." Baylor, Norton wrote, "is such another, tho I pity him most having a far less share of understanding." As we shall see, Norton was wrong about Baylor's academic potential, but was right about Baylor's lack of business savvy, which ultimately led to Baylor's undoing.[7]

While at Cambridge, Baylor, like his father, had his portrait painted (Fig. 2), but in a very different setting and context. Instead of donning rich Georgian finery, as would be typical of a young gentleman's portrait at the time, Baylor posed in his academic cap and a waistcoat-style gown worn over a simple gray flannel jacket and high-collared shirt. In a stylized pose then common (if somewhat trite) in English portraiture, his right hand (the injured one) is tucked inside his jacket. He looks studious and serious; his lips, slightly parted, seem poised as if about to speak. Baylor's scholarly mien and sober attitude seem intended to prove, perhaps to his parents and his skeptical uncle—and possibly even to himself—that he was indeed a worthy Cambridge undergraduate.

After he returned to Virginia in the summer of 1772, Baylor worked with his co-executors in an attempt to reduce the indebtedness of his father's estate, and his efforts bore some short-term relief. Lacking his father's sentimental attachments to elite horseflesh, he closed Newmarket's stud farm and sold off most of its high-priced thoroughbreds. Along with his brothers George and Robert, he petitioned the Virginia House of Burgesses to dock (i.e., break) the entail on the real estate they had inherited from their father so they could sell one-fourth of Newmarket's vast acreage to satisfy some of their father's debts. He also sold the first of what would much later become almost all his slaves.[8]

**Fig. 2. The worthy Cambridge student: John Baylor IV (1750-1808)
at about age 20. Courtesy Carter B. Filer.**

Yet before even a year had lapsed following his return to Virginia,
the still-unmarried Baylor was itching to go back to England. John
Norton's sister, Susanna Norton Turner, had predicted as much in
a letter she wrote to Baylor's cousin John Hatley Norton not long
after Baylor departed for Virginia: "[Y]our Cousin Baylor is gone
home full fraighted but not glutted with all these pastimes that
are now in Vogue; indeed he has drank so plentifully of Comus'
Cup that I wish he does not thirst after more Draughts of the same
sort in his own Country," she observed. And, "in my opinion," she
sniffed, "England has render'd him an unhappy Man," meaning that
Virginia would be a startling letdown compared to the pleasures of
London and the solemn dignity of Cambridge. She believed that if
Baylor had received definite news of his father's death, rather than a
message that he was very ill, "no one could have prevail'd on him to
have quitted England & all its alluring temptations."[9]

Susanna Turner was correct in her perceptions. Young men

from the American colonies, having spent a significant portion of their formative years attending British schools and reveling in the pleasures of London, were often ambivalent about returning home, particularly if their home was in the backcountry. The brilliant but exasperating Arthur Lee (1740-92) of Stratford Hall, for example, left Virginia at age eleven to attend Eton and remained in Britain following his 1764 graduation from the world-renowned University of Edinburgh medical school. Two years later, in a letter to his older brother Richard Henry Lee (1732-94), he wrote, "I cannot help wishing to settle in England," which he described as "the Eden of the world and the land of liberty and independence." After Arthur Lee, at his brother Richard Henry's urging, returned to Virginia, his friend Edmund Jennings Jr. attempted to console him by suggesting that his reverse culture shock on coming home was normal: "I find that you have been disappointed in your Expectations & that you sigh after the Enjoyments & that delightful Variety which London affords. I am not surprised at it[.] [N]ot one of my countrymen but have done so before on the[ir] first arrival in America." Jennings added, "Mr. [Daniel] Dulany [II] of Maryland in particular was the [most] miserable Man imaginable on his first return Home." Unlike Baylor, Arthur Lee was a younger son with no patrimony who consequently was not under the same familial duty to return and live out his days in Virginia. As it turned out, Lee, bored and alienated in Williamsburg amid bitter personal and political controversies, returned to Britain and later became part of the American diplomatic mission in Paris during the American Revolution.[10]

Girls were no less susceptible to deep disappointment in Virginia following years abroad in London. William Lee (1739-95), another of Arthur's older brothers, acknowledged that an "English Education" was "superior," but recalled his daughters to Virginia anyway because the "manners & customs of the Ladies in England are so extremely different from the Ladies here that I never knew an instance of a Young Lady Educated in England who live[d] happily here."[11]

To be sure, London, with its profound extremes of wealth and poverty and of high culture and vice, was intimidating to American colonial students at first. John Dickinson (1732-1808), who left

Delaware to study law at the Inns of Court in the mid-1750s, arrived in London during an especially dreary January and informed his mother, "I found myself in a social wilderness ... I was surrounded with noise, dirt and business." But most American students grew to appreciate if not become enamored of the city, perhaps giving credence to the old adage, "London conquers most who enter it." Four months after his arrival Dickinson concluded in a letter to his father that: "It would be impossible to enumerate all the benefits to be acquired in London, but it cannot be disputed that more is learnt of mankind here in a month than can be in a year in any other part of the world." In a subsequent letter, Dickinson wrote his father that "London is the place where a person may learn Truth" about human nature.[12]

Moreover, by the early 1770s London was vastly different from the mephitic metropolis Baylor's father had known a half century earlier. The city's main thoroughfares, once unpaved and "obstructed by mountains of filth" and refuse, were finally paved and largely cleaned up by the time Baylor arrived. The Fleet River, previously a "stinking and offensive ditch," had been covered over in 1737 and the Stocks Market—the source of much of the stench and offal in the river—was closed. Westminster Bridge opened in 1750, and seven years later London Bridge was widened and the decrepit medieval houses that were encrusted upon it like ancient barnacles were pulled down. For most of the eighteenth century, London invariably compared poorly to Paris, but by the last quarter of the century, many cosmopolitans regarded London as the superior city in which to live.[13]

In November 1772 Baylor hosted a ball in Williamsburg, attended by George Washington and other notables, but Williamsburg paled in comparison to London, and Baylor was bored and discontented. He dropped a note to his former don, William Bond (1745-1832), requesting readmittance to Caius College, but Bond coyly demurred. Failing to take the hint, Baylor made another appeal to Bond, but was turned down again, in polite but unremittingly firm terms. "[T]he usual time for scholastic exercises," Bond dryly replied, "was past with you," though Baylor was merely twenty-two years old. "[Y]our best employment," Bond advised, "would be a careful observance

of men and things together with as much judicious reading as
could be spared from the attention necessary to the culture and
improvement of your inheritance." Baylor, he asserted, was now a
"Man of the World" who could achieve "but little of importance in
the occupations of a seminary of boys." Bond further observed that
"by study and a few well-chosen books it as easy to increase one's
knowledge in Virginia as in Cambridge," and added, "I would rather
tell you painful truths than sooth you with fair speeches." Baylor's
Cambridge days were decidedly over.[14]

Baylor lingered restlessly in Virginia another two years. In
October 1775 he departed for Philadelphia, where he remained
until the following spring. His brother George W. Baylor (1752-
84) had been appointed by George Washington as his first aide-de-
camp when Washington's Continental Army was organized in the
summer of 1775. (Due to his debilitating injury, military service for
John Baylor IV was out of the question.) Baylor met his brother in
Philadelphia later that year before making his way farther north to
Boston, and from there he sailed to Glasgow the following October
or November. After touring Scotland and revisiting his old haunts
and communing with his friends in England, Baylor paid court to
his first cousin in London, Frances Norton (1759-1815). Nine years
younger than her American cousin, Frances (Fig. 3) was petite and
somewhat frail looking, with a long, aristocratic nose, small mouth,
and narrow chin. Baylor had known her since his days at Putney,
when she was scarcely seven years old. Nothing about her education
or upbringing survives, but her later correspondence indicates she
was cultivated, charming, and deeply loyal to her family. Despite
some initial reluctance on her part—family tradition has it that she
was in love with a military officer—they were engaged by the spring
of 1777.[15]

**Fig. 3. John Baylor IV and Frances Norton Baylor.
Courtesy Carter B. Filer.**

Five

A European Sojourn

Having secured his betrothal, Baylor left soon afterwards for France and remained there until January 1778 for reasons that are not clear. Circumstantial evidence suggests that he may have been involved in the convoluted swirl of intrigue and espionage associated with the American effort to obtain French assistance in the struggle for independence from Britain. In November 1775 the Continental Congress established the Committee of Correspondence (soon renamed the Committee of Secret Correspondence), the nation's first intelligence apparatus. The committee appointed three commissioners, including Benjamin Franklin, who were sent to Paris to solicit aid from Louis XVI's government. The commissioners, having but little to offer France in exchange for help, struck an agreement with the consortium of French businessmen that controlled the French tobacco monopoly whereby America would supply the monopoly with 5,000 hogsheads of tobacco. "Tobacco," proclaimed Arthur Lee, one of the three commissioners, "was the most weighty political engine we could employ with the French court." With the powerfully effective British shipping blockade in the Atlantic, however, this was much more easily said than done, and in the end very little tobacco actually reached France.[1]

Because Baylor was a major tobacco planter, his likely role, if indeed he had one, would have been to help secure the transshipment of tobacco from Virginia to France. In the summer of 1777, Baylor removed from Paris to Nantes, the spy-infested port city from which French matériel and munitions were shipped to America and to which tobacco and other American commodities would be sent, if only they could get through the British blockade. In August 1777, William Lee, who had recently been appointed by the Continental

Congress as its agent in Nantes, wrote a letter to his younger brother Arthur in Paris in which he mentioned that "Mr. Baylor presents his compliments and begs you will send to the Hotel d' York, Rue Jacob, and inquire if any letters have come there for him, and get them forwarded here to the care of Mr. Schweighauser." Jean-Daniel Schweighauser (ca. 1714-81), a Swiss-born merchant, had been appointed by William Lee as an American commercial agent in Nantes, where he was instrumental in procuring supplies for the American war effort. Baylor's cavorting with the Lee brothers and Schweighauser, as well his extended stay in Nantes, suggests that he had, or perhaps wanted to have, some connection with American war-related activities in France.[2]

At least one of the letters—now lost—that Baylor received in France was from his brother George. George Baylor, it will be recalled, was Gen. George Washington's first aide-de-camp, but his bravado and skills as an expert horseman far exceeded his utility as a secretary and letter writer. In 1777, upon Washington's recommendation, George Baylor was given command of the 3rd Continental Dragoons, a small regiment of light horse called "Baylor's Dragoons." Baylor wrote his brother George a letter of introduction for a Swiss nobleman. "The Bearer of this," Baylor began, "Baron of Bonstetten has served in the Danish and Prussian Wars, desires a Letter of recommendation to some of our officers in America as he is [a] man[,] as I am informed, of Character and is willing to enter into the Cause of Liberty and the service of the American State." Alluding to the turbulent milieu of diplomacy and chicanery in France, Baylor added: "The subject of Politics, a subject of the first importance to an American I must totally neglect, although I could write many sheets with pleasure." Baylor closed his letter by advising his brother that he "hope[d] to [be] in our Quarter this Winter."[3]

In January 1778, Baylor, accompanied by a personal servant from Germany, sailed from Le Croisic, a small port town near Nantes, on the *Thamas Koulikan*, a French merchant ship that was supposedly bound to Santo Domingo (now Haiti) in the French West Indies. The ship, built in Amsterdam and christened the *Pacifique* before it was mysteriously renamed the *Koulikan* by its Parisian owners, was a fine vessel of about 410 tons. Designed for speed and strong defense, the ship carried fourteen cannon, each a tweleve-pounder, armament more typical of a privateer than a merchant vessel. In her cargo hold were large quantities of tea, hundreds of yards of fabric (much of it buff and blue colored and suitable for American military uniforms), brandy, and several tons of salt, a commodity more precious and scarce than gunpowder in revolutionary America. Colonial Americans, who used salt to preserve meat and fish, imported nearly a million bushels of salt annually just before the Revolution, most of it from British sources, and the sudden disruption of the vital mineral was a major problem for the Americans. Lund Washington, George Washington's cousin who managed Mount Vernon while Washington commanded the Continental Army, secreted a stash of salt at Mount Vernon and, when confronted by agitated neighbors who asked him if could spare any, lied and "told them he had none." Even before the Americans declared their independence from Britain armed marauders pillaged salt and other valuables in several Virginia counties. In December 1776, Nicholas Cresswell, a British visitor in Virginia, wrote in his diary that he had seen "a Dutch mob of about 40 horsemen ... on their way to Alexandria to search for Salt." And "[i]f they find any," he noted, "they will take it by force."[4]

Also stuffed on board the *Koulikan* were hardware, lead shot, hosiery, haberdashery, cordage, sail cloth, and a dozen ship's anchors. During the ten-month period before the *Koulikan* sailed, Silas Deane, one of Benjamin Franklin's fellow commissioners in Paris, had repeatedly mentioned to French officials and merchants that these items were among those most needed in America. "No Article sells better," he wrote one correspondent, "then Salt & Coarse Goods & Sail Cloth, Cordage, &c." In a June 1777 memorandum from Benjamin Franklin to Deane, Franklin enumerated some of the "things proper to carry to America" as "Cannon, Cordage, Sailcloth, Salt, Anchors."[5]

Even before the *Koulikan* sailed, the British already knew all about her interesting cargo and dubious provenance, thanks to their vast and extraordinary network of spies in France. At the time, no European nation was blessed with better intelligence about its most dangerous enemies than Britain. Often, however, valuable information about Franco-American machinations forwarded by William Eden, later Lord Auckland (1745-1824), the brilliant head of the British Secret Service, was so prodigious and detailed that an incredulous George III refused to believe much of it and thus failed to fully exploit it. In a letter to Lord North, for example, the harried British monarch smugly informed his minister that he "was quite settled in my opinion" that every American spy in France "only gives intelligence to deceive [Britain]." But to Baylor's misfortune, on this occasion Lord North and the British navy, then the largest and most powerful in the world, made quite effective use of their intelligence resources. North instructed the First Lord of the Admiralty, the Earl of Sandwich, that his naval captains "should be expressly directed to take the *Pacifique* if they can."[6]

Four British warships prowled the Bay of Biscay off the western coast of France searching for vessels suspected of aiding the American rebels despite France's official position of neutrality. At the same time, the British navy was also on the lookout for American or French vessels laden with Chesapeake tobacco for the French market. Tobacco imports from America to Britain plummeted from 101 million pounds in 1775 to about 2.4 million pounds by 1777. According to historian Jacob M. Price, during the American Revolution more than 60 percent of Britain's tobacco came from admiralty prize seizures. John Lloyd (1735-1807), a British-born merchant who moved from Charleston, South Carolina, to Nantes in 1777, observed: "The french Ports have been and are still so carefully watched, that its scarce possible for a vessel going out, or coming in to avoid being examined."[7]

One of the British ships lurking in the Bay of Biscay, the *Hector*, a 74-gun British man-of-war, was under the able command of Sir John Hamilton (1726-84), a Welsh-born Canadian who had been made a baronet by George III in recognition of his services at the siege of Quebec in 1759. On board the *Hector* was Joseph Hynson, a villainous Maryland sailor who, just three months earlier, had intercepted and turned over to his British spymaster a large packet of ultrasecret correspondence from Benjamin Franklin and his fellow commissioners in Paris intended for the Continental Congress in Philadelphia. (Ironically, Hynson was one of the spies whom George

III wrongly suspected was an American plant.) In the early morning of Sunday, January 11, 1778, Hynson recognized the *Koulikan* as the *Pacifique*, a ship intended for trade with the American rebels, and alerted an officer on board. Taking full advantage of a strong wind that turned into a fierce squall, the *Hector* gave chase. Shortly after eleven o'clock that evening, the *Hector* fired two cannon shot across the bow of the *Koulikan*. Unable to immediately board the captured vessel due to the still-raging storm, on the following morning Sir Hamilton sent one of his lieutenants and twenty-two other men to take control of his prize and guide her into the massive naval harbor at Portsmouth, England. Upon their arrival in Portsmouth, the *Koulikan's* captain, crew, its four passengers, including Baylor and his servant, were all detained and the ship and her cargo were seized. A London newspaper heralded the capture of the "frigate built" French ship "laden with cloathing, cannon, &c and an American Gentleman [Baylor]."[8]

Imprisoned aboard the *Koulikan*, a greatly exasperated Baylor lodged a protest with Admiral Sir Thomas Pye, but to no avail. Finally, on February 5, 1778, the day before the American commissioners signed treaties of friendship and commerce in Paris formalizing the Franco-American alliance, Baylor appealed to British prime minister Lord North. Complaining that he found his confinement "by no means agreeable," Baylor denied the accusation he said had "just heard" that he had in his "possession a Treaty of Commerce to be established between the Court of France and the Congress, particularly relative to a supply of Tobacco" from Virginia. "I do candidly declare," he implored, "that I have not in my possession any such Treaty, nor have I ever had, nor yet have, any concern whatsoever in the ship." Baylor was eventually released, but was soon summoned back to give testimony in the Prize Court proceeding regarding the seizure of the *Koulikan* and her cargo under the Prohibitory Act enacted by Parliament in December 1775 in response to the American rebellion. If the court found—as its captain and crew swore was the case—that the *Koulikan* was simply conducting legitimate trade with Santo Domingo, a French colony, it would be released back to its owners. On the other hand, if the court determined that the vessel's ultimate destination was America, then the ship and her cargo would be sold off and the proceeds divided among His Majesty's treasury and Sir Hamilton and his crew (an aspect of the law that led John Adams to denounce the Prohibitory Act as the "piratical" or "plundering" act).[9]

One of the *Koulikan's* putative owners, Henri-Maximilien Grand (1757-1827), was on board the ship when she was seized. Grand, just twenty years old but full of easy bluff and self-assurance, was the son of the wealthy, Swiss-born Rodolphe-Ferdinand Grand (1726-94), Benjamin Franklin's neighbor at Passy and an important banker and fiscal agent for the American delegation in Paris. The elder Grand held and disbursed the bulk of the millions of livres loaned or given by the French government to the Americans, and he and his son were probably nominee owners of the *Koulikan* on behalf of the American commissioners. Grand and the ship's captain paraded before their captors bills of lading, letters of credit, and dozens of other ship's papers, all of which appeared legitimate and which, as Grand confidently noted in an intercepted letter to his father, "were perfectly in order" for Santo Domingo. And they were—not a single document found by the British on board the ship mentioned America. But Grand's cooperation ended there. He huffed at the suggestion that there was more to the voyage than a simple trading excursion to the French West Indies, and he remained stonily silent during his interrogations by British officials. Later, on the advice of Emmanuel-Marie-Louis, Marquis de Noailles, the French ambassador to Britain, Grand asserted his status under international law as a noncombatant passenger and French citizen on a private vessel and declined to appear at the Prize Court proceeding. Noailles had previously filed a formal protest with the British government regarding the French ship's seizure, which can "only be regarded as illegal," he fumed.[10]

In fact, Grand had much to hide. The truth was that the *Koulikan* was sailing for America. The purported stop in Santo Domingo was merely a pretext, a cover for the real destination. In late November 1777, when the *Koulikan* (i.e., the *Pacifique*) was being fitted out at Le Havre for her trans-Atlantic journey, Grand received from Silas Deane a transmittal note accompanied by letters of introduction from Deane to Benjamin Harrison V (1726-91), a Virginia planter and member of the Committee of Secret Correspondence, and to

Patrick Henry, then governor of Virginia. Deane's letter to Harrison described Grand as "a young gentleman who visits America to obtain acquaintance in the Country, and, if he find it agreeable, to establish himself in Commerce, or … the Purchase of Lands." Deane added that he wished that Virginia would "answer his [Grand's] Expectations here." Deane's cover letter also offered the names of contacts in New York and New England to whom Grand might turn for assistance, as well as this caution: "[T]he present Situation of the Country you are going to requires that you should constantly be on your Guard, and not to put Confidence in any one without his being well recommended to you by some one on whom you can rely."[11]

If Grand had these letters with him while the *Koulikan* was being pursued by the *Hector*, he destroyed them or threw them overboard—all in accordance with what by then had become the standard playbook for Franco-American smuggling operatives in the run-up to France's formal entry into the American war. A few months before the *Koulikan* departed from Nantes, Silas Deane had given orders to Pierre Landais, a French naval officer who covertly transported military supplies to America, to pretend his vessel was headed to Santo Domingo and to dispose of any incriminating documents if captured: "My advice is that you clear out in form for Saint Domingo, & be careful that you have no Papers on board that may shew the contrary except what are in your own Power, & these have always ready to be sunk in case of an attack or danger in a search."[12]

Baylor, too, initially refused to submit to interrogation. On at least two occasions, he "positively refused," according to British officials, to give any testimony. Baylor, of course, was in an untenable position—he was undoubtedly afraid of being imprisoned along with some four hundred other Americans who had been caught privateering or accused of "treason" against Britain and been thrown into dank, fetid holds across Britain. At the same time he did not want to cause Grand or any his crewmen to lose their liberty or to suffer the loss of their expensive ship and cargo. But if Baylor, at least for the time being, maintained his silence, his fellow American passenger, Alexander Boyd, was all too ready to spill his story to British interrogators.[13]

Boyd, a twenty-five-year-old native of New London, Connecticut, was an experienced sailor and ship's pilot who had relocated to Georgetown, South Carolina. Grand seriously doubted Boyd's intelligence, and in any case, Boyd, as master of the *Freeman*, an American merchant schooner, had been captured once before by the British navy in 1777 for illicit privateering, but later informed Silas Deane that he had escaped. This time around Boyd no doubt feared prolonged imprisonment. (Boyd's fears were not without justification: at Lord North's urging, in March 1777 Parliament enacted legislation authorizing captured American sailors, who were deemed—in current parlance—unlawful enemy combatants, to be imprisoned without bail or trial and without recourse to the writ of habeas corpus.) Indeed, as Grand noted, Boyd was so visibly shaken when Sir Hamilton's men boarded the *Koulikan* on January 11 that they took him aside for separate questioning. Boyd's resolve, if he had any at all, quickly melted, and before the day was over he signed a self-incriminating declaration in which he acknowledged that the ship was headed to America. At his subsequent deposition, on Friday morning, February 13, 1778, Boyd testified that the *Koulikan* was bound for Charleston, South Carolina, and that as a ship's pilot closely familiar with the South Carolina coastline he was supposed to "assist the Commander of the said Ship with his Advice and Endeavors to navigate her safely to Charles Town." Boyd said under oath that the *Koulikan*, after unloading her cargo in Charleston, was supposed to sail north to Virginia and take on a full load of tobacco before proceeding back to France.[14]

Unbeknownst to Boyd, Joseph Hynson, the American traitor, had alerted his British spy handler in November 1777 that Boyd would be on board the ship for the purpose of assisting in a voyage to America. A week later, in a memorandum labeled "Most Confidential" from Viscount Stormont, the British ambassador to France, to Lord Weymouth, the British Secretary of State, Stormont derisively referred to the arrangement for the ship as "double captains."[15]

The following month, while Grand and Baylor were in Britain cooling their heels as the Prize Court proceedings played out, Baylor apparently sought guidance from Grand about what testimony he ought to give in the case. Grand fired back an odd reply:

Your surprise is not well grounded at all. I have been threatened all along that if I would not speak or cause to speak I should go to Prison. [B]ut they have been generous enough as to take in consideration that it was a matter of Impossibility for me to do it, without running the chance of going to the Bastille for the remainder of my days if I disobeyed my Sovereign; & how can you require I should advise you to speak [?] No I can't. You may do just as you think proper. [F]or once more don't mind me any more in that affair but act for yourself & in every case let us remain good Friends.[16]

By this point the lawyer Grand's father retained to represent his interests in the Prize Court proceeding against the *Koulikan* had advised him that someone—either a crewman or passenger—on the *Koulikan* had testified under oath that the ship was bound for an American port in order to trade with the rebels. The report, based on unnamed sources at the Prize Court and made on February 10, 1778, must have been heard by the younger Grand before he wrote his letter to Baylor more than six weeks later (although there is no indication Baylor was given the information). Given Boyd's devastating confession, Grand likely decided that any effort to coordinate stories with Baylor was useless, and that the best he could do was cut his losses and get back to France as quickly as possible.[17]

Baylor was deposed on March 28, the same date as Grand's patronizing and unhelpful letter. Having been essentially abandoned by Grand, and probably aware by then of the substance of Boyd's testimony, this time Baylor did not hold back the truth. He conceded that the *Koulikan* was going to Charleston, not Santo Domingo, even though he was aware the ship's documents were made out for Santo Domingo. Pressed on what he knew regarding any disposition of papers on board the ship, Baylor admitted that "just before" the crew of the *Hector* boarded the *Koulikan*, he saw one of the crewmen, the brother of the ship's captain, throw overboard a parcel of letters and documents addressed to residents of Charleston. Finally, he acknowledged that Alexander Boyd's purpose on the ship was to help navigate the ship as the vessel approached South Carolina. The *Koulikan* and her cargo were condemned by the British government.[18]

There is no evidence that Baylor was detained following his testimony, and in any event he soon returned to Gould Square, London, where he lived at the home of his intended, Frances Norton, and her mother. (John Norton had died in October the prior year.) Baylor's activities in Britain during the rest of 1778 are largely unknown, except for his curious acquaintance with Granville Sharp (1735-1813), the brilliant and eccentric antiquarian and indefatigable antislavery activist. Sharp, an archdeacon's son who was apprenticed to a London linen draper at age fifteen, taught himself Greek and Hebrew and became so proficient at the former that he authored a seminal work of important grammatical principles still accepted today in translating text from the Greek New Testament. He was the driving force behind the *Somerset* decision (1772), in which Chief Justice Lord Mansfield famously held that an African-born Virginia slave transported to Britain could not be compelled by his slave master to leave Britain. (The decision did not, as many have mistakenly believed, end slavery in Britain, but it was an important moral victory for Sharp and his fellow abolitionists.) Sharp was highly sympathetic to the American cause and resigned his post at the government's Ordnance Department, declaring that he could not perform his "duty whilst a bloody war is carried on, unjustly as I conceive it, against my fellow-subjects."[19]

Beginning in 1777 Sharp lobbied relentlessly for American representation in Parliament, hoping such a concession would end the hostilities. (It was, of course, far too late for that.) In May 1778 he introduced Baylor, "a gentleman of fortune in Virginia," to Charles Lennox, the third Duke of Richmond (1753-1806). Lennox, sometimes called the "radical duke" because of his progressive mindset, strongly advocated British parliamentary reform, including complete manhood suffrage, and also worked toward a compromise with the Americans. "The Duke endeavoured to persuade Mr. Baylor," Sharp recorded in his diary, "that it would be advantageous to America if she would admit the constitutional connection with this kingdom by the Crown, under due limitation." But Baylor, despite his strong ties to England, would have none of it. "Mr. Baylor defended the American cause," Sharp wrote, "and could not think that dependence was at all either necessary or expedient."[20]

Preparations for Baylor's wedding to Frances Norton later that year were jolted by tragic news from America about his brother George. On September 28, 1778, Col. George Baylor, in command of the 3rd Continental Light Dragoons, was bayoneted repeatedly, including savage thrusts through his chest and lungs, during a vicious nighttime assault by British Major General Charles ("No Flint") Grey and his troops in Bergen County, New Jersey. Grey was dubbed "No Flint" because one of his favorite tactics was ordering his men to remove their musket flints, thus preventing any shots being fired, and to stealthily attack startled American rebels at night with bayonets and sabers. In what soon became known as "Baylor's Massacre," Grey's redcoats executed the maneuver with barbarous perfection, just as they had done a year earlier upon another American detachment of sleeping soldiers near Paoli, Pennsylvania. Under cries of "Skiver them!" and "Give no quarter!" Grey's redcoats mercilessly clubbed and stabbed dozens of Baylor's men even after many of them had surrendered and begged for their lives. Then, like common thugs rather than professional soldiers, some of Grey's men robbed the Americans' dead or dying bodies of money and personal effects. Despite Grey's orders that no rebel prisoners be taken, some of his junior officers, repelled by the gratuitous slaughter after about a third of Baylor's regiment had been killed or wounded, halted the bloodshed and took some prisoners anyway. According to an official American account, sixty-seven of Baylor's 104-man regiment were killed, wounded, or taken prisoner. Grey's men unceremoniously dumped the bodies of the dead into nearby tanning vats, where a few of them were excavated nearly two centuries later in 1967. Most of the badly wounded were simply left to die, except Col. Baylor, who, though barely clinging to life, was taken prisoner along with a few of his officers. (He was later exchanged but died from his wounds in Barbados in 1784.)[21]

On Wednesday, November 18, 1778, John Baylor IV and Frances Norton were married at St. Olave Church on Hart Street, near Tower

Hill, a tiny medieval church that survived the Great Fire of London in 1666 only to be completely gutted in the 1941 German blitz (it was not restored until 1954). The seventeenth-century writer and diarist Samuel Pepys regularly worshiped within its ancient stone walls and was buried there along with his wife. Frances's father, John Norton, was also interred there following his death in October 1777.

On the Saturday following their wedding the Baylors left London, never to return, and made their way to the Netherlands to book passage to America. They were likely stuck in Amsterdam longer than they wished—it was not until March 1779 that they finally sailed to St. Eustatius, a tiny, mountainous island in the Netherlands Antilles that served as America's indispensable arsenal during the American Revolution. The merchants of St. Eustatius, who were predominantly European Jews, supplied the rebellious colonies with tons of gunpowder, arms, and other critical supplies. The Baylors arrived in Philadelphia in May 1779, bringing with them many trunks full of books purchased by Baylor during this three-and-a half-year odyssey. More than six decades later, Baylor's son summarized his father's European adventure as follows: "His resources, Education, and friends enabled him to mix with the Leading circles of the day both in England and on the Continent, and on his return from abroad [he] brought with him a fine private Library."[22]

Ironically, when Baylor arrived back in his homeland, his loyalty to America was called into serious question, and his property, liberty, and reputation were all at stake as a result. He obtained written testaments of his indubitable allegiance from his brother George and from family friend and neighbor Edmund Pendleton (1721-1803), then chairman of the Caroline County Committee of Correspondence. Pendleton, a highly esteemed attorney and public servant, probably prepared the 1779 petition filed on Baylor's behalf before the Virginia House of Delegates in order to clear his name. The legislative committee that considered his petition found that "at the time of the battle of Lexington" Baylor had "manifested his attachment to the American cause," and that his "voyage to England was in consequence of an honourable engagement he had entered into with his present lady." (In fact, Baylor had not become engaged to Frances Norton until some months after he arrived in Britain.) "[D]uring his residence in England," the committee noted, his correspondence "on both sides of the Atlantic" suggested he had been a "warm advocate for the rights of America" and "a friend of the declaration of independence." Following Baylor's seizure "by a British man of war in an attempt to reach his native country" and his appearance before a British admiralty court, the legislators further observed, Baylor made a "bold avowal of his being a subject of the State of Virginia and he refused to answer any interrogatories to the prejudice of the vessel and cargo wherewith he was captured, being the property of our French allies."[23]

Interestingly, the committee report said nothing about Baylor's extended stay in France (perhaps because Baylor, by not disclosing the full story, let the legislators believe that he had gone to France only to obtain passage back to America). Moreover, the statement that Baylor "refused to answer any interrogatories" was not entirely true either, for although Baylor initially kept his silence under undoubted threats and intimidations, after he learned or suspected that Boyd had sold everyone out and Henri Grand had abandoned him, he did admit in his deposition that the ship's purported *raison d'être* was an elaborate lie. Nevertheless, because of the ongoing hostilities with Britain there was no ready way to know what Baylor had said in his deposition, so the committee members—very much aware of Baylor's elite socioeconomic status and the sacrifices his valiant brother George had made for his country—must have taken Baylor's explanation at face value. The committee resolved that Baylor had "uniformly acted as a friend to the interests of America," and he was able to resume life at Newmarket.

Six

Classics and History

John Baylor IV's library of twelve to thirteen hundred volumes was an assemblage of his father's library, the books he purchased in England and France, the books he acquired in America, including Williamsburg and Philadelphia, and finally the books he ordered through British merchants as his father had done. Because, as discussed below, Baylor's library was hurriedly sold off to satisfy creditors in the months just before his death, no catalogue of his entire library exists, in contrast to the book collections of Thomas Jefferson, William Byrd II, and Robert Carter of Nomini Hall, who owned, respectively, the three largest private libraries in colonial Virginia. Fortunately, four surviving sources reveal roughly a third of the contents of Baylor's library: (1) his father's business letterbook, which includes some of Col. John Baylor III's book orders from his British merchants; (2) his father's estate inventory; (3) the *Virginia Gazette* daybooks, as discussed above; and (4) a handwritten catalogue of mostly French and European authors and titles. The books mentioned in these sources are listed in the Appendix.

Colonel Baylor's letterbook has been used by historians since it became publicly available in the 1920s, mostly for the rich detail it imparts about the life of a major (and heavily indebted) Virginia tobacco planter, but curiously not as a source for private Virginia libraries or studies regarding the reading habits of the Virginia gentry. His estate inventory was previously unknown because most of the early probate records of Caroline County, Virginia, where it was recorded, were destroyed during the Civil War. A copy of it was filed by John Baylor IV's administrator, Thomas R. Rootes III, in *Daingerfield v. Rootes*, one of the many suits filed against John

Baylor IV's estate following his death, and a duplicate was found by the author in 2006 among the pleadings in the case.[1]

The most intriguing, and in many ways the most confounding, source is the French and European author-book catalogue, which became available to scholars in the 1940s as part of the University of Virginia's 2,000-item "Baylor Family Papers," but which appears to have been completely overlooked. The two-page catalogue, unsigned and undated—tucked within a folder labeled "Miscellaneous"—sets forth the names of leading French and European Enlightenment figures generally in order of their dates of death, beginning with astronomer Pierre Gassendi (1592-1655) and ending with French historian Abbé Raynal (1713-96). Most of the items on the list, which does not appear to be in John Baylor IV's handwriting, include anglicized short titles next to the authors' names. In many cases the list appears to refer to a collected-works edition of the authors' works.[2]

Of course, the most obvious question is, what was the purpose of this list? Was it some kind of academic exercise or perhaps a Virginia planter's pretension on a forgotten winter's evening? The evidence, though admittedly circumstantial, would suggest otherwise. Certain notations on the list refer specifically to a particular published version of the author's work, as if made from an actual book collection (rather than a mere list of book titles). For example, the entry for François Eudes de Mézeray mentions an "Abridgement" of Mézeray's *Histoire de France*. Similarly, the short title associated with French dramatist Pierre Corneille is "30 Dramatic Pieces." Moreover, the historical context associated with John Baylor IV— his having spent more almost a year in France (where he acquired "a fine private library," his son later recalled) and the fact that the quantity of books he inherited from his father composed less than a third of his entire library—indicate that the catalogue was almost certainly made with reference to his library at Newmarket. Finally, as we shall see, John Baylor IV had a pronounced predilection for aesthetic and cultural grandeur, and his acquisition of the works mentioned on the author-book catalogue was entirely consistent with this aspect of his character.[3]

Because these sources permit reconstruction of less than a third of John Baylor IV's library, one must of course be circumspect in forming interpretations or drawing broad conclusions about the collection as a whole, especially regarding the literary inclinations or reading habits of its owners. Moreover, any specific subject matter classification, as is usually performed when studying historic private libraries, would be inherently suspect. On the other hand, there are more than enough titles among the sources that merit some discussion and observations.

*   *   *

Much of the known Baylor library was typical of an eighteenth-century elite Virginia planter's book collection. The library included the usual Roman classics and Latin books, such as Caesar's *Commentaries*, Gordon's *Tacitus*, Lily's *Grammar*, Ovid's *Metamorphoses*, and works by Virgil, Livy, and Juvenal. Lily's *Grammar*, perhaps the most common of these books in colonial Virginia, was remembered by Virginia governor and planter John Page as an "insipid and unintelligible book," though subsequently, with the benefit of a "faithful and ingenious young" instructor, he acknowledged that it was an "excellent Key to the Latin Language."[4]

Regarding Greek-language books, as Wilberforce noted regarding his Scottish-influenced education, "with Greek we did not much meddle," nor does it seem the Baylors did either, for no Greek titles, either in translation or otherwise, appear within the sources for their library except Ann Dacier's French translation of the *Iliad* (1699). Contrary to some scholarly assertions that facility in Greek was, for example, "considered essential for preserving and manifesting the amenities of a cultivated life" among Virginia gentlemen, only a tiny handful of the Chesapeake elite bothered with ancient Greek in its original lexicon after they completed their formal education.[5]

Apparently some scholars, blinded by the lexicographical brilliance of a few colonial Virginians, have failed to realize the exceptionalism of these men. Richard Lee II (1647-1715) kept his diary notations in Greek, Latin, and Hebrew. William Byrd II, who had studied Greek and owned more Greek-language books than anyone else in colonial Virginia, composed his sappy marriage proposal to his second wife in that language, admitting that he "went completely crazy" over her after he learned that that she was conversant in Greek, the "tongue of the Muses" (though strangely he requested that she reply in English in care of his London coffee house). Laboring under the mistaken belief that Homer had "invented" ancient Greek, young Ben Carter of Nomini Hall cursed the blind poet and "wished that he might kick Him" while his tutor Philip V. Fithian sought to conduct his Greek lesson. Thomas Jefferson, under the tutelage of classical scholar Rev. James Maury (1719-69), was often seen "with his Greek Grammar in his hand" while his fellow students played. Two years later Jefferson read law at the College of William and Mary under the direction of the brilliant and learned George Wythe (1726-1806), who was said to have had a "perfect knowledge of the Greek language."[6]

Much, too, has been made of the influence of ancient Greek writers and philosophers upon the Founders, as if most of the venerated generation who cited Plato, Euripides, Herodotus, Thucydides, Aristotle, Xenophon, Polybius, or Plutarch in their writings translated directly from the language of Homer. But the reality is that Lee, Byrd, Jefferson, and Wythe were by far the exceptions in Virginia and Maryland. If they owned books by ancient Greek authors at all, most of the Chesapeake gentry, like the majority of their elite counterparts elsewhere in colonial America, preferred them in Latin or English translation. Indeed, of the 148 titles recommended by Thomas Jefferson for a busy gentleman's library, he listed only four titles by ancient Greek authors, all in English translation: Alexander Pope's *Iliad* (1715-1720) and *Odyssey* (1725-1726); Sarah Fielding's *Xenophon's Memoirs of Socrates* (1762); and Elizabeth Carter's *Epictetus* (1758). During the period 1736-80, the *Virginia Gazette* published retail book advertisements for fourteen classical Greek authors, including Aesop, Homer, Plato, Isocrates, Thucydides, and Xenophon. Although several of the advertised books were Greek-Latin editions (such as Samuel Clarke's *Homeri Opera Omnia* [1743]), most were in English translation. Plato's works were available only in an abridged English edition, translated from Anne Dacier's French version. Moreover, all of these titles were published in Britain and imported, suggesting no one in Virginia had the ability or the inclination to publish a Greek-language book. The same was true elsewhere in eighteenth-century colonial America: only 28 books were published in Latin, and only three were published in Greek (two of which were reprints of Greek grammars first published in Britain).[7]

Although Jefferson did not suggest any Greek-language books to Robert Skipwith, he firmly believed that high proficiency in Greek was necessary for the learned professions, including medicine and law. Writing from Paris in 1785, Jefferson exhorted his nephew Peter Carr (1770-1815), who lived at Monticello, to study more than two dozen Greco-Roman authors and to read "every thing in the original and not in translation." Similarly, in the 1770s he advised Bernard Moore, a "young friend" about to embark on his legal education, to read ancient history in "the Greek and Latin originals." Jefferson revered ancient Greek as "the finest of human languages," but despite his passion for the language very few of his American contemporaries actually read full-length books by ancient Greek authors in their original lexicon.[8]

Jefferson's attitude about classical language studies was almost certainly influenced by his boyhood teacher, Rev. James Maury. Maury held that "[a]n Acquaintance with the Languages, anciently spoken in Greece & Italy" was "absolutely necessary" in order to cut a "reputable Figure in Divinity, Medicine or Law." He also believed that concentration in Greco-Roman languages was "delightful, ornamental & useful, nay even necessary" for those "in some other Parts of the World [who] turn in more exalted Spheres of Life," such as the British aristocracy. But Maury, anticipating a strain of pragmatism that has run through American education since the Revolution, rejected heavy immersion in Greek and Latin for most of the Virginia gentry. The problem was time or, more precisely, a lack of it. While the British aristocracy were true creatures of leisure, the Virginia gentry, for the most part, needed to dedicate a significant amount of their time to actively managing their business affairs. "[P]rudent Management of a large Virginia estate," Maury wrote, "requires so frequent & close an Inspection" in order to successfully operate it that once a planter's son assumes control of it he "can expect but little of that Leisure & Repose, which are requisite for a pleasurable or successful Engagement in such Parts of Literature, as the Languages, Criticism, & curious & deep Researches into Antiquity."[9]

Richard Ambler (1690-1766), a prosperous Yorktown merchant who sent two of his sons to English boarding schools in the late 1740s to obtain the fine education he thought he lacked, completely agreed with Maury's belief that children of Virginia planters must be taught the classics as well as more practical subjects. "I do not mean to confine you to any part or branch of Learning," Ambler informed his sons, adding that he was willing to allow both of them to pursue "any branch of learning which suits your genious or inclination." But at the same time Ambler had a core curriculum in mind: "Latin, French, writing and Accounts especially the latter, must by no means by omitted, as it is likely it may fall to one or both your lots to be concern'd in Trade or Commerce but that will be left to your choice."[10]

This is not to suggest that college-educated or well-tutored colonial Americans eschewed ancient Greek entirely or did not have basic familiarity with certain Greek writings. After all, most had little choice in the matter. Harvard required successful applicants to demonstrate an ability to "read, construe, and parse" selected Greek texts, such as the New Testament. Yale and the College of New Jersey (later Princeton) had similar requirements. King's College (later Columbia) insisted that its matriculants be able "to render into English, *Caesar's Commentaries of the Gallic War*, the four orations of Cicero vs. Catiline; the first four Books of Vergil's *Aeneid*, and the Gospels from the Greek." The charter for the College of William and Mary's grammar school, which required four years of Latin and two of Greek, peremptorily declared, "[L]et the Latin and Greek Tongues be well taught." William and Mary's grammar school students who wished to go on to its college (called the philosophy school) were required to demonstrate to the president and faculty of the college they had "made due progress in their Latin and Greek."[11]

Though many children of the Virginia gentry were, like the Baylors, required to have some Greek-language education, very few made much of an effort to retain their facility in Greek after the end of their formal education except for intellectuals such as Lee,

Byrd, Jefferson, or Wythe, each of whom had a lifelong passion for classical learning. Jacky Custis, who had studied ancient Greek at the very learned Rev. Jonathan Boucher's school for elite boys, owned a few Greek lexicons and grammars among his nearly 600 volumes when he died, but he owned only one other book written in the ancient language, a Greek New Testament. Likewise, John Mercer, George Washington's attorney, esteemed author of an abridgment of Virginia laws and master of a library of between 1,500 and 1,800 books, owned a Greek grammar and a Greek New Testament, but no other Greek-language titles. Virginia's first state governor, Patrick Henry, who apparently had a solid education in Latin and Greek as a lad under his university-educated father's tutelage, said that he had "not looked into a Latin book" since he was fifteen. When, as a rising statesman and unrivaled public speaker, Henry wanted a volume of speeches by Demosthenes, the ancient Athenian orator, he chose Thomas Leland's popular English translation, *Orations of Demosthenes* (1763). At his death, the only Greek-language books he owned were a few Greek grammars and lexicons from his childhood and a Greek New Testament.[12]

Scholars debate the influence of Greco-Roman authors upon the Founders. In his important study of the most influential political pamphlets in the run-up to the American Revolution, Bernard Bailyn concluded that "often the [classical] citations appear to have been dragged in as 'window dressing with which to ornament a page or a speech and to increase the weight of the argument.'" Carl J. Richard, on the other hand, believes "the classics exerted a formative influence upon the founders, both directly and through the mediation of Whig and American perspectives." As Carl J. Richard, Forrest McDonald, and other historians have posited, the weight of the evidence supports the view that Greco-Roman authors indeed had a profound impact on the Founders' thinking, but two important points should also be borne in mind: the majority of the Founders read and understood the ancients, particularly the Greeks, in translation, and the Founders tended to draw upon the ancients in much the same way appellate lawyers rely on useful legal precedents in preparing their briefs— selectively, sometimes out of context, and, most importantly, with an avowed intention to win the argument rather than in a philosophic search for the truth.[13]

*   *   *

The Baylors owned what might be described as the core trinity of religious books in colonial America: the Bible; the *Book of Common Prayer* (1549); and Richard Allestree's *Whole Duty of Man* (1658). Aside from the Bible, Allestree's moral guidebook was the most popular religious tract in English in the seventeenth and eighteenth centuries. (The book's subtitle clearly reveals Allestree's purpose in setting down his religious precepts "in a plain and familiar way, for the use of all, but especially the meanest reader.") Along with the Bible and the *Book of Common Prayer*, *Whole Duty of Man* was an ubiquitous fixture in even modest colonial Chesapeake households. Sarah Ball, for example, who died in Lancaster County, Virginia, in 1742, is recorded as owning only these three books and no others. Likewise, the only books held by Sarah Jones (d. 1720) of Northumberland County, Virginia, were a Bible, a primer, and *Whole Duty of Man*. The personal library of Sabine T. Marshall (d. 1768) of Charles County, Maryland, consisted of only a Bible, a prayer book, a book of sermons, a four-volume edition of *Don Quixote*, and a copy of *Whole Duty of Man*. The *Virginia Gazette* bookstore always had ready copies of *Whole Duty of Man* available for purchase, and it was one of the very few book-length titles the *Gazette* printed (other than official publications for the Virginia colonial government). In a study of 1,911 Maryland probate inventories covering the period 1718-47, *Whole Duty of Man* was one of the most frequently listed books. An analysis of eighteenth-century probate inventories in Northumberland County, Virginia, indicated that *Whole Duty of Man* was the most popular devotional book after the Bible.[14]

The Baylors also owned a few other religious books published in Britain, including: *A Treatise on the Passions and Faculties of the Soul of Man*, first published by Edward Reynolds (1599-1676) in 1647; *History of the Reformation* (1679-1714), by Scottish theologian and historian Gilbert Burnet (1643-1715); and *New History of the Holy Bible* (1737), by Thomas Stackhouse (1677-1752). Stackhouse, the vicar of Beenham Parish in Berkshire, England, who turned to writing in order to climb out of poverty, was especially fond of drink and reputedly wrote his *New History* largely in a booth of his local pub.[15]

In contrast to their apparently small collection of religious works, the Baylors owned a number of "useful" titles for both plantation operations and sport, including: *A New System of Agriculture* (as noted above); *Farriery Improv'd* (1737-40); *The Art of Farriery* (1758); *A New Treatise on the Diseases of Horses* (1751); *A New and Complete System of Practical Husbandry* (1762-65); *The Modern Husbandman* (1750); *The Complete Farmer* (1776); *Sportsman's Dictionary* (1735); and Cheny's and Heber's annual horse racing calendars mentioned above. Though not formally educated in the law, John Baylor IV, like his father, served as a justice of the peace in Caroline County after the Revolution, but if he owned any Virginia law books (his father owned at least three) they were sold in the creditor's liquidation of his personal assets.

Like their Virginia peers, the Baylors were immensely fond of histories and biographies. They owned a half set of Gibbon's six-volume *Decline and Fall of the Roman Empire* (1776-87), all four volumes of Lord Lyttelton's *Life of King Henry the Second* (1767-71), and the eight-volume revised edition of David Hume's *History of England* (1763). Colonel Baylor III's estate inventory mentions the Earl of Clarendon's *History of the Rebellion and Civil Wars in Ireland* (1719), but curiously not Clarendon's far more popular *History of the Rebellion and Civil Wars in England* (1702-03). Baylor owned at least half of the highly-esteemed twenty-one-volume *Universal History* (1747-51), by George Sale and others, and all or most of the series' subsequent forty-four volumes published under the title *The Modern Part of An Universal History* (1759-66), whose principal contributor was Tobias Smollett (1721-71). Smollett, a Scottish surgeon and prolific author best known for his novel, *Peregrine Pickle* (1751), also wrote a five-volume *Continuation* (1760-65) of his earlier *Complete History of England* (1757-58). The Baylors also owned Smollett's *Continuation*. The *Universal History* series was popular among the literate who could afford it in colonial America, and Smollett's *Modern Part* was sold by booksellers in New York, Boston, Philadelphia, Williamsburg, and Charleston.[16]

In addition to Smollett, the Baylors owned other important works by Scottish historians who were well known to the Virginia gentry and the Founders. Thomas Salmon (1697-1767), a Scottish geographer and historical writer, published his massive thirty-two-volume *Modern History* between 1725 and 1739. Colonel Baylor III ordered an indeterminate number of volumes of Salmon's *magnum opus* from one of his London tobacco merchants, and he purchased Salmon's two-volume *Universal Traveler* (1752-53), along with William Robertson's two-volume *History of Scotland* (1758-59), from the *Virginia Gazette*. Along with David Hume and Edward Gibbon, William Robertson (1721-93) was one of the leading historians of the Scottish Enlightenment, and his *History of Scotland* was popular in both colonial New England and the South.[17]

"To the eighteenth century colonist," wrote Trevor Colbourn, "the study of history was a prestigious and a practical pursuit." Colbourn, historian and author of a now-classic study of the use and interpretation of history by the Founders, argued that colonial Americans established much of the intellectual foundation for their rebellion against their mother country on their close, albeit highly selective, reading of history, particularly "Whiggish" histories of Britain. Broadly speaking, eighteenth-century British historiography was largely divided into two intellectual camps: "Tory" and "Whig" (in this context, neither refers to political party affiliation, but rather to a point of view). Whig history emphasized a romanticized version of pre-Norman, Anglo-Saxon England, in which land was owned outright (rather than held under the yoke of a feudal lord) by liberty-loving farmers whose monarch was not an absolute ruler and who governed themselves through representative assemblies that prefigured Parliament. Tory history, on the other hand, did not find ancient antecedents for Parliament among the Saxons and exalted post-Norman law and order and benevolent but powerful monarchs.[18]

One of the most important eighteenth-century Whig historians was Paul de Rapin-Thoyras (1661-1725), a French Protestant and historian who fled France for England after revocation of the Edict of Nantes. Rapin performed military service for Britain in Ireland and was granted a stipend by William III that enabled him to toil for seventeen years on his *Histoire d'Angleterre* (1724-27), a ten-volume history of England from the Roman invasion to the death of Charles I. Drawing upon Tacitus's works, Rapin wrote that the Anglo-Saxons were descended from the ancient German tribes who migrated to England and brought with them democratic institutions, including an elected king and legislative assembly called a *witenagemot*. Rapin's *Histoire d'Angleterre*, which was also published in a popular English translation (*History of England*), greatly influenced other eighteenth-century historians of Britain and was a major source of the "Saxon myth," as it is called today, of the simple purity and superiority of ancient Saxon government, a historical viewpoint that persisted well into the nineteenth and even the early twentieth centuries. In colonial America, Rapin's "radically Whiggish" interpretation of British history, as Bernard Bailyn referred to it, was well known and widely accepted among the elite, especially Thomas Jefferson, who read his father's copy as a young boy. Even as late as 1825, Jefferson believed that "[t]here is as yet no general history [of Britain] so faithful as Rapin's," which was by then a century old. Among the Chesapeake elite, William Byrd II, Daniel Dulany I, Charles Carroll of Carrollton, and Robert Carter of Nomini Hall all owned a copy of Rapin's *History* in English. John Baylor IV, along with Byrd and Jefferson, owned a French-language edition.[19]

If Jefferson greatly admired Rapin's *History of England*, he utterly detested David Hume's work of the same name—which the Baylors also owned—with a censorious vehemence that has made Jefferson's biographers blush. Though generally known today as a brilliant and important Scottish philosopher and political economist, Hume (1711-76) was more renowned during his life as a historian. He published his best-selling *History of England* in four installments from 1754 to 1762, covering the period from the Roman invasion of Britain to the Glorious Revolution in 1688. Jefferson assailed Hume's "Tory" interpretation of British history that the supposed representative democracy of the Anglo-Saxons did not really exist and that the causes of the English civil wars lay as much in the illicit and unprincipled usurpations of authority by the House of

Commons as in the monarchical despotism and intransigence of the Stuarts. In particular, Hume challenged the historical basis of the most fundamental tenet of the Whigs—the existence of an "ancient constitution" that supposedly predated Parliament, and even the common law itself.

Hume's skepticism did not make him a Tory apologist; in fact, his *History* was far more accurate and balanced than Rapin's. "The truth is," Hume revealed to a correspondent while writing his first volume, "there is so much reason to blame and praise, alternately, king and parliament, that I am afraid the mixture of both, in my composition, being so equal, may pass sometimes for an affectation, and not the result of judgment and evidence." Hume insisted, "I am of no party, and have no bias." Indeed, just as he had feared, in his effort to spread "blame and praise" fairly Hume managed to offend a number of Tories and Whigs alike. Still, according to his modern biographer, Hume's *History* accomplished for his era "a broad sweeping narrative of the national developments, philosophically coherent, artistically ordered, and pre-eminently readable."[20]

Voltaire pronounced Hume's *History* as "perhaps the best ever written in any language." Jefferson, too, acknowledged that, compared to Rapin's work, Hume's version of British history was much better written, but for Jefferson that was precisely the problem. Hume's *History* "is so plausible & pleasing in it's style and manner," Jefferson wrote, "as to instil it's errors and heresies insensibly into the minds of unwary readers." In fact, Hume's prose was so insidiously elegant and convincing, so full of "poison," as Jefferson snidely put it, that as he planned a library for the University of Virginia Jefferson was genuinely fearful that impressionable young students would be taken in by Hume's artful verse and become unwitting Tory dupes unless they were properly guided otherwise. Jefferson's paranoia notwithstanding, Hume's *History of England* quickly displaced Rapin's version in Britain and America and remained the leading history of its kind until the publication of Macaulay's *History of England* (1848-55).[21]

One of the most interesting items in the Baylors' library was a manuscript copy of the *Letters of Junius* (1772). Under the pseudonym "Junius," a clever and well-informed British government insider wrote a series of sardonic letters that accused, with much justification, several of George III's ministers, especially the Prime Minister, the third Duke of Grafton, of corruption and immorality. The letters, which were almost certainly written by war office employee Philip Francis (1740-1818) (later knighted), were published in a London newspaper, the *Public Advertiser*, from January 1769 to January 1772. Junius's letters, as well as rampant speculation over their authorship, created a powerful buzz that raged through London's coffee houses and taverns and that eventually stormed through Whitehall, leading to Grafton's resignation in 1770.[22]

Precisely how—and why—John Baylor IV acquired or produced the manuscript, which appears to be in his handwriting, is unknown. In a memorial composed many years after Baylor's death, his son, John Baylor V (1785-1865), said his father was the "Bosom friend of Junius" and was so impressed with the letters as they appeared in the *Public Advertiser* that he faithfully copied them all into a folio journal. Interestingly, Baylor's son also suggested that his father revered Junius's letters primarily because they eloquently revealed the true cause of colonial American resentment toward the British— the arrogance, intransigence, and venality of their government ministries. A second explanation of the manuscript comes from Virginia historian Robert A. Brock (1839-1914), who understood from a later generation of Baylor's descendants that John Baylor IV befriended Sir Philip Francis, the putative author of the letters. Following Baylor's marriage to Frances Norton in London, Baylor and his bride were, Brock wrote, houseguests at Sir Philip's home, where he reportedly handed over his holographic copy of the letters as a gift to Baylor, presumably on condition that Baylor not disclose their author's identity. The account of Baylor's son, who inherited the manuscript and was closer in kinship and time to its original owner, is probably the correct one. The story of Baylor's acquaintance with Sir Francis, however, is also entirely plausible, and it is quite possible that such a relationship, if it existed, was convoluted with the origin of the manuscript, as so often happens over multiple generations of family history.[23]

The Baylors' known collection of British literature is relatively scant, but still typical of the Virginia gentry. They owned

Miscellaneous Works: In Verse and Prose by Joseph Addison, co-founder of *The Spectator*, which included *Cato, A Tragedy*, his Roman-era play that was first performed in London in 1713 to the wide adulation of Tories and Whigs alike. *Cato* eventually became even more popular in colonial America than in Britain, especially among the Founders. Patrick Henry's incendiary roar, "Give me liberty or give me death," was derived from lines in the play. Nathan Hale's supposed final utterance from the gallows, "I regret that I have but one life to give for my country," paraphrases another line from *Cato*: "What a pity it is that we can die but once to save our country." *Cato* was George Washington's favorite play, and he quoted from it often. During the brutally harsh winter of 1777-78, Washington had it performed repeatedly for his beleaguered soldiers at Valley Forge to boost their morale.[24]

In 1759 Laurence Sterne (1713-1768), an Anglican minister, anonymously published the first two-volume installment of his comic masterpiece, *Tristram Shandy*, which Col. Baylor III ordered from London by the following year. *Tristram Shandy*'s heavy but clever use of innuendo and constant double entendre created a sensation, and when it became known that the bawdy novel's author was a clergyman, a scandal erupted. One contemporary critic acknowledged the author's "original and uncommon abilities" in writing style, but denounced the book as "indecent" and full of "downright gross and obscene expressions." In fact, Sterne's slyly salacious style was anything but gross, and as literary critic Brooke Allen has pointed out, Sterne's avant-garde work was imbued with a strikingly modern free-thinking liberalism and deep self-consciousness that has inspired writers such as Vladimir Nabokov and Salman Rushdie. Sterne had his detractors in America, too, but he also had a number of intense admirers, especially Thomas Jefferson and his wife, Martha Wayles Jefferson.[25]

As Martha Jefferson lay dying in 1782, she paraphrased one of their favorite passages from the ninth and final volume of *Tristram Shandy* on a scrap of paper: "Time wastes too fast: every letter I trace tells me with what rapidity life follows my pen. The days and hours of it are flying over our heads like clouds of [a] windy day never to return more[.] [E]verything presses on[.]" Jefferson completed the passage where she left off: "[A]nd every time I kiss thy hand to bid adieu, every absence which follows it, are preludes to that eternal separation which we are shortly to make!" After his wife's death Jefferson folded the paper with a lock of her hair inside and stashed the cherished memento in a secret drawer beside his bed, where it remained for forty-four years until his death. "The writings of Sterne," Jefferson declared to his nephew some years after Martha's death, "form the best course of morality that was ever written."[26]

Patrick Henry was known to have read *Tristram Shandy* for "several hours together, lying with his back upon a bed." George Washington's correspondence indicates that he was familiar with and had probably read at least some of *Tristram Shandy*, but no copy of it was found within his vast library at Mount Vernon after his death, perhaps because his staid sense of proprietary prevented him from actually possessing a copy of such a smutty book, however much he might have privately enjoyed it.[27]

The Baylors owned a collection of works by Jonathan Swift (1667-1745), as well as the Earl of Orrey's biography of Swift, *Remarks on the Life and Writings of Jonathan Swift* (1751), which a recent authority has denounced as "dull and malicious" and a "Judas-biography ... by someone who once claimed the writer as a close friend." They also owned Dryden's *Virgil* and a set of Shakespeare's works, as well as collected works by Charles Churchill (1731-64) and Edward Young (1683-1765). Churchill, a fierce satirist and poet now known chiefly among British literary scholars, emerged from obscurity in Britain with the publication of his poem *Rosciad* in 1761. Several years later he was so popular among the Virginia gentry that when, for example, Richard Henry Lee asked Landon Carter in a letter postscript whether Carter "[c]ould spare ... for a short time, Churchill's prophecy of famine, and his poem on retirement," no further description was necessary. In 1768 Anglo-American bookseller James Rivington (1724-1802) published an enormously successful edition of Churchill's complete poems in which he listed some 2,200 North American subscribers, most of whom were from the Chesapeake.[28]

Edward Young, also virtually unheard of today, was an immensely popular British dramatist and poet during his life and throughout the eighteenth century. Young's most famous poem, *Night Thoughts*, went through forty-eight authorized editions during his lifetime (including compilations) and was illustrated by William Blake in 1797. Thomas Jefferson wrote out long passages from *Night Thoughts* in his commonplace book and quoted the poem in his correspondence with John and Abigail Adams.[29]

Given that Col. Baylor III sent his daughters to boarding school in England, he undoubtedly had serious regard for their reading habits and education. Although no extant records indicate for certain that he bought any particular books for his wife or daughters, it appears from at least one of his *Virginia Gazette* book orders that he had them in mind when he bought books. In February 1764 he purchased: Eliza Haywood's periodical, the *Female Spectator* (1744-46); Frances Brooke's epistolary novel of sensibility, *The History of Julia Mandeville* (1763); Lady Mary Wortley Montagu's *Letters of the Right Honourable Lady M——ry W—— M——e* (1763); John Langhorne's now entirely forgotten epistolary novel, *The Effusions of Friendship and Fancy* (1763); and Jean-Jacques Rousseau's *Eloisa* (1761) and *Emilius and Sophia* (1762), both in English translation. A month later he purchased from the *Gazette* Tobias Smollett's novel *Roderick Random* (1748) and Voltaire's *Candide* (in English) (1759).[30]

Interestingly, with the exception of *The Female Spectator* and Langhorne's novel, each of these works appeared on the list of books recommended by Thomas Jefferson to his future brother-in-law Robert Skipwith as the critical components of a "gentleman's library." To be sure, these books were read by men and women alike, but they appear to have been more popular with women, especially France Brooke's and Lady Montagu's works. On a pallid September morning in 1787, Lucinda Lee, daughter of Thomas Ludwell Lee, wrote in her journal that she "spent this morning in reading *Lady Julia Mandeville* and was much affected" by it. "Indeed," she confided, "I think I never cried more in my life reading a Novel: the stile is beautiful, but the tale is horrid."[31]

Protofeminist Lady Montagu (1689-1762), the eldest daughter of the Earl (later Duke) of Kingston, eloped with Edward Wortley Montagu, MP, in 1712 and accompanied him to Istanbul four years later when he was appointed British ambassador to the Ottoman Empire (now Turkey). Her book, often called the *Turkish Embassy Letters*, was based on her journal and the letters she wrote in Istanbul and Austria, which she subsequently revised and liberally embroidered into an epistolary travel account of her journey and experiences.[32]

It is also worth noting that, as was the case with hundreds of other books, the *Virginia Gazette* had Frances Brooke's and Lady Montagu's works available for sale within months after they came off the press in London, and that Col. Baylor III, who no doubt read about them in the *Monthly Review* and *Gentleman's Magazine*, acquired them less than a year following their publication. So prevalent was the culture of secular books and printed matter in Virginia's capital (at least for those who could afford them) that an early-twentieth-century student of the *Gazette* concluded: "Literary London was far nearer Williamsburg than Boston."[33]

Given their British educations and socioeconomic status, as well as the other books they were known to have owned, the Baylors probably also held other works of literature by authors such as Chaucer, Milton, Pope, and Johnson, but these may have been disposed of in the creditor's sale of John Baylor IV's assets.

Seven

The Enlightenment Books

In addition to its size, the Baylor library stood apart from most other private libraries in the Chesapeake due to its large assortment of books by French and European authors. French was not widely spoken or studied in British colonial America, particularly in the South. France and England had been enemies for centuries and fought a succession of wars in the eighteenth century, and the French and Indian War, which ended in 1763, left many Americans with only bitter feelings about the French. Prior to the Revolution, Harvard College categorically refused gifts of French books for its library, even monumental accomplishments such as Pierre Bayle's *Dictionnaire historique*. Silas Deane, a lawyer and Yale graduate who, as noted in Chapter 5, was part of the American delegation in Paris during the Revolution, complained in a letter to Ezra Stiles, Yale's president, that while in Paris he had "experienced the many difficulties & embarrassments which a man doing Business abroad labors under who is ignorant of any modern Language except his own." Deane, whose frank admission makes him sound as if he were the original "ugly American," urged President Stiles to "establish a Professor of the French Language" at Yale and to assemble a "collection of the Writings of their most celebrated Authors for your Library." But fearing "Popery," among other reservations, Yale's governing trustees wanted no part of French-language education, and it was not until 1825 that Yale officially offered French as a course of study. Prior to his diplomatic service in Paris, Thomas Jefferson recommended a number of works by French authors to Robert Skipwith, including Molière, Fénelon, Rousseau, and Voltaire, but he specifically suggested each in English translation.[1]

Richard Beale Davis bullishly declared: "French appears to have been read with relative ease from Maryland to Georgia." Professor Davis based his conclusion upon the significant presence of French dictionaries and grammars in eighteenth-century estate inventories and surviving book lists from the colonial South. The most popular of these lexicons were Abel Boyer's English-French *Royal Dictionary* (1699) and *The Complete French-Master* (1694), both of which were reprinted in numerous editions. The estate inventories and book lists Davis relied on, however, typically indicate a French dictionary or grammar book accompanied only by a very few French-language books, and sometimes none at all. The more likely explanation is that many educated readers kept a French dictionary on hand in order to help them translate the occasional French phrase or quotation, especially in law books, which still contained many expressions in Norman French. For instance, Maryland attorney Philip Thomas Lee (1736-78), who had been trained at the Middle Temple in London, owned a copy of Boyer's *Dictionary* and some three hundred other volumes, about a third of which were legal treatises, but not a single French-language book. Similarly, Dr. Nicholas Flood, who, as noted in Chapter 2, possessed a library of more than nine hundred volumes, owned Boyer's *Dictionary* and a few works by Voltaire and Fénelon in English translation, but nothing in French.[2]

Books advertised in the *Virginia Gazette* also seem to bear this out. Of thirty-nine French literature titles offered for sale in the *Virginia Gazette* during the years 1736-80, including works by Voltaire, Molière, and Montaigne, only four were in French (Chambaud's *Fables choisies*, Fénelon's *Télémaque*, Goudar's *L'espion chinois*, and Le Sage's *Gil Blas*). Montesquieu's *De l'esprit des lois* (*The Spirit of the Laws*), indisputably the most important French book among the Founders, was available only in Thomas Nugent's popular English translation.[3]

To be sure, as historians Howard Mumford Jones and Paul Merrill Spurlin have ably demonstrated, there were some notable exceptions to the paucity of those who could speak or read French in colonial America, such as Huguenot émigrés and early New England divines (including Cotton Mather) who were steeped in Calvinist tracts published in French. In addition, after the Franco-American alliance in 1778, there was increased interest in America for French language and culture, and Founders such as George Washington, John Adams, George Mason, and others remarked on the importance of acquiring some facility in the language of the nation's new ally. Still, by 1780, when a French fleet sailed into Boston harbor, the "want of a knowledge of the French language" was "a matter of regret with every gentleman in the town," according to one firsthand observer. The Babel-bumbled Bostonians ended up communicating with their French guests in Latin through a local physician sufficiently conversant in the ancient language. Marquis de Chastellux (1734-82), a major general with the French expeditionary forces in America, confirmed that knowledge of the French language, even in Boston, was "far from being common." The situation had not changed several years later when another Frenchman, J. P. Brissot de Warville (1754-93), who spent six months touring Boston, New York, Philadelphia, Maryland, and Virginia, observed that "[e]ven the best" French books "will not sell here," because "[v]ery few people know French."[4]

James Madison, as chair of a Congressional committee appointed in 1782 to recommend a "list of books to be imported for the use of the United States in Congress Assembled," compiled a list of recommended books and maps composed of some 547 titles and more than 1,600 volumes. Madison's list included many obvious choices, such as histories, geographies, and travel narratives, as well as many works on law, politics, and international treaties, and diplomacy. In addition, Madison, who had studied French under his tutor Donald Robertson and also at Rev. John Witherspoon's College of New Jersey (later Princeton), suggested a surprising number of French-language books. Topping the list was Charles-Joseph Panckoucke's *Encyclopédie méthodique*, the first volume of which had appeared in Paris just months before Madison submitted his catalogue to Congress. Beginning in 1782, the *Encyclopédie méthodique* was published over the next half century in 166½ volumes of text and 51 of illustrations. Madison, Thomas Jefferson, Benjamin Franklin, and James Monroe subscribed to it, along with the College of William and Mary and the American Philosophical Society.[5]

In addition to Panckoucke's Polypheme-proportioned *Encyclopédie*, Madison recommended works by, as one of his biographers put it, "European heretics, freethinkers, antimonarchists and Catholic skeptics," including Barbeyrac, Bayle, Millot, Vertot, and Voltaire. Madison's book list bears the undoubted influence of Thomas Jefferson, who roomed with him in a Philadelphia boarding house while Madison completed his bibliographic burden and Jefferson worked on his own massive catalogue of books that he owned and those he wanted to purchase. As it turned out, Madison's efforts were completely wasted—Congress overwhelmingly rejected his entire list in 1783, and when Congress finally procured its first book collection for the Library of Congress from a London bookseller in 1800 (by which time Franco-American relations were tense), it acquired only 158 titles, consisting of 728 volumes—only one of which, a dictionary, was in French.[6]

The most prominent of those who had studied and could read French (though he stumbled for years before he could tolerably speak it) in colonial America was, of course, Thomas Jefferson. In May 1784 Jefferson received a Congressional commission to assist John Adams and Benjamin Franklin at Paris in their efforts to negotiate treaties of amity and commerce with European nations. Jefferson became minister to France upon Franklin's departure the following year. "While residing in Paris," Jefferson later recalled to a Georgetown bookseller, "I devoted every afternoon I was disengaged, for a summer or two, in examining all the principal bookstores, turning over every book with my own hand, and putting by everything which related to America, and indeed whatever was rare and valuable in every science." During his five-year tenure in Paris, Jefferson purchased some twenty-three hundred volumes, most of them in French, and nearly doubled the size of his personal library. He continued to order books from his favorite Parisian bookseller, Jacques François Froullé (d. 1794), for years after his return to Monticello.[7]

Fellow Virginian William Short (1759-1849), who was related to Jefferson by marriage and whom Jefferson referred to as his "adoptive son," followed Jefferson to Paris in 1784 and served as Jefferson's dutiful private secretary. Short, who studied law under George Wythe at the College of William and Mary and was a co-founder and president of the Phi Beta Kappa Society, remained in

Paris when Jefferson departed in 1789 and was promoted to *chargé d'affaires*. Though Jefferson clearly expected his protégé would succeed him as minister to France, President Washington appointed Short to other diplomatic posts, first as minister to the Netherlands in 1792, and subsequently as minister to Spain, though Short never officially took office in Madrid and was replaced following a bitter political mêlée not of his own making. Humiliated, Short retreated to Paris, where he was again grievously disappointed, this time in a long-running *affaire du coeur* with Rosalie de la Rochefoucauld, whose aristocratic husband Duc Louis Alexandre de la Rochefoucauld had been murdered in the French Reign of Terror. Loveless and forlorn, when he finally returned to America for good in 1810 at age fifty-one, Short had precious little to show for what began as a brilliant diplomatic career other than some 1,850 volumes of fine books he had acquired in Europe. Short settled in Philadelphia, where he became a wealthy businessman, and when his library was sold off piecemeal in the 1930s in a Washington, D.C., bookshop, an observer noted that it had grown to more than three thousand volumes, which he described as "predominantly French works."[8]

John Adams, who, like his fellow treaty commissioner Jefferson, died on the fiftieth anniversary of the Declaration of Independence, left a library of 2,756 volumes (by his own count), including some four hundred French-language titles, representing about a third of his entire collection. Virginian James Monroe (1758-1831), later fifth U.S. president, followed Adams and Jefferson in Paris as minister to France in 1794. Monroe's introduction to the French, however, began much earlier when he was a twenty-year-old officer in George Washington's army and he befriended the Marquis de Lafayette and his fellow soldier, Pierre S. DuPonceau (1760-1844). According to Monroe's biographer, DuPonceau "brought Monroe into direct contact, for the first time, with the world of the *philospophes*." Monroe's Francophilia and regard for Enlightenment ideals intensified as he came under the strong influence of Jefferson, who sold Monroe some thirty-six French language books in 1784 before Jefferson departed for Paris. During his diplomatic assignments in Paris, Madrid, and London, Monroe acquired a remarkable French library, including works by Bayle, Buffon, Diderot, Montaigne,

Raynal, and Voltaire. By the time he died in 1831, Monroe had amassed an impressive collection of nearly three thousand volumes, more than a quarter of which were in French.[9]

But the undisputed owner of the most French-language books in eighteenth-century America was not Jefferson, Short, Adams, or Monroe. It was their colleague and fellow diplomat Benjamin Franklin. According to the reconstruction of Franklin's library compiled by Edwin Wolf 2nd and Kevin J. Hayes, as many as two-thirds of Franklin's four thousand volumes were in French. According to Hayes, Franklin's French library "may have been the largest collection of French titles south of Quebec."[10]

Aside from Jefferson and Monroe, the largest collections of French-language titles in the Chesapeake were owned by William Byrd II and Charles Carroll of Carrollton. Byrd, who believed French historians freely and inextricably mixed fact and romantic fiction and consequently regarded his French books as "chiefly entertainment," owned about 240 French-language titles, consisting of some 542 volumes. Charles Carroll of Carrollton (1737-1832) was probably the richest man in Maryland and was the only Catholic signer of the Declaration of Independence (as well as the last of the signers to die). Carroll's father, known as Charles Carroll of Annapolis (1702-82) to distinguish him from his son and other related Charles Carrolls, sent him to France for a thoroughly Jesuit education when he was eleven years old. The younger Carroll remained in France until he was twenty-two and then spent five years studying law in London before returning to Maryland in 1764. While abroad, Carroll set out to significantly expand his father's already-large library, and the sixteen-year correspondence between father and son during this period, though mutually respectful and warm, was, as one historian characterized it, "astonishingly bookish."[11]

The Carrolls frequently discussed the books they were reading or wanted. In 1758, for instance, Carroll asked his father to send him a catalogue of all his French books so that he would avoid purchasing any duplicates. His father's list, which was heavily weighted with historical works, revealed that he owned twenty-six French-language titles and 138 French-language volumes, a very large foreign-language library for colonial America. Knowing how exorbitantly expensive books were, even for the wealthiest family in Maryland, Carroll sought to reassure his father as he undertook his book-buying mission: "I intend only to buy such as are useful & entertaining & the most esteemed in the french language, for example their best Dramatick poets & some others as Boileau[,] Rousseau &c." While in Europe and probably afterwards at home, Charles Carroll of Carrollton acquired an additional ninety-five French-language titles, totaling some 365 volumes.[12]

John Baylor IV, according to his author-book list, owned about fifty French titles comprising about one hundred fifty volumes. Because Baylor's list does not indicates which editions he owned, it is impossible to determine how many volumes he owned with any precision. Perhaps a few references to various short-title descriptions of "Voltaire's works" in private libraries will illustrate the challenge: Virginia Gov. Lord Botetourt owned a set of *"Oeuvres de Voltaire,"* which comprised six volumes; Jacky Custis, Washington's stepson, owned a thirty-six-volume edition of "Voltaire's works"; and William Short owned a French edition of Voltaire's *Oeuvres complètes* in ninety-two volumes. Moreover, each of these editions of "Voltaire's works" was published in different years by different publishers. In many instances the titles on Baylor's book list were anglicized and abbreviated, but since he acquired all or nearly all of his books by French and European authors in France, it is reasonable to assume they were original-language editions rather than English translations. Moreover, since Baylor lived in Paris and Nantes for almost two years, he must have acquired some level of proficiency in French.[13]

George Mason V (1753-96), who lived in France from 1779 to1783 in an ultimately unsuccessful attempt to restore his ruined health, died at age forty-three at Lexington, his Virginia estate, leaving behind a library of nearly three hundred volumes, including about forty French titles comprising some 124 volumes. Mason's father, George IV of Gunston Hall, who has justly been called one of America's "forgotten Founders," was quite well read and possessed a large library, no doubt having been inspired by his bibliophile uncle, John Mercer of Marlborough, who had become Mason's co-guardian when he was a boy of ten. In 1779 George Mason IV arranged for his close friend George Washington to write a letter introducing his son to Benjamin Franklin in Paris. Washington's letter requested that Franklin extend his "friendly countenance & civilities" to the younger Mason. Franklin faithfully complied with the request, paving an enviable entree for the young Virginian into Franco-American society.[14]

Mason, like Baylor, had no fixed address or remunerative occupation while in France, but did have access to a generous line of credit established for him by his father, which left him with plenty of time and money to buy books. Daniel Dulany II of Annapolis, Maryland, who attended Eton and Cambridge University and became an enormously successful lawyer and politician like his Irish-immigrant father, owned "95 French Books" at his death, but unfortunately no title list survives. Unlike Franklin, Jefferson, Short, Adams, Monroe, Baylor, and Mason, each of whom purchased the bulk of their French books while living in France, Byrd acquired his French books from London, and Dulany acquired his in Annapolis and London. Although the numbers of French volumes owned by Baylor, Mason, and Dulany pale in comparison to the quantities held by Franklin, Jefferson, Short, Byrd, Monroe, or Adams, the former three men nevertheless stood far apart from the bulk of their Chesapeake gentry brethren in the size of their French book collections. In the Gunston Hall probate sample, for instance, no one else owned more than a dozen or so French books (and in most cases they appear to have been English translations). Without question, the 325 affluent estates analyzed in the Gunston study were far more likely to have French plate or brandy than French books.[15]

If a Virginia planter owned any books by French authors the most likely title was *The Adventures of Telemachus*, the English version of François Fénelon's *Les avantures de Télémaque* (1699). Fénelon (1651-1715), a French archbishop, was hired in 1689 as the tutor to Louis, the arrogant and intractable Duke of Burgundy, the eldest son of Louis, *Le Grand Dauphin*, heir to the French throne. In his didactic novel, which Fénelon wrote while employed as the young Dauphin's teacher, he tells the tale of Ulysses's son Telemachus and of his instruction by Mentor, the goddess Minerva in disguise, who teaches him the virtues of courage, patience, humility, and restraint, all of which Telemachus—and by implication Louis also—would need when he became king. Fénelon's manuscript, which he circulated to a select few in the French court and which was published without his consent, was a thinly veiled criticism of the despotic absolutism and wretched excesses of Louis XIV, the Duke of Burgundy's grandfather, who was still very much on the throne and who immediately banned it.[16]

Télémaque had a significant influence upon Montesquieu, who pronounced it a "divine work," and upon later generations of republican-minded intellectuals, such as Thomas Jefferson, who were attracted to its "doctrine of what constitutes the good ruler," as Howard Mumford Jones put it. *Télémaque*, in one of its innumerable English, French, or bilingual editions, was the most popular French novel in colonial America, including among the 325 gentry whose estates were studied by Gunston Hall Plantation, though fewer than a dozen in that group owned it. On a "rainy and disagreeable" fall day in 1787, Lucinda Lee, daughter of Thomas Ludwell Lee, spent the entire morning and afternoon reading *Telemachus*, which she found "really delightful, and very improving." The *Virginia Gazette* office imported *Télémaque* in both French and English versions and sold the novel in Williamsburg. John Baylor IV owned a French-language edition of Fénelon's collected works, including *Télémaque*.[17]

While *Télémaque* was probably the most popular French novel in colonial America, Voltaire was the most widely read French author, though curiously his histories were more popular in America and in Britain than his other works. Voltaire, who had been exiled by Louis XV, died four months after Baylor left France in 1778, but the bulk of his prolific work had already been published in numerous multivolume editions in French, English and other languages, one of which (presumably a French edition) Baylor scooped up before he departed France. Baylor also acquired one of the numerous editions of Rousseau's and Boileau's collected works, as well as compendia of the French dramatists Molière, Racine, Pierre Corneille and his younger brother Thomas. George Smart noted that only a few colonial Virginia libraries contained works by these playwrights, an observation that was also true for the rest of colonial America, though of this group of writers Molière was the most common. Moliere's comedies were performed—in English—more frequently in colonial America than the works of any other French writer, and collected versions of his plays were sold in Williamsburg.[18]

Baylor, like Charles Carroll of Carrollton, collected a number of books by seventeenth- and early eighteenth-century French religious writers and sermonists, most of whom had an association with the court of Louis XIV. Jacques-Bénigne Bossuet (1627-1704), a French bishop and pulpit orator who tutored the dull-witted Louis, Louis XIV's eldest son (i.e., *Le Grand Dauphin* mentioned previously), published *Discours sur l'histoire universelle* (*Discourse Upon Universal History*) in 1681. Bossuet's *Discours*, which traced human history from its biblical beginnings to the reign of Charlemagne, was an attempt to reaffirm divine providence in human history in response to the theories of René Descartes about the importance of deductive reasoning. In addition to Bossuet's *Discours*, Baylor owned his *Oraisons funèbres* (*Funeral Orations*) (1689), a collection of the more than a dozen funeral orations for royalty and other notables that Bossuet gave during his lifetime, including three that are considered his greatest orations, delivered at the funerals of Henrietta Maria, widow of Charles I of England; her daughter, Henrietta, duchess of Orleans; and Henri II, Prince de Condé.[19]

Baylor owned *Sermons du Père Bourdaloue* by Louis Bourdaloue (1632-1704), a Jesuit priest noted for his grim homilies of astonishing verbosity, and a collection of sermons and panegyrics by Esprit Fléchier (1632-1710), a French writer and bishop. Jean-Baptiste Massillon (1663-1742), another great French pulpit orator whose works Baylor acquired, was selected by both Voltaire and D'Alembert in their respective *Encyclopédie* as the most eloquent French sermonist over all others, including Bossuet, who had previously been regarded as the best. "Massillon," one authority noted, "effected by pathos, indignation, or exhortation, what Bourdaloue had effected by force of logic and declamation." Jacques Saurin (1677-1730), a French Protestant whose family abandoned France following revocation of the Edict of Nantes, was, like Bossuet, Bourdaloue, and Massillon, a great pulpit orator, but he produced his great sermons in the Netherlands, where he settled in 1705, rather than at Louis XIV's court. Baylor owned a collection of Saurin's works, probably either his *Sermons sur divers textes de l'Escriture Sainte* (*Sermons on Various Scriptural Texts*) (1708-49) or his *Discours historiques, critiques, theologiqués, et moraux sur les événements les plus mémorables du Vieux et du Nouveau Testament* (*Speeches, Historical, Critical, Theological and Moral on the Most Memorable Events of the New Testament*) (1728-39). Less well known, then as now, was French bishop Jules Mascaron (1634-1703), whose *Oraisons funèbres* (*Funeral Orations*) (1666) Baylor also owned.[20]

One of the most erudite—and probably one of the oddest— French clerics in the seventeenth century was Adrien Baillet (1649-1706). Baillet, a priest, librarian, and writer who composed voluminous biographies, histories, and compendia on a variety of secular and religious subjects, was one of the most obsessive bibliophiles who ever lived, a man who "lived and died for books" and had "no life apart from them." But as much as loved books, he was also deeply afraid of them. In 1685 Baillet warned that the "multitude of books which grows every day in a prodigious fashion" would soon overwhelm Western civilization, leaving it in a "state as barbarous" as that which followed the fall of the Roman Empire. In order "to prevent this danger," Baillet advised, the best and most useful books should be separated from the others, which should be discarded or left to "oblivion." To this end, Baillet wrote his nine-volume *Jugemens des sçavans* (*Judgment of the Learned*) (1685-86), in which he set forth his assessment of what he regarded as Europe's most important authors. The principal eighteenth-century edition of Baillet's *Jugemens*, which was probably the one Baylor owned, was an eight-volume set published in Amsterdam in 1725. Robert Carter of Nomini Hall owned all eight volumes of this edition.[21]

In addition to Fénelon, Voltaire, and Boileau, Baylor collected other works of French literature far less common in colonial America. Jean de La Bruyère (1645-96), a French lawyer of bourgeois origins who much preferred literary pursuits, created a scandal with his delectable satire, *Les Caractères de Théophraste, traduits du Grec, avec les caractères et les moeurs de ce siècle* (*The Characters of Theophrastus, Translated From the Greek, With the Characters and Manners of This Century*) (1688), which Baylor owned. Bruyère's book consisted of his French translation of a work by Theophrastus, an ancient Greek writer, to which he annexed hundreds of personal maxims and reflections illustrated by supposedly fictional character sketches that bore remarkable similarity to a number of his powerful and influential contemporaries. Not surprisingly, they were outraged despite Bruyère's persistent denials that the resemblance was purely coincidental. One of the most popular books that appeared during the French Enlightenment was Duc de La Rochefoucauld's *Maximes* (*Maxims*) (1665). Born into one of the most prestigious French aristocratic families, by age forty La Rochefoucauld had suffered financial ruin, treacherous political reversals, and bitter personal betrayals. *Maximes*, which La Rochefoucauld expanded and revised in four subsequent editions during his life, is a collection of his pithy, insightful, and penetrating reflections on human nature, many of which appear today as starkly modern, if somewhat cynical.[22]

Somewhat similar in style to La Rochefoucauld's *Maximes*, but quite different in content, was Blaise Pascal's *Pensées de M. Pascal sur la religion* (*Thoughts Upon Religion*) (1670), which Baylor owned. Pascal (1623-62), a brilliant French mathematician, inventor, and philosopher, jotted down his private musings about God, religion, and various aspects of human behavior that were selectively edited and arranged by his Jansenist friends after his death in order to emphasize their religious aspects. The earliest French author whose works Baylor owned was François Rabelais (ca. 1494-1553), a French monk, classics scholar, and author of numerous works, who is best known for his five-volume novel, *La vie de Gargantua et de Pantagruel* (*The Life of Gargantua and Pantagruel*) (1532-1564).[23]

The French Enlightenment also produced several important female authors whose works appear in Baylor's library. Anne Lefèvre Dacier (1654-1720), or Madame Dacier as she was called, was a French scholar and linguist who was highly regarded for her translations of classical Greco-Roman poets, particularly *Les comédies de Terrence* (*Terrence's Comedies*) (1688) and her translations of the *Iliad* and *Odyssey*, *L'Iliade d'Homère* (1699) and *L'Odyssee d'Homère* (1708). Following the lead of Boileau, Madame Dacier plunged into a heated intellectual debate, known in France as "*la querelle des anciens et des modernes*" ("the quarrel of the ancients and the moderns"), between French poet and fairy tale author Charles Perrault (1628-1703) and his adherents, who believed that the literary and artistic achievements of France under Louis XIV had surpassed the ancients, and Boileau, Dacier, Racine, and their followers, who regarded the lofty and sublime works of Homer and other ancient writers as far superior to seventeenth-century French literature, which they dismissed as decadent and degraded in comparison.[24]

Less accomplished academically than Madame Dacier but no less fascinating and brilliant was Madame de Sévigné (1626-96). Orphaned at age seven, Madame de Sévigné married a caddish French aristocrat at age eighteen with whom she had a son and daughter before he was killed in a duel over one of his mistresses six years later. Rejecting a train of attractive suitors from France's top elite, including the Duc de La Rochefoucauld, who became one of her closest friends and admirers, the young widow spent the rest of her long life in the service of her children. She was a regular figure at court and at the best salons in Paris, where she was considered an especially witty conversationalist. She wrote over eleven hundred letters, mostly to her daughter, that eloquently displayed her charm and intellect. After her death and well into the eighteenth century, numerous editions of her letters—some of which were unauthorized—appeared, one of which Baylor acquired in France. Baylor also owned an edition of poems by Antoinette Deshoulières (1638-1694), who, like Madame de Sévigné, was well known in Parisian salons, but who was far less known in colonial America.[25]

Baylor collected important medical and scientific books from the late seventeenth and eighteenth centuries. He owned botanical treatises by Paolo Boccone (1633-1704) and Herman Boerhaave (1668-1738). Boerhaave, a Dutch physician and scientist at a time when botany was considered part of medicine, published his *Index Plantarum* (*Index of the Plants*) (1710), a catalogue of more than six thousand plant species, many of which he studied in a large botanical garden he maintained in Leyden. Boerhaave was far more renowned, however, as a physician whose famous lectures at the University of Leyden drew thousands of medical students from across Europe and Britain during his tenure there. His medical theories held sway in colonial America well into the eighteenth century, leading Dr. Benjamin Rush to declare in 1760 that "the system of Boerhaave governed the practice of every physician in Philadelphia." In eighteenth-century Virginia, Boerhaave's treatises on chemistry and medicine were sold in Williamsburg and were an elemental fixture in physicians' libraries. An earlier figure in the development of medicine, Théophile Bonet (1620-1689), a Geneva physician and anatomist, described nearly three thousand abnormalities encountered in dissections and autopsies in his principal work, *Sepulchretum* (1679), for which he is regarded as a pioneer in medical pathology. Baylor owned one of Bonet's books, most likely his *Sepulchretum*.[26]

Thomas Jefferson, who seems to have established nearly every bibliographic record in eighteenth-century America, owned at least thirty-five titles on astronomy. Jefferson, like his close friend John Page, had a keen, life-long interest in astronomy, and he owned a number of fine astronomical instruments, including a telescope made by Jesse Ramsden, London's premier maker of optics and scientific apparatus. Jefferson's telescope was considered the best of its kind in America at the time. Unlike Jefferson, Baylor is known to have owned only three astronomy books, but the titles he had set his library apart from those of his Virginia contemporaries. Except for Jefferson and Byrd, no one else in colonial Virginia is recorded as having owned *Institutio Astronomica* (1647) by French philosopher, mathematician, and astronomer Pierre Gassendi (1592-1655).[27]

Christiaan Huygens (1629-95) was an important Dutch mathematician, astronomer, and physicist who, among his many scientific accomplishments, formulated the wave theory of light and discovered the true nature of Saturn's rings. In his *Cosmotheoros* (1698), which he wrote during the last year of his life, Huygens set down his Copernican-based philosophic views of the universe, including his speculations about the possibility of life on other planets. Huygens wrote his book in Latin and gave it a cumbersome Greek title in order to limit its reach to academics. "I would not want to tell this [his book] to everybody," he explained. "I wish to choose readers of my own taste, to whom astronomy and philosophy are not yet unfamiliar." Ironically, within a few years of Huygens's death, his *Cosmotheoros* was translated into English, French, Dutch, and other languages, and it was widely read among the literate classes in Europe, though very few copies of it made their way to colonial America. Baylor owned a compendium of Huygens's works, including, presumably, his *Cosmotheoros*. One of Huygens's collaborators was Giovanni Domenico Cassini (1625-1712), an Italian mathematician and astronomer who discovered several of Saturn's moons and ring features, and later became Louis XIV's royal astronomer and astrologer in Paris. Baylor owned either Cassini's *Les elemens de l'astronomie* (*The Elements of Astronomy*) (1684) or, more likely, Cassini's collected works published after his death, *Divers ouvrages d'astronomie* (*Various Works of Astronomy*) (1731).[28]

Several of the most important historians of the French Enlightenment also appear in Baylor's library. Baylor owned the seventeen-volume *Histoire de France* (*History of France*) (1713), by Father Gabriel Daniel, a Jesuit priest who wrote numerous theological and historical works and was appointed as the historiographer of France by Louis XIV. Henri de Boulainvilliers (1658-1722), a French historian, political writer, and aristocratic reactionary who glorified medieval French feudalism, was one of the earliest historians of the modern period to view history systemically and as something from which present leaders could draw lessons from by studying the mistakes of their predecessors. Boulainvilliers's most important historical works were all published posthumously, including his *Histoire de l'ancien gouvernement de la France* (*History of the Ancient Government of France*) (1727), which is probably the title Baylor acquired. Baylor also owned Abbé Vertot's histories of the revolutions in Spain, Portugal, Sweden, and ancient Rome, which were quickly translated into English and made their way to colonial America. Vertot's histories were available from the *Virginia Gazette* for more than two decades before the American Revolution. As with Rollin's *Ancient History* (discussed below), one would not immediately expect American colonials to be much interested in a French cleric's somewhat romanticized account of political revolutions in ancient Rome, Sweden, Spain, or Portugal, but, as Edwin Wolf 2nd noted, Vertot's works "expressed a liberal view of history, the mutability of kings and States, in an era when the rights of rulers were being increasingly questioned."[29]

By far the most popular work of history in eighteenth-century America was Charles Rollin's *Ancient History*. Rollin (1661-1741), a French professor and historian, first published his massive thirteen-volume *Histoire ancienne des Egyptiens, des Carthaginois, des Assyriens, des Babyloniens, des Mèdes et des Perses, des Macédoniens et des Grecs* (*Ancient History of the Egyptians, Carthaginians, Assyrians, Babylonians, Medes and Persians, Macedonians and Grecians*) from 1738 to 1741. Rollin was a follower of Jansenism, a branch of Catholicism that, somewhat like Calvinism, subscribed to an especially dark view of human nature based on strict Augustinian notions of predestination and the fundamental depravity of mankind. Rollin's didactic *Ancient History* attributed the ruin that swept over ancient empires, such as Egypt, Carthage, and Rome, to the avarice, perfidy, and degeneracy of their leaders and elite supporters. It was an "indisputable principle," Rollin declared with supreme righteousness, that the "providence of the Almighty has from all eternity, appointed the establishment, duration, and destruction of kingdoms and empires."[30]

At first blush, it would seem surprising that so many readers in eighteenth-century America, the Founders and common readers alike, would embrace such a dismal and dreary history of ancient empires that had crumbled into dust millennia before. In fact, the colonial Americans' "view of antiquity was highly selective, focusing on decline and decadence," according to historian Gordon S. Wood. Colonial Americans, more rustic and religious than their cousins in the mother country, found in Rollin's *Ancient History* moral support for their growing republicanism. Like the ancient Spartans and early Romans so much admired by Rollin in his work, their provincialism, their "simplicity, frugality, industry," as historian William Gribbin described it, could be seen as republican virtues. "What better texts," Gribbin rhetorically inquired, "could have been provided a young American of meager means and tattered clothing than those which assured him that his very poverty ennobled him, that the habits of a hardworking proletarian could make him a republican freemen?"[31]

As tensions with the British Parliament and the Board of Trade escalated, growing numbers of republican-minded Americans began to look at Georgian London, with what they perceived as its rampant materialism, its cultural snobbery and decadence, its venal aristocracy, and its arrogant, even tyrannical government, as imperial Rome, or worse, Sodom itself. Thompson Mason, writing as a "British American" in 1769, asserted that Britain had "sunk to the lowest state of venality and corruption," and that Britain's nobility cared only about "who shall share the greatest dividend of her [Britain's] treasures" rather than what was best for the nation and its colonies. Charles Lee declared to his friend Robert Morris: "Great Britain is so sunk in corruption and stupidity that she is no longer fit to be the presiding power." Most colonial Americans who perused Rollin's *Ancient History*, as curious as they might have been about the popular work, were not about to slog through thirteen volumes in its original turgid French prose; instead, they opted for one of the many abridged English-language editions. Even John Adams, who possessed a massive collection of French books, owned his Rollin volumes in English. A relative few, including Jefferson, Monroe, Baylor, and Landon Carter, owned a French edition.[32]

In addition to Voltaire, who, as noted above, was regarded by colonial Americans primarily as a historian, Baylor owned several important works by French Enlightenment encyclopediasts and philosophers. One of the earliest of these was Louis Moréri (1643-80), a French priest and theologian. Moréri published his one-volume *Le grand Dictionnaire historique* (*The Great Historical Dictionary*) in 1674. Baylor likely owned one of the numerous multivolume revisions of Moréri's *Dictionnaire* that continued to appear well into the eighteenth century. Nicholas Malebranche (1638-1715), a French priest and Cartesian philosopher, was lauded by his contemporary Pierre Bayle as the "premier philosopher of our age." His most important work, *De la recherche de la vérité* (*The Search after Truth*) (1674-75), was probably the one Baylor owned (Baylor's book list refers to it as Malebranche's *Philosophy*). Baylor also owned *Dictionnaire historique et critique* (*Historical and Critical Dictionary*) (1697) by Pierre Bayle (1647-1706), a Huguenot who had also embraced Cartesian philosophy and was one of the most erudite men of his generation. In his *Dictionnaire*,

Bayle espoused a profound skepticism about metaphysics and the irrationality of traditional Catholic doctrine that greatly influenced later French *philosophes*, including Diderot and Voltaire, the latter of whom pronounced Bayle's work the "arsenal of the Enlightenment." Bayle, who spent most of his adult life in Holland, also believed in religious toleration, then considered a radical, heretical idea in his native France, and his ideas informed John Locke's views regarding toleration.[33]

One of the most important achievements of the French Enlightenment, which Baylor owned, was *Histoire naturelle* (1749-1788), a thirty-six-volume natural history by Georges-Louis Leclerc, comte de Buffon (1707-88) (eight additional volumes were published after his death). In 1739 Buffon, a brilliant French naturalist, became *intendant* (director) of the *Jardin du Roi* (the Royal Garden) in Paris, a position he held until his death. The *Jardin du Roi* included the "King's cabinet," a natural history collection that Buffon greatly enlarged in his effort to "encompass the whole range of the kingdoms of nature, vegetable, animal, and mineral." With equal passion, Buffon sought to capture in his *Histoire naturelle* all that was known about the natural world. Benjamin Franklin, Thomas Jefferson, and John Adams befriended Buffon and admired his work—except for Buffon's theory of degeneracy. Noting obvious differences in animals between the Old World and the New, Buffon posited that animals in the New World were usually inferior and smaller than their counterparts in Europe. For example, Buffon pointed to the tapir, which he referred to as the "elephant of America," noting that it was merely the size of a small cow. Buffon also held that domestic animals transplanted to America from Europe degenerated over time. The reasons for this phenomenon, Buffon asserted, were the greater moisture and lower temperatures in America compared to the Old World (clearly Buffon was unaware of the oppressive climates in the American South and West).[34]

As ridiculous and bizarre as this "theory" seems today, it was accepted as doctrinal truth by the European *cognoscenti* of the Enlightenment. Buffon was lauded not only in Europe but in America as well. Indeed, in 1768—two years after publication of the fourteenth volume of his *Histoire naturelle* that included his theory of animal degeneracy—he became the first Frenchman elected to the American Philosophical Society. If one subscribed to Buffon's theory of animal degeneracy in the New World, it did not take much of an intellectual leap to apply the notion to the people who lived there, which is what happened when two European clerics extended Buffon's thesis to Americans, natives and immigrants alike.[35]

In the same year Buffon was lionized by the American Philosophical Society, Abbé Cornelius De Pauw (1739-99), a Dutch philosopher, published the first tome of his two-volume *Recherches philosophiques sur les Américains* (*Scientific Researches on the Americans*) (1768-69). De Pauw argued in no uncertain terms that the native populations of the Western Hemisphere were decayed and degenerate. While De Pauw focused mostly on indigenous peoples, Abbé Guillaume Raynal (1713-96), another of Buffon's disciples, claimed that the same climatic elements that adversely affected American Indians would also ruin European immigrants. With unattributed assistance from Diderot and other collaborators, Abbé Raynal set down his arguments in his *Philosophique et politique des établissements et du commerce des Européens dans le deux Indes* (*Philosophical and Political History of the Establishment and Commerce of Europeans in the Two* [East and West] *Indies*) (1770), which Baylor owned. Raynal's book, usually referred to as *Histoire de deux Indes* (*History of the Two Indies*), postulated that Europeans who emigrated to America would become stunted and debased just like the aboriginal inhabitants and animals whose environment they shared. The climate and soils of America, Raynal believed, sapped those who lived there of their strength, their vigor, and even their intellect and character. "One must be astonished," Raynal sneered, "that America has not produced one good poet, one able mathematician, one man of genius in a single art or science." As a testament to the power of ideas, even absurd ones, Raynal's *Histoire* had gone through more than twenty editions by the mid-1780s, including an English translation published in Edinburgh in 1776 and in the London the following year.[36]

Raynal's canard was not only insulting; it was also dangerous because its fast-spreading popularity and alarming acceptance among many in Europe who had never been to America threatened to endanger the brand-new nation's reputation and prospects for immigration, trade, and investment. Oliver Goldsmith, in his eight volume *History of the Earth and Animated Nature* (1774), endorsed the Buffon-Raynal hypothesis and propagated it to a large British and American reading public. Something had to be done, and Thomas Jefferson, the principal author of the Declaration of Independence, took up the weapon he knew best—his pen. In his *Notes on the State of Virginia* (1785), which Jefferson began in Virginia in 1780 in response to a set of queries about Virginia from the secretary of the French legation at Philadelphia, he rebutted Buffon's and Raynal's theories with a heavy barrage of facts and logic.

Though Jefferson's refutation is detailed and—as one might call it today—wonkish, it is, like his Declaration, an eloquent statement of American identity. How is it that "nature is less active, less energetic, on one side of the globe than she is on the other," Jefferson posed. "As if both sides," he continued, "were not warmed by the same genial sun; as if a soil of the same chemical composition, was less capable of elaboration into animal nutriment; as if the fruits and grains from the soil and sun, yielded a less rich chyle [a digestive body fluid], gave less extension to the soils and fluids of the body.... The truth is, that a Pigmy and a Patagonian, a Mouse and a Mammoth, derive their dimensions from the same nutritive juices."[37]

But his *Notes* was just the beginning of Jefferson's combat against the degeneracy theorists. Among Buffon, De Pauw, and Raynal, Buffon was the most respected among the European intelligentsia (and the one whom Jefferson most admired), and it was Buffon's climatic suppositions upon which De Pauw and Raynal established their own positions. Thus, Jefferson, animated by the "spirit of both national pride and scientific accuracy," directed his campaign almost entirely towards Buffon. Jefferson arranged for a copy of his *Notes* to be delivered to Buffon along with a large panther skin that Jefferson had purchased in Philadelphia (in order to demonstrate that large animals really did inhabit the American continent). Buffon responded by inviting Jefferson for dinner, and though Jefferson found the Frenchman engaging and amiable, Buffon remained entirely unpersuaded by Jefferson's reasoning.[38]

Undaunted, Jefferson realized that he needed irrefutable proof that American animals were not the sorry, retrograde critters Buffon insisted they were. In an over-the-top gesture unique in the annals of American diplomacy, Jefferson decided it was time to trot out to the pertinacious Parisian *philosophes* an unassailable Exhibit A in the biological battle royale—the largest American quadruped he knew of—a moose—or at least the remains of one. He engaged an acquaintance, General (later Governor) John Sullivan of New Hampshire, to send him "the skin, the skeleton, and the horns of a moose," which, Jefferson added, "would be an acquisition here, more precious than you can imagine." Sullivan, a vain and controversial former Revolutionary War officer with a reputation for driving men and horses to the point of collapse, had led a now infamous scorched-earth campaign against the Iroquois nation in New York in 1779. Sullivan and his team of some twenty battle-hardened war veterans spent days on end traipsing through the White Mountains in bitter winter cold tracking down and eventually bagging Jefferson's quarry. The hunt was the easy part—it took Sullivan and his men an entire fortnight to drag the putrefying mammal more than twenty miles through almost impenetrably dense woods until they reached the nearest road. Sullivan reported that the gruesome task of preparing the moose carcass in accordance with Jefferson's detailed specifications was "both Expensive and Difficult," as it "was never before attempted, in this Quarter." Nevertheless, Sullivan did the best he could and crated up what was left of the moose and sent it to Paris, along with deer, elk and caribou horns, and a detailed invoice for £47.[39]

Sullivan's strange package arrived in Paris in late September 1787, much worse for the wear after its five-month journey. "A good deal of the hair of the Moose had fallen off," Jefferson sighed, but he was still thrilled to have his large if grisly evidence finally in hand. Less than a week afterwards and with undoubted childlike enthusiasm, Jefferson presented his prized moose skeleton to Buffon, along with a variety of other horns and specimens that he had received from other American correspondents. Jefferson hoped Buffon would add these American "spoils" to the "treasures of nature" under Buffon's care at the *Jardin du Roi*. Though not immediately convinced, Buffon did come around and, as Jefferson recalled to Daniel Webster many years later, he "promised in his next volume to set these things right ... but he died directly afterwards." Jefferson's remarkable efforts had thrown considerable doubt upon the theory of New World degeneracy, but it still persisted among some European intellectuals throughout the nineteenth century.[40]

In addition to his large collection of French Enlightenment authors, Baylor also owned several works by important figures in the Italian Enlightenment. Within the legal or political realm, the most important of these was Cesare Beccaria (1738-94). In his *Dei delitti e delle penne* (*On Crimes and Punishments*), which he first published anonymously in Livorno, Italy, in 1764, Beccaria advocated revolutionary penal reform, rejecting torture, inhumane prison conditions, disproportionate sentences, and capital punishment. Despite a papal ban and the derision of traditional European jurists, Beccaria's book flew threw six editions within two years, including a French edition in which Voltaire heaped anonymous praise upon it, and was translated into English by 1767. In America, Beccaria's radical book soon became highly influential among the Founders, especially Adams and Jefferson. At the criminal trial of eight British soldiers following the Boston Massacre in 1770, John Adams, their defense attorney, melodramatically opened his summation to the jury with an out-of-context quote from Beccaria in which Adams prayed that he might be "the instrument of preserving one life," even if it brought down upon him the "contempt of all mankind." Of all the Founders, Thomas Jefferson was the most affected by Beccaria's treatise, which profoundly informed his views about human rights and criminal justice and which became, according to historian Gary Wills, the "principal modern authority for revising the [criminal] laws of Virginia."[41]

Marcello Malpighi (1628-94) was an Italian anatomist and professor at the University of Bologna who used an early microscope to make a number of pioneering observations and important findings regarding the anatomy and physiology of plants and animals, particularly his discovery of the circulation of blood in capillaries. Baylor owned an unspecified title of Malpighi's, probably one of the many compendia of his works published in the late seventeenth or early eighteenth centuries. Pietro Trapassi (1698-1782), known by his pseudonym, Metastasio, was a grocer's son of modest means who, thanks to his adoption by a brilliant scholar of law, linguistics, and classics, became the most important lyrical poet and librettist of the Italian Enlightenment. Trapassi abandoned his legal career to compose more than seventy melodramas, as well as numerous oratorios, *cantate*, *canzonette*, and other works. In 1730 he became the imperial poet in Vienna, a post he retained until his death. Baylor owned one of the collections of Trapassi's works, probably in Italian or French.

Eight

What to Make of The Library

What are we to make of John Baylor IV's library? What impelled him to assemble such a collection of books so remarkable for an eighteenth-century Chesapeake library? Baylor seems to have been intent on creating the perfect French and European Enlightenment library in much the same way his father wanted the perfect thoroughbred. Even if scholars could agree on which titles and editions were required for such a "perfect" library, Baylor's collection would fall far short of the mark. But his efforts and his collection were nevertheless quite extraordinary for his time and place.

Who—or what—guided Baylor in his book selections? As the Enlightenment swept through French intellectual circles in the second half of the seventeenth century, two related and overlapping phenomena also arose: *bibliophily* (a passion for books, but with primary regard for their content rather than their particular edition or appearance); and *bibliomania* (a madness for books—which one author described as "bibliophilia inordinately pursued"—often manifested with an obsession for collecting the finest or rarest editions, but with relatively little concern for a serious study of their content). As German bibliographer Hanns Bohatta put it, "The bibliophile is the master of his books, the bibliomaniac their slave." Thomas Jefferson confessed, "I labour grievously under the malady of Bibliomanie." But there was a definite method to Jefferson's seeming madness for books, and in reality he was probably a *bibliophile extraordinaire* rather than a true bibliomaniac.[1]

When Baylor arrived in Paris in 1777, the city was home to 129 booksellers. In addition, dozens of bibliographic guides for book buyers had been published in France in the eighteenth century. One of the most important of these was *Bibliographie instructive: ou traité de la connaisance des livres rares* (*Instructive Bibliography, or, Treatise of Knowledge of Rare Books*) (1763-68), a seven-volume series published by Parisian rare book dealer Guillaume-François Debure le Jeunne (1731-82). Recognizing the limitations imposed by time, space, and resources, some guides were highly selective and sought to recommend their authors' conception of the very best books. For example, *Conseils pour former une bibliothequè peu nombreuse mais choisie* (*Advice for Forming a Small but Select Library*) (1746), by French-German Huguenot Jean-Henri-Samuel Formey (1711-97), listed about one hundred books for an essential library of religion, literature, classics and rhetoric, history, and philosophy. A large number of the French books Baylor purchased, including several by authors whose prominence had seriously lapsed by the middle of the eighteenth century (such as François Mézeray), were mentioned in Formey's book. Whether Baylor consulted any of these guides in not known, but it is a virtual certainty that he was assisted in his selections and purchases by one or more Parisian booksellers.[2]

In 1785 Walker Maury (1752-88) wrote Thomas Jefferson a letter while Jefferson was in Paris serving as the American minister to France. Maury, the son of Rev. James Maury, Jefferson's boyhood teacher, had been invited by the College of William and Mary to establish a grammar school in Williamsburg, and he wanted Jefferson to send him "a list of the french authors of most merit." Like his recommendations to Robert Skipwith for a busy Virginia gentleman's library, Jefferson's reply was not generally surprising. Fénelon's *Télémaque*, by far the post popular work of fiction by a French author in colonial America, was at the very top of the list. More than half of the titles were histories, including Vertot's histories of ancient Rome, Sweden, Spain, and Portugal; Voltaire's historical works; and Pufendorf's *Histoire Universelle*. Despite Jefferson's avowed fight against the theory of degeneracy in the New World, he also recommended Raynal's *Histoire le deux Indes* and the entire edition of Buffon's *Histoire naturelle*. As for literature, here again Jefferson chose the authors most popular in America—Molière and Racine, as well as the Corneille brothers, Boileau, and various works of travel literature. Finally, Jefferson included several French grammars and dictionaries, including *Dictionnaire de l'Académie Française*, the official dictionary of the French language published by the French Academy since 1694 and then in its fourth edition (1762) (it is still published today—the ninth edition, begun in 1986, is currently under way).[3]

Compared to Jefferson's list of books for Maury, John Baylor IV's library holds up well except, perhaps, for travel literature. However, Baylor's assemblage had other, more significant gaps, the most glaring of which is his puzzling failure to acquire any portion of the thirty-five-volume *Encyclopédie* (1751-80), edited primarily by Denis Diderot (1713-84) and Jean le Rond d'Alembert (1717-83). The *Encyclopédie*, which contained some 72,000 text entries and 2,885 plates by more than 270 writers and artists, was the greatest literary achievement of the French Enlightenment. It was a profound and eloquent manifesto—an act of sublime intellectual worship—to the supremacy of reason over religion. Its definitional article about *philosophes* proudly declares: "*La raison est à l'égard du philosophe, ce que la grace est à l'égard du chretien. La grace détermine le chrétien à agir; la raison détermine le philosophe.*" ("Reason is to the philosopher what grace is to the Christian. Grace determines the action of the Christian; reason determines that of the philosopher.") Predictably, in 1759 Pope Clement XII banned the *Encyclopédie* and ordered that any Catholic who already owned the wicked title must have it burned by a priest or face excommunication.[4]

Jefferson, as governor of Virginia in 1780, ordered a set of the very expensive *Encyclopédie* for public use (and then held on to it at Monticello until the Virginia Council finally ordered him to give it back), but did not mention the *Encyclopédie* in his letter to Maury. Benjamin Franklin, John Adams, James Madison, and James Monroe owned copies of the *Encyclopédie*, as did Charles Carroll of Carrollton, who owned an entire set in duodecimo published in Lausanne, but hardly any other Americans did. In his studies of the importation of French books for sale in eighteenth-century New York and Philadelphia, Howard Mumford Jones noted scarcely any interest in the work. "It is … curious," he concluded, "that Diderot and D'Alembert seldom figured in the book lists." It may well have been that although many literate Americans were eager to read histories, political ideas, plays, and comedies by French authors, as a group they were far less interested in abstruse French philosophic structures or systems, a phenomenon Alexis de Tocqueville noted during his tour of America in the 1830s. In addition to Diderot and D'Alembert, the Marquis de Condorcet (1743-1794), generally considered the last of the important French Enlightenment *philosophes*, is nowhere in evidence in Baylor's library, though it should be noted that Condorcet's major works were published years after Baylor left France.[5]

To what extent did Baylor read or learn from his French books? Did they influence his intellectual development or outlook, or were they just staggeringly expensive academic accoutrements to impress his friends or stroke his vanity? "It hardly need be said," Paul Merrill Spurlin rightly observed, "that while the presence of French books in private libraries may indicate interest, their presence does not necessarily imply influence." Charles Carroll of Carrollton, who spent so many years at school in France while thoughtfully augmenting his family's library of French books, encountered the phenomenon of "show books" first hand. He offered his spendthrift son, Charles Carroll of Homewood (1775-1825), described by one historian as "[h]andsome, charming, sensitive, alcoholic, [and] amoral," $10,000 to enable him to build a fine Maryland home. At the time, such an amount was more than enough to accomplish the task. But in erecting his Georgian edifice the younger Carroll went over his allotment by almost four times, "a most improvident waste of money," his father groused. Finally, when the younger Carroll sent his father an invoice amounting to nearly £50 for imported books the old statesman erupted: "If you would really read and acquire useful knowledge by studying and writing, this would be money well laid out." But "these books," he carped, "which you have imported without my knowledge ... were intended more to decorate your book-case than for you."[6]

So was Baylor's collection of extraordinary books intended merely for ostentation, or did he have a serious, substantive interest in his books? We'll never know for sure, but it appears that Baylor was motivated by both flamboyance and genuine intellectual interest.

In September 1783, Nathanael Greene (1742-86), a distinguished major general in George Washington's Continental Army, traveled through Virginia, where he "lodged at Mr. John Baylor's, a man of considerable property, naturally very covetous and yet ostensibly generous." Greene took an immediate and intense dislike of his host. Baylor, he jeered in his journal, was a "great macaroni in dress, and was once the head of the Macaroni Club in London." (*Macaroni Club* was a derisive term used, mostly in Britain, to describe young fops in London who affected Continental dress and habits.) "He possesses middling abilities," he wrote, and "rather a morose temper." Greene found Baylor's wife Frances "a very agreeable woman," but wrote that Baylor "treated his wife very ill" while Greene was at Newmarket.[7]

Apart from however Baylor might have seemed or behaved to merit this harsh rendition, it must be noted that Greene was a man highly predisposed to dislike Baylor before he even laid eyes upon him. A bright son of a Rhode Island ironmonger, Greene grew up in a strict Quaker household, "amongst the most supersticious sort," he later regretted, in which ostentation or ornament of any kind was severely frowned upon. Greene never attended college and had little formal schooling. Except for the Bible, his childhood home had almost no books because his father would not permit them. One of his deepest disappointments, he later confided to his friend Samuel Ward Jr., son of a Rhode Island governor and prominent statesman, was his "want of a liberal education." In fact, Greene had spent much of his adult life carefully studying essentially the same books he would have read if he had had a solid formal education, but his experience left him with a serious chip on his shoulder. It is not surprising, then, that he despised a 33-year-old Cambridge-educated Virginia aristocrat clad in an elegant London bespoke suit, who was master of a genteel mansion house stuffed with fashionable Georgian furnishings (including a spectacular library) and lord of a vast tobacco plantation.[8]

Even if Baylor was motivated in part to own a great Enlightenment library for the sheer pleasure of beholding its gilt-leather tomes and showing them off to visitors, it would be inaccurate to conclude that Baylor did not also have a serious interest in his books or a significant appreciation of their content. Prior to Baylor's matriculation at Caius

College, Cambridge University, it will be recalled that his British cousin, John Frere, suggested in a letter to John Norton that Baylor was an academic lightweight, and Norton concurred that Baylor might not excel there if he did not improve. Baylor was admitted to Caius College on March 28, 1770, and, contrary to Frere's and Norton's expectations, he was awarded an academic scholarship from Michaelmas term that year (October through December) until March 1772, when he left to attend to his dying father in Virginia. Though Baylor may have fallen short of Frere's extravagant expectations, Baylor was clearly a man of real intellectual ability.[9]

John Frere (1740-1807), who matriculated at Caius College twelve years before Baylor, was also awarded a scholarship to the college, where he achieved very high academic distinction. He obtained his master of arts degree there in 1766, and was also admitted to the Middle Temple at the Inns of Court. A serious-minded intellectual, in 1771 he became a fellow of the Royal Society and later a member of Parliament for Norwich. In 1797 he made important scientific findings regarding some flint weapons from the Lower Paleolithic era that were found near his home. His contributions lay chiefly in his meticulous notations of the geologic context in which the implements were found, his recognition that the flints were primitive weapons fabricated by human hands, and his gentle speculation that perhaps the geologic strata in which they were found, and therefore the earth itself, were older than had been previously thought. Frere, despite (or perhaps because of) his intellectual attainments, was also an inveterate snob insofar as Americans were concerned.[10]

Frere's letters to Baylor, more than a dozen of which survive, are full of remarks reflecting his conviction that American students had habitual difficulty performing well at British grammar schools and universities and that perhaps they would do better by just staying home. During the Napoleonic Wars, he believed that American statesmen were second-rate minds who would be outfoxed by the French at every turn. In a June 1800 letter to Baylor he wrote: "I hope the true sense you entertain of the genuine interest of your country, will be more generally diffused & not overset by the perfidious arts & bribes of France, who will never want the means of gaining over needy factious scoundrels, who in a government of so popular [illeg.] as yours must have too many means of influencing the minds of the *sovereign People*." A month later he was even more blunt: "I am in great apprehension about your country—French intrigue will certainly be an overmatch for you." Frere seems to have forgotten the successes of Benjamin Franklin, one of the greatest minds of the Enlightenment, who, as the head of America's diplomatic legation in Paris, played his cards brilliantly against impossible odds, not to mention cunning and intractable French diplomats and officials.[11]

If Frere's view of Baylor—and his fellow countrymen—was biased, another question still remains: If Baylor in fact read and appreciated the books in his extensive library, did he mention or make reference to them in his writings? This question cannot be answered because, unfortunately, very few of Baylor's writings survive. Due to Baylor's childhood injury, we know that, for him, the act of writing was extremely uncomfortable and eventually became almost impossible. His surviving letters tend to be terse (in an age of florid epistolary writing), they are usually consumed with his pressing business and legal headaches, and they became nearly indecipherable in the final years of his life as his health declined. Moreover, unlike, say, Landon Carter or John Adams, who left prodigious if occasionally scathing marginalia in their books, the dispersal of Baylor's library following his insolvency leaves us unable to assess his thoughts as he journeyed through his books.

Nine

Gone

Cut off from the tobacco trade with Great Britain during the Revolution, farmers and planters in the Chesapeake, including Baylor, lost most of their usual income from tobacco exports, in addition to suffering severe depredations from British forces, seizures by American troops, and slave desertions by the thousands. After the war ended in 1781, things went from bad to worse, as the Virginia Commonwealth, along with most of the newly formed nation, underwent a "truly disastrous" economic decline, as two historians have characterized it. Then there was the matter of £5 million in prewar indebtedness owed by Americans to British creditors. Incredibly, nearly half of this sum was owed by Virginians. In a major (though hardly unexpected) blow to Virginia planters, the Treaty of Paris (1783) between Britain and the United States reaffirmed all British debts (including accrued interest) contracted before the war.[1]

Despite the clear mandate of the treaty, Virginia courts and juries did their best to delay or block the claims of British creditors. According to a British collection agent living in Virginia, the place was a "rascally State" in which the courts were dominated by "Villainous Lawyers and Packed Juries" who sought to deny British creditors their due. Baylor, too, sought to avoid his British debts by retaining the finest legal talent in Virginia—including John Marshall, the future Chief Justice, John Taylor of Caroline, and Edmund Randolph, former member of the Continental Congress and subsequently the first U.S. Attorney General. Finally, in 1796, the U.S. Supreme Court held that all legitimate British claims must be collectible through the state and federal courts. Two years later, John Backhouse's widow sued John Baylor IV over his father's unpaid pre-Revolutionary debt, along with more than two decades of accrued interest, and obtained a judgment for $17,662.51, a fantastic sum at the time. Numerous other suits and judgments followed, from both British and Virginia creditors. According to his neighbor and friend Edmund Pendleton Jr., Baylor was always "prest for money" and "very frequently sued for debts he owed."[2]

Though few, if any, in Baylor's situation could have managed to save his holdings, in Baylor's case his chances for staving off disaster were especially dim given that he had no head for business. In a letter written twelve years after Baylor's death, one of his lawyers, John Taylor of Caroline, bluntly informed Baylor's son: "Your father was not calculated to manage such [business] affairs." Like an ensnared animal struggling to escape its steely trap by gnawing away at its forepaw, Baylor continued to hack away at his patrimony, his only income-generating capital, by selling off more land and slaves in an ultimately futile effort to eliminate his debts. Of Newmarket's original 12,000 acres, Baylor was forced to mortgage or sell off all the land except for the 2,000 entailed acres that surrounded his house. He also sold thousands of acres in Orange County that were part of his father's 1726 land grant. And Baylor denuded much of his remaining land by felling trees and selling lumber.[3]

Despite his efforts, creditors continued to swarm around him in the last decade of his life. One of Baylor's most humiliating financial headaches was a £6,771 judgment that George Washington, as executor of Jacky Custis's estate, obtained in 1786 against Col. Baylor III's long since-depleted estate in connection with a bond Col. Baylor had given as an accommodation to his friend Bernard Moore. Dr. Robert Wellford (1753-1823), George Washington's esteemed Surgeon General during the 1790s, accused John Baylor IV of being "mean [i.e., ill-bred] and dishonest" regarding a debt he owed. It was during this period that Baylor, a lifelong dreamer and unflagging optimist, seems to have become utterly detached from the economic realities of his life as he embarked on a scheme of delusional grandiosity to build the finest home in America.[4]

Among the many books that Baylor brought back with him from Europe was *The Architecture of M. Vitruvius Pollio* (1771), an English translation of the first five volumes of *De architectura libri decem* (*Ten Books of Architecture*), a treatise by Marcus Pollio Vitruvius, an ancient Roman architect. The translator, William Newton (1735-90), was a talented British architect best known today for his design of the reconstructed Chapel at Greenwich Hospital. Newton had apparently befriended Baylor while the latter was in England and prepared a concept design for him for a new mansion to be built at Newmarket. (Newton's work was displayed at the Royal Academy of Arts in London, which may be how Baylor learned of him.) The design, a carefully wrought watercolor (Fig. 4), is tipped into the endpaper of Baylor's copy of *Vitruvius*. It reveals the elevation of an English-style grand country house on a breathtaking scale larger and more elaborate than any private residence then built in America. The main portion of the three-story residence was drawn with five massive bays (rather than the usual three bays commonly found in large American mansions at the time) and an enormous square cupola in the center with a skylight that rose yet another story above the palatial structure. The neoclassical portico depicted on the drawing features a decorated pediment supported by four large Corinthian columns. An enormous double door is set underneath a Palladian window and flanked by sculptural niches nearly equal in dimension to the doors.[5]

Fig. 4. The dream of sublime madness: "Baylor's Folly," Newmarket, Virginia. Courtesy Carter B. Filer and Virginia Historical Society.

Much of Baylor's inspiration for his palatial home no doubt came from the great country estates he saw and visited in England, but his romantic vision for the perfect Virginia mansion likely began at home. John Page's Rosewell (ca. 1737) was the "largest and finest of American houses in the Colonial period," according to a noted architectural historian. Baylor's brother George had married Lucy, John Page's sister, and Baylor had visited Rosewell many times. Baylor no doubt admired, and possibly envied, Rosewell's stunning size and magnificence, its beautiful mahogany stairs, which were wide enough for eight persons to stand or pass abreast and were "unrivaled as the finest of all American examples," its floor-to-ceiling wood paneling, and its marble mantels and floors.[6]

But as large and elegant as Rosewell was, neither it nor its architectural or cultural peers in Virginia—Stratford (ca. 1740), Westover (ca. 1736), Nomini Hall (ca. 1729), Sabine Hall (ca. 1740), or Carter's Grove (1755)—or for that matter anywhere else in colonial America, measured up to any of the great English estates. As historian Bernard Bailyn has reminded us, even the richest colonial Americans were mere provincials compared to their British counterparts. In comparing the largest houses in eighteenth-century America to the grand estates in Britain, places such as Blenheim, Chatsworth, or Longleat, "[t]here is no possible correspondence, no remote connection, between these provincial dwellings and the magnificent showplaces of the English nobility," he emphasizes. The design, scale, decoration, and furnishings of these English properties were all much superior.[7]

At the time Baylor embarked on his plan, the most qualified person in Virginia capable of rendering an informed opinion about how well the Commonwealth's mansions measured up to Britain's was probably Benjamin Henry Latrobe (1764-1820). Latrobe, an enormously talented British architect who emigrated to Virginia in 1796 following the death of his wife, later designed a number of important buildings in America, including the Bank of Pennsylvania in Philadelphia, portions of the U.S. Capitol in Washington, D.C., and the Basilica of the Assumption in Baltimore. During his years in Virginia (1796-98), Latrobe ingratiated himself with dozens of the Virginia gentry, including the Pages and the Randolphs. Though

Latrobe admired the usually unfailing hospitality he received from his elite hosts, he was profoundly unimpressed with their mansion houses. In Amelia County, for example, Latrobe commented that he "could have again fancied himself in a society of English Country Gentlemen (a character to which I attach everything that is desirable as to education, domestic comfort, manners and principles) had not the shabbiness of their mansions undeceived me." Following his visit to Mann Page III's Mannsfield, a Georgian mansion that was, at least by American standards, large and elegant, he remarked to his journal that it was "built of Stone of a good but coarse grit in the Style of the Country Gentlemen's houses in England of 50 Years ago." It is "a tolerably good house," he sniffed, "but the taste is indifferent." Latrobe was similarly dismissive of George Washington's Mount Vernon, which was, he wrote, "extremely good and neat, but by no means above what would be expected in a plain English Country Gentleman's house of £500 or £600 a Year."[8]

From his many years abroad in Britain and in France, Baylor also understood the relative shortcomings of American domestic architecture, and when he obtained his conceptual scheme from Newton he was determined to construct the first edifice in Virginia, and in America, that was truly comparable to a grand English home. He wanted the perfect mansion for his perfect library. Incredibly, despite his worsening economic misfortunes, Baylor began construction on his dream house around 1800, but the project, which soon became known as "Baylor's Folly," did not get very far before he had to stop. Ellen Bruce Carter Baylor (1858-99), a Virginia historian and wife of one of Baylor's descendants, later recorded: "[T]he walls and foundations were completed, but there the building ceased," and some years after Baylor's death "they were pulled down and the bricks used for other purposes." Three decades before Baylor began his folly, his uncle John Norton suggested that Baylor was a "perfect Quixotte," and, as it turned out, he was right.[9]

Baylor was determined to remain an Anglo-Virginia gentleman to the end, even as he was forced to sell off furniture and possessions at Newmarket to satisfy scavenging creditors. "[T]o the last," according to Ellen Bruce Carter Baylor, he "kept up a great deal of form and ceremony in his household, having his hair powdered and himself dressed carefully each day for dinner, and requiring that no overseer or employee [i.e., household slave] should approach him with his head covered or with anything but the most exaggerated tokens of respect." In her description we can readily imagine this sad and pathetic fourth-generation squire of Virginia, in fusty dress frock and wig, his pockets empty and his dreams irretrievably shattered, shouting at his listless household slaves to observe proper decorum and formality, while his ragged voice echoed aimlessly along Newmarket's empty walls and down its barren halls.[10]

As Baylor's health and financial situation deteriorated amidst the ruin of "Baylor's Folly," his creditors forced him into debtor's prison, where he died, a beaten and broken man, on February 5, 1808, the thirtieth anniversary of his appeal to Lord North while confined within another prison, the hold of the *Thamas Koulikan*. Thomas R. Rootes III (1785-1820), a distinguished Fredericksburg, Virginia, attorney and the administrator of Baylor's estate, reported that in the months before Baylor died his "whole personal estate & even household furniture" had been liquidated in order to reduce his debts. Rootes further recounted that he had sold the bulk of Baylor's precious library prior to Baylor's death for $227 (an average of less than a quarter per book), leaving Baylor with only with "a few volumes of books." Baylor's will, drawn on October 30, 1807, just months before he died, says nothing about his grievous financial condition and simply directs that his library be divided between his sons John and George. In a state of apparent denial regarding his circumstances, he specifically mentioned his library of "twelve to thirteen hundred volumes," despite the imminent liquidation of his personal estate. His will also contained his last book order: he directed that his sons "import from London" a "well bound Family Bible and prayer Book" for each of his five daughters. As for Baylor's Folly, the unfinished rubble of sublime madness that littered Newmarket, Baylor bequeathed to his son John "the mansion house and brick improvements which I have commenced" without any further comment or stated wishes.[11]

Baylor's son John V was the first in five successive father-son generations, each with an eldest son named John, not to be educated in Britain, a fact that must have done incalculable damage to

Baylor's Virginia gentry and familial pride. Though Baylor could not afford to send any of his children abroad for their education, he hoped, in vain, to resurrect the tradition in the next generation. "[I]t is my desire," he entreated in his will, that the eldest sons of his sons John and George be sent to grammar school at "Eton, Westminster, Harrow or Winchester and then ... to University at Cambridge," one to his alma mater, Caius College, and the other to Trinity or St. John's College. Baylor never stopped dreaming, even as his life ebbed away, his landed empire crumbled, and his remarkable library was packed up and sold off.[12]

Even if Baylor could have afforded to send his progeny to Britain for their education, he failed to realize that an English education was a fantastic extravagance no longer necessary or desirable for a Virginia gentleman. His sociocultural worldview—like his once fancy but now faded and threadbare London wardrobe—had long since become outmoded and out of fashion in a postcolonial, republican Virginia. He, like the rest of the pre-Revolutionary Virginia gentry still clinging to survival in the early Republic, was a living anachronism, a spent and tragic ghost of an era forever gone—from Virginia and from America.[13]

Appendix

Unless otherwise indicated, all books listed here are from the following sources: John Baylor IV's list of French and European books, Baylor Family Papers, Albert and Shirley Small Special Collections Library, University of Virginia, Charlottesville (**BL**); letterbooks of Col. John Baylor III, 1749-65, Baylor Family Papers, Virginia Historical Society (**BLB**); *Virginia Gazette* Daybooks, 1750-52 and 1764-66, University of Virginia (**VG**); and the list of books in the estate inventory of Col. John Baylor III, in *Daingerfield v. Rootes*, Superior Court of Chancery, Fredericksburg, Va. (1809-23) (**IL**).

The title as it appears in the source is given first; the actual title, if known or fairly discernable, appears next in brackets. In almost every instance, it is impossible to tell which edition the Baylors owned, which is typical of private library lists in colonial America; therefore, the first edition is given except as otherwise noted. A few entries on the source lists were not legible.

Addison, Joseph [1672-1719]. *Addison's work* [*The Works of the Right Honourable Joseph Addison, Esq.* or *The Miscellaneous Works, in Verse and Prose, of the Right Honorable Joseph Addison, Esq., ...*]. The first collection of Addison's works appeared two years after his death under the title *The Works of the Right Honourable Joseph Addison, Esq.*, 4 vols. (London, 1721). The edition the Baylors probably owned was *The Miscellaneous Works, in Verse and Prose, of the Right Honourable Joseph Addison, Esq.*, 4 vols. (London, 1765). IL.

_____. *Remarks on Italy* [*Remarks on Several Parts of Italy ... in the Years 1701, 1702, 1703*]. Addison's first edition of his *Remarks* appeared in 1705 (London). IL.

[Allestree, Richard] [1619-81]. *Whole Duty of Man* [*The Whole Duty of Man Laid Down in a Plain and Familiar Way...*]. Allestree, a royalist supporter of Charles I and later professor of divinity at Christ College, Oxford, anonymously published the first edition of this work under the title *The Practice of Christian Graces, or, The Whole Duty of Man...*, in London (1658). VG and IL.[1]

Anonymous. *A New System of Agriculture or an Easy and Speedy Way of Growing Rich* [*A New System of Agriculture; or, A Plain, Easy, and Demonstrative Method of Speedily Growing Rich...*]. Published in London and Dublin in 1755 under the stated authorship of a "Country Gentleman," this book, now very scarce, may have been written by Edward Weston (1703-70), editor of the *London Gazette*, who published several other books in which he identified himself as the author and a "Country Gentleman." BLB.

Anonymous. *New Week's Preparation* [*The New Week's Preparation for a Worthy Receiving of the Lord's Supper...*]. 2 parts. London, 1737-38. VG.

Anonymous. *Sportsman's Dictionary* [*Sportsman's Dictionary; or, the Country Gentleman's Companion, in all Rural Recreations...*]. First published in a two-volume octavo edition in 1735 (London), the protracted subtitle of this book amply describes its contents: *With Full and Particular Instructions for Hawking, Hunting, Fowling, Setting, Fishing, Racing, Riding, Cocking. With the Method of Breeding, Curing, Dieting, and Ordering of Horses, Dogs, Pigeons, Cocks....* 2 vols. IL.[2]

Atlas of the United States [details unknown]. The inventory list of Col. Baylor III's estate mentions "3 volumes of the world," which may have included this atlas or others. IL.[3]

Baillet, Adrien (Adrian) [1649-1706]. *Judgment of the Learned, Biography, &c* [*Jugemens des sçavans sur les principaux ouvrages des auteurs*; other titles not specified]. 9 vols., Paris (1685-86). The best edition of Baillet's *Jugemens* was revised and expanded by M. de la Monnoye and published in Amsterdam in 1725 (8 vols.). BL.

Bartlet, John [ca. 1716-72]. *Bartlet's Farriery* [*The Gentleman's Farriery: or, A Practical Treatise, on the Diseases of Horses*]. First published in 1753 in London, Bartlet's *Gentleman's Farriery* appeared in more than twenty editions by the 1790s. Colonel Baylor III bought the fifth edition (London, 1764) from the *Virginia Gazette* in 1764. VG.

Bayle, Pierre [1647-1706]. *Historical and Critical Dictionary* [*Dictionnaire historique et critique*]. Bayle's *Dictionnaire* was first published in Rotterdam in 1697 (4 parts in 2 vols.), and was subsequently published throughout the eighteenth century in a number of French, Dutch, and English editions. BL.[4]

Beccaria, Cesare Bonesana, Marchese di [1738-94]. *Dissertations on Crimes and Punishments* [*Dei delitti e delle penne*]. Beccaria's *Dei delitti e delle penne* was first published, anonymously, in Livorno, Italy, in 1764 and in a significantly altered French edition that appeared in Paris the subsequent year. The first English edition was issued in 1767 under the title *An Essay on Crimes and Punishments Translated from the Italian; with a Commentary Attributed to Mons. De Voltaire Translated from the French* (London), which went through four editions by 1775. Numerous editions of Beccaria's book, many not faithful to Beccaria's original text, followed in western Europe, Britain, and America throughout the eighteenth and early nineteenth centuries. BL.[5]

[Bernard, Jean Frédéric] [1690-1752]. *Praises of Hell* [*Éloge de l'énfer: ouvrage critique, historique et moral*]. Authorship of this odd and extremely scarce book is often attributed to Jean Bernard Frédéric, a French Huguenot who established himself in Amsterdam as a writer, publisher, and bookseller. Published in 1759 (2 vols., The Hague), *Éloge de l'énfer* is a satirical work in which the reader is taken on a tour of hell where things are not so bad at all. The first English version appeared in two imprints published in London in 1760 (2 vols.). One was published by G. Kearsly under the title *The Praise of Hell: or, a View of the Infernal Regions*.... The other appeared under the imprint "M. Cooper" (n.d. [1760]) as *The Praise of Hell: or, a Discovery of the Infernal World*.... Based on surviving records, the Baylors appear to have been the only holders of a copy of this book in the colonial Chesapeake (and possibly in all of colonial America). IL.[6]

Bible. Described as "1 Large bible." IL.

Bickham, George [1684-1758]. *Round Text* [*Round-Text: A New Copy-Book*]. According to the *English Short-Title Catalogue*, Bickham's *Round-Text* was printed in London about 1712; no subsequent editions are indicated. If this was the title purchased decades later by Col John Baylor III in 1764 from the *Virginia Gazette*, it would seem likely that there was a subsequent edition. VG.[7]

[Bland, Richard] [1710-1776]. *Col. Dismounted* [*The Colonel Dismounted: or, the Rector Vindicated*]. Pamphlet. Williamsburg, Va., 1764. VG.

Boccone, Paolo [1633-1704]. *Natural History* [probably *Recherches et observations naturelles*]. Boccone was a Sicilian botanist who published a number of books in his lifetime, including his first book, *Recherches et observations curieuses sur la nature...* (Paris, 1671). His subsequent work, *Recherches et observations naturelles de monsieur Boccone...* (Paris, 1674), was more widely known and thus more likely to have been the one purchased by John Baylor IV. BL.

Boerhaave, Herman [1668-1738]. *Botany &c* [*Index Plantarum* or *Historia Plantarum*]. Boerhaave published *Index Plantarum...* (*Index of the Plants*) in 1710 (Leyden). An expanded edition with copperplate engravings of Boerhaave's garden was published in 1720 under the title *Index alter Plantarum...*, 2 vols. in 1 (Leyden).

A collection of Boerhaave's lectures and materials on botany was published in 1727 under the title *Historia Plantarum...*, 2 parts in 1 (Rome). BL.

Boileau-Despréaux, Nicolas (usually referred to as Boileau) [1636-1711]. *Satire, Art of Poetry, Epistles, the Lutrin &c* [probably a posthumous compendium, e.g., *Oeuvres de Boileau Despréaux*, that included *Satires, L'Art Poétique, Epistles, Le Lutrin*, etc.]. During his lifetime, Boileau published a dozen individual satires, which were first assembled in a compendium edition in 1716 (Paris). Similarly, he published individual epistles that were first collected and published as a set in 1701 under the title *Epitres*. His theoretical tract on poetry, *L'Art poétique*, was published in 1674 (Paris), and *Le Lutrin*, a mock heroic epic, was published serially between 1674 and 1683. Numerous French editions of Boileau's collected works were published in the eighteenth century under the title *Oeuvres de Boileau Despréaux*. 2 vols. BL.

Bonet, Théophile [1620-89]. [no title specified] [possibly *Sepulchretum*]. Bonet, a Geneva physician and anatomist, published his principal work, *Sepulchretum sive anatomica practica, ex cadaveribus morbo denatis*, in Geneva in 1679 (2 vols.). BL.

Bossuet, Jacques-Bénigne [1627-1704]. *Discourse Upon Universal History* [*Discours sur l'histoire universelle*]. Paris, 1681. BL.

_____. *Funeral Orations* [*Oraisons funèbres*]. Paris, 1689. BL.[8]

Boulainvilliers, Henri de, comte de Saint-Saire [1658-1722]. *History* [possibly *Histoire de l'ancien gouvernement de la France*]. Boulainvilliers wrote numerous books and tracts on French history, but most were not published until after his death, including: *Histoire de l'ancien gouvernement de la France...*, 3 vols. (The Hague and Amsterdam, 1727); *État de la France...*, 3 vols. (London, 1727-28); and *Histoire de la pairie de France...*, 2 vols. in 1 (London, 1753). John Baylor IV most likely owned Boulainvilliers's general history of ancient France, *Histoire de l'ancien gouvernement de la France*. BL.

Bourdaloue, Louis [1632-1704]. *Sermons* [*Sermons du Père Bourdaloue de la Compagnie de Jésus...*]. In the two decades following Bourdaloue's death, a number of editions of his collected sermons appeared in French under the title *Sermons du Père Bourdaloue de la Compagnie de Jésus...* (Paris, 1709). BL.

Boyer, Abel [1667-1729]. *The Complete French Master for Ladies and Gentlemen*, 18th ed., London, 1756.[9]

Boyle, John, Earl of Orrery [1707-62]. *Orrey's Life of Swift* [*Remarks on the Life and Writings of Jonathan Swift*]. Lord Orrery, as he was known, published his *Remarks* in London in 1751. The book was popular and went through a number of editions. IL.

Bracken, Henry [1697-1764]. *Bracken's Farriery* [*Farriery Improv'd: or, A Compleat Treatise Upon the Art of Farriery...*]. Bracken, a physician and mayor of Lancaster, England, first published his *Farriery Improv'd* in London in 1737 and added a second volume in 1740. A number of subsequent editions were published in London, Dublin, and Philadelphia throughout the eighteenth century, and the book was very popular among the Chesapeake gentry. Colonel Baylor III purchased the ninth edition (2 vols., London, 1763) from the *Virginia Gazette* in 1764. VG and IL.

Brice, Andrew [1690-1773]. *Brice's Geographical Dictionary* [*A Universal Geographical Dictionary; or, Grand Gazetteer...*]. Brice, a printer, simultaneously published his two-volume *Geographical Dictionary* in London and Exeter, England, in 1759 under the title, *The Grand Gazetteer, or Topographic Dictionary*. VG and IL.

Brooke, Frances [ca. 1724-89]. *Lady Julia Mandeville's Letters* [*The History of Lady Julia Mandeville*]. 2 vols. London, 1763. VG.

Bruyère, Jean de La [1645-96]. *Characters* [*Les Caractères de Théophraste, traduits du Grec, avec les caractères et les moeurs de ce siècle*]. Paris, 1688. BL.

[Buchanan, James] [fl. 1753-73]. *British Grammar* [*The British Grammar: or, an Essay, in Four Parts, Towards Speaking and Writing Language Grammatically, and Inditing Elegantly*]. London, 1762. VG.[10]

Buffon, Georges-Louis Leclerc, comte de (usually referred to as Comte de Buffon) [1707-88]. *Natural History* [*Histoire naturelle, générale et particulière, avec la Description du Cabinet du Roi*]. 36 vols. Paris, 1749-88. Following Buffon's death, another French naturalist, Bernard-Germain-Étienne de La Ville-sur-Illon, comte de Lacépède, published eight additional volumes to Buffon's *Histoire naturelle* (Paris, 1788-1804). BL.

Burnet, Gilbert [1643-1715]. *Burnett on the reformation* [*History of the Reformation of the Church of England*]. Burnet, a Scottish theologian, historian, and Bishop of Salisbury, published the first volume of his *History of the Reformation of the Church of England* in 1679, followed by the second and third volumes in 1689 and 1714 (London). Numerous reprints and subsequent editions were produced throughout the eighteenth century. 3 vols. IL.

[Burt, Edward] [d. 1755]. *Letters from the north of Scotland* [*Letters from a Gentleman in the North of Scotland to His Friend in London*]. Burt, a British army officer, published his epistolary account of his experiences in the Scottish Highlands in 1754 (2 vols., London). IL.

Caesar, Gaius Julius [100 BC-44 BC]. *Caesar's Commentaries* [*Caesar's Commentaries on the Gallic and Civil Wars* or similar title]. Numerous eighteenth-century editions were published in London in both English and Latin. One of the most popular English translations was William Duncan's, published in London in 1753. IL.

Camm, John [1718-1778]. *Camm's Pamphlet* [*A Review of the Rector Detected: or the Colonel Reconnoitred*]. Pamphlet. Williamsburg,

Va., 1764. VG.

Cassini, Giovanni Domenico [1625-1712]. *Astronomy* [either *Les elemens de l'astronomie* or *Divers ouvrages d'astronomie*]. Cassini published several works during his lifetime regarding his astronomical observations in Latin, Italian, and French. His most popular work was *Les elemens de l'astronomie...* (Paris, 1684). A collection of his works was published in Paris after his death in 1731 under the title *Divers ouvrages d'astronomie*. BL.

Champion, John [1709-65]. *The Penman's Employment* [*The Penman's Employment: A New Copy Book, Containing* [a] *Choice Variety of Examples in all the Hand*[s] *of England*]. Beginning in 1759, Champion, a teacher to nobleman and gentry, produced forty-four beautifully wrought folios for his *Penman's Employment*, which he published in London in 1762. A second edition followed in 1763, and a third in 1765 (both London). A boarding school master and contemporary of Champion's declared the *Penman's Employment* a "grand and elaborate work." VG.[11]

Cheny, John [fl. 1729-50]. *An Historical List of All Horse-Matches Run and of All Plates and Prizes in England and Wales*. Cheny, the founder of the modern horse racing calendar, published twenty-four issues covering the years 1727-50 (1728-51, London). His list was continued by Reginald Heber (see below). BLB.

Church of England. *Book of Common Prayer*. BLB.[12]

Churchill, Charles [1731-64]. *Poems* [probably *Poems*]. Churchill published his poems separately during his lifetime, except for a partial collection that appeared in 1763 (2 vols., London). Following his death, numerous editions of his collected poems appeared in Britain and America. IL.

Cicero, Marcus Tuillius [106-43 BC]. *Cato Major* [probably *Cato Major; or, a Treatise on Old Age...*]. London. VG.

_____. *Letters* [exact title unknown]. The Baylors probably owned a Latin edition published in London. 3 vols. IL.[13]

Clarke, John [1687-1734]. *Clarke's Introduction* [*An Introduction to the Making of Latin...*]. Clarke, a schoolmaster and classical scholar at Hull, published his *Introduction* in London in 1721. By 1800, more than thirty editions of his popular Latin grammar had been issued. VG.

_____. *Clarke's Cordery* [*Corderii colloquiorum centuria selecta; or, A Select Century of Cordery's Colloquies...*]. Clarke edited one hundred of the instructional Latin dialogues of Maturinus Corderius (1479-1564) into a Latin-English work he entitled *Corderii colloquiorum* (often called "Clarke's Cordery"), which was published in York in 1718. By the end of the eighteenth century, Clarke's *Corderii colloquiorum* had been published in more than forty editions in London, Dublin, Boston, and Philadelphia. VG.[14]

Coles, Elisha [1624-1680]. *Coles dictionary* [*An English Dictionary Explaining the Difficult Terms that are Used in Divinity, Husbandry...*]. Coles, an English schoolmaster, published his *Dictionary* in London in 1676. It remained very popular throughout the eighteenth century and is still regarded as an important historical resource for lexicographers today. VG and IL.[15]

Corneille, Pierre [1606-1684]. *30 Dramatic Poems* [exact title unknown]. Corneille, a French dramatist and poet, wrote thirty-two plays that were published during his lifetime, both individually and as compendia. BL.[16]

Corneille, Thomas [1625-1709]. *Tragedies* [exact title unknown]. A French dramatist, Corneille was the younger brother of Pierre Corneille. He published his dramatic poems and tragic plays during his lifetime, and following his death numerous editions of his tragedies appeared in French and English. BL.[17]

Country Magazine [*The Town and Country Magazine, or Universal*

Repository of Knowledge, Instruction, and Entertainment]. *Town and Country Magazine* was published in London from 1769 to 1796 in twenty-eight volumes [specific volumes not specified]. IL.

Dacier, Anne (née Lefèvre) [1654-1720]. *Trans. of Terence &c* [*Les comédies de Terrence*]. Mme. Dacier published her three-volume translation of Terentius's works, with annotations, in Rotterdam in 1717. BL.[18]

_____. *Translation of Homer* [*L'Iliade d'Homère*]. Dacier published her translations of the *Iliad* in 1699 and the *Odyssey* in 1708 (both in Paris). Numerous editions of both followed throughout the eighteenth century. BL.

Daniel, Gabriel [1649-1728]. *History of France* [*Histoire de France*...]. Father Daniel's *Histoire de France* was first published in Paris in 1713 (17 vols.). His *Histoire* went through numerous editions, and was subsequently abridged by the author into an eight-volume edition that was translated into several languages. The best edition of his *Histoire* is a seventeen-volume quarto edition published in Paris in 1755-60, which is most likely the one the Baylors owned. BL.

Deshoulières, Antoinette (née Antoinette du Ligier-de-la-Garde) [1638-94]. *Poetry.* [*Les poésies de Madame Deshoulières*]. Madame Deshoulières published the pastoral poems for which she became most renowned, including "Les Moutons" and "Le Ruisseau," during her lifetime. Her *Les poésies* was published in Paris in 1687, and the first complete collection of her poems was published a year after her death. BL.[19]

Dilworth, W. H. [or possibly others]. *The Life of the Duke of Marlborough* [possibly *The Life and Heroic Actions of John Churchill, Duke of Marlborough*...]. In addition to numerous elegiac poems, ephemera, and illustrations produced after the death of John Churchill, Duke of Marlborough (1644-1722), in a cultural apotheosis similar to that which followed George

Washington's passing, numerous similarly-named biographies of Marlborough were published in the eighteenth century. One of the earliest, *The Life of the Late Victorious and Illustrious Prince, John Duke of Marlborough*, was published anonymously under the sobriquet "Impartial Hand" in London and Dublin a year after the Duke's death. Jean Dumont, baron de Carlscroon (1667-1727), published a biography of Churchill in French in 1729 under the title, *Histoire Militaire du Prince Eugenè de Savoye, du prince et Duc de Marlborough...* (Paris). Dumont's work was translated into English and published in London as *The Military History of the Late Eugene of Savoy, and of the late John Duke of Marlborough...*, 2 vols. (1736-37). A subsequent English translation of Dumont's work, which dropped Prince Eugene from its title, was published in 1753 as *The Life and Military History of His Grace the Duke of Marlborough* (London). Thomas Lediard (1685-1743), published his three-volume *The Life of John, Duke of Marlborough, Prince of the Roman Empire* in 1736 (London). In 1741, John Bancks (1709-51) published *The History of John Duke of Marlborough* (London), which was followed by W. H. Dilworth's *The Life and Heroic Actions of John Churchill, Duke of Marlborough* in 1758 (London). The Marlborough biography owned by the Baylors could have been any of these, but was most likely Dilworth's. IL.

Dryden, John [1631-1700]. *Virgil* [*The Works of Virgil*]. The first edition of Dryden's translation of Virgil's works was published in London in 1697. IL.[20]

Duhamel Du Monceau, Henri-Louis [1700-82]. *Duhamel's Husbandry* [*A Practical Treatise of Husbandry*]. Duhamel, the most important French botanist of his day, wrote a number of important works, including *Traité de la culture des terres...* (6 vols., 1750-61, Paris), which was edited and translated into English by John Mills and published in London in 1759 under the title *A Practical Treatise of Husbandry*. Colonel Baylor III purchased the second English edition (London, 1762) from the *Virginia Gazette* in 1764. VG and IL.

Ellis, William [ca. 1700-58]. *Modern Husbandman* [*The Modern Husbandman: or, the Practice of Farming: as it is Now Carried on by the Most Accurate Farmers in Several Counties of England*]. Ellis, a farmer living near Hertfordshire, began publishing his monthly serial, *The Modern Husbandman*, in 1742. In 1744, loose sheets of his publication for 1742 and 1743 were assembled in four volumes, and in 1750 he published an eight-volume reprint edition (London). 7 vols. IL.

Erasmus, Desiderius [1466-1536]. [no title specified]. Erasmus, a Dutch theologian and classical scholar, published several important works in his lifetime, including *Collecteana adagiorum* (*Adagia*) (1500), *Encomium moriae* (*The Praise of Folly*) (1509), and *Colloquia* (1519). BL.

Fénelon, François de Salignac de la Mothe [1651-1715]. *Telemachus, Dialogues of the Dead*, and *Demonstration on the Reign of God &c* [probably a compendium of collected works, including *Les avantures de Télémaque, Dialogues des morts composez pour l'education d'un prince*, and *Demonstration de l'existence de dieu*]. Fénelon published his *Les avantures de Télémaque* in 1699 (The Hague), his *Dialogues des morts composez pour l'education d'un prince* in 1712 (Paris), and his *Demonstration de l'existence de dieu...* in 1713 (Paris). John Baylor IV likely owned one of the French editions of Fénelon's collected works published after the author's death. BL and IL.[21]

Fléchier, Esprit [1632-1710]. *Sermons, Funeral Orations, &c* [no titles specified]. Fléchier, a French bishop, writer, and poet, published separate books of his funeral orations (*Oraisons funébres*), his sermons (*Sermons de morale*), and his panegyrics of select saints (*Panigyriques des saints*) during his life. John Baylor IV probably owned one of the many eighteenth-century editions of Fléchier's combined works. BL.

[Francis, Philip] [1740-1818]. *Letters of Junius*. Manuscript consisting of hand-copied letters published under the pseudonym

"Junius" in the *Public Advertiser* (London) from January 1769 to January 1772. Baylor Family Papers, Albert and Shirley Small Special Collections Library, University of Virginia, Charlottesville.

François VI, duc de La Rochefoucauld [1613-80]. *Maxims [Reflexions ou sentences et maximes morales]*. First published in Paris in 1665, de La Rochefoucauld's *Maximes* went through five editions in his lifetime. The first English edition appeared in London in 1706 under the title *Moral Reflections and Maxims, written by the Late Duke de La Rochefoucauld*. BL.

[Franklin, Benjamin] [1706-90]. *Interest of Great Britain [The Interest of Great Britain Considered, with Regard to Her Colonies, and Acquisition of Canada and Guadaloupe]*. Franklin's pamphlet was first published anonymously in London in 1760 and reprinted in Philadelphia, Boston, and Dublin the same year. A second London edition followed in 1761. VG.

Gassendi, Peter (Pierre) [1592-1655]. *Astronomy [Institutio Astronomica, jiuxta hypothesis tam vetervm...]*. The first edition was published in Paris in 1647; the first English edition appeared in London in 1653. At least six editions were published between 1647 and 1702 in London, Paris, and The Hague. BL.

Gibbon, Edward [1737-94]. *The Roman History [The History of the Decline and Fall of the Roman Empire]*. The first volume of Gibbon's celebrated *History* appeared in 1776 (London), and quickly went through three editions. The second and third volumes were published in 1781, and the fourth, fifth, and sixth volumes finally appeared in 1788. The Baylors owned three volumes, presumably volumes 1-3. IL.[22]

Gibson, William [1680?-1750]. *Gibson on Horses [A New Treatise on the Diseases of Horses]*. Gibson, a surgeon, wrote several books about horses, including *The Farrier's New Guide* (London, 1720), but he is most known for his *A New Treatise on the Diseases of Horses*, published posthumously in 1751 (London) and in a revised second edition in 1754 (2 vols.). Because this is a book that Col. Baylor III would have wanted immediately, and since his estate inventory reflects only a single volume, he probably owned this work in its first edition. IL.[23]

[Gittins, Daniel] [d. 1761]. *Barkley on the Quakers* [probably *Remarks on the Tenets and Principles of the Quakers, as Contained in Theses Theologicae of Robert Barclay*]. Robert Barclay (1648-90), a Scottish Quaker who had been imprisoned for his religious beliefs, wrote a number of tracts about the religion of the Society of Friends, including his most famous work, *The Apology for the True Christian Divinity*, which sets forth the basic tenets of Quakerism. He wrote his first version of the *Apology* in Latin, *Theologiae vere Christianae apologia* (Amsterdam, 1676), and translated the work into English two years later (Aberdeen and London, 1678). Despite the title *Barkley on the Quakers* on Col. Baylor's inventory list (which was likely taken directly from the book's binding), this volume was probably the tome written by Rev. Daniel Gittins, *Remarks on the Tenets and Principles of the Quakers*, which was published anonymously in 1758 (London). IL.[24]

Gordon, Thomas [d. 1750]. *Gordon's Tacitus* [*The Works of Tacitus*]. Gordon's translation of the writings of the ancient Roman senator, Cornelius Tacitus, was first published in 1728 (2 vols., London), and in a corrected second edition in 1737 (4 vols., London). 5 vols. BLB and IL.[25]

[Haywood, Elizabeth (Eliza)] [ca. 1693-1756]. *The Female Spectator*. 4 vols., London, 1744-46. Haywood, one of the most important and prolific female authors of the eighteenth century, wrote popular plays and novels. Her *Female Spectator* (unrelated to *The Spectator*) was intended for a female audience and contained romantic tales and advice on how to manage domestic matters, especially children and husbands. VG.[26]

Heber, Reginald [d. 1769]. *Race List* [*An Historical List of Horse-Matches Run and of Plates and Prizes Run in Great Britain and*

Ireland]. 18 vols. (1752-69, London). Heber began his important annual chronicle of elite horse races in Britain and Ireland in 1751 and continuously published it until his death in a lunatic asylum in 1769. BLB and IL.[27]

Hederich, Benjamin [1675-1748]. *Patricks Lexicon* [*M. Beni. Hederici Lexicon manuale graecum...*]. The first edition of Hederich's Greek lexicon was published, in Latin, in Leipzig in 1722. Dr. Samuel Patrick (1684-1748), an English schoolmaster, prepared a subsequent edition that first appeared in London in 1727, followed by a second edition in 1739. A revised third edition was published in London in 1755, which is most likely the edition owned by the Baylors. IL.

Herbelot, Barthélemy de Molainville d' [1625-95]. *Bibliothèque orientale* [*Bibliothèque orientale, ou dictionnaire universel contenant tout ce qui regarde la connoissance des peuples de l'Orient*]. D'Herbelot's *magnum opus*, an unfinished bibliography of ancient Arabic manuscripts and books, was completed by Antoinne Galland and published in Paris in 1697. Subsequent European editions were published in the eighteenth century, the most important of which was a four-volume edition published in The Hague (1777-99). BL.

Hume, David [1711-76]. *History of England* [*History of England, from the Invasion of Julius Caesar to the Revolution in 1688*]. Hume's *History of England* was published in four installments from 1754 to 1762 (6 vols., London). A revised, eight-volume edition, published in 1763 (London), was apparently the edition the Baylors owned because they owned eight volumes of this work. 8 vols. IL.[28]

Huygens, Christiaan [1629-95]. *Mathematics and Astronomy* [probably *Cosmotheoros*]. Huygens's *Cosmotheoros, sive, de terris cœlestibus earumque ornatu conjecturae* was first published posthumously in Latin in The Hague in 1698 and in an English translation the same year under the title, *Celestial Worlds Discover'd: or, Conjectures Concerning the Inhabitants, Plants and Productions of the Worlds in the Planets* (London). BL.[29]

Hyde, Edward, Earl of Clarendon [1609-74]. *Clarendon on the rebellion in Ireland* [*The History of the Rebellion and Civil Wars in Ireland* and *An Historical View of the Affairs of Ireland*]. Hyde, the first Earl of Clarendon, is more commonly known for his classic history of the English civil wars, published posthumously as *The History of the Rebellion and Civil Wars in England, Begun in the Year 1641*, 2 vols. (London 1702-1703). Hyde completed his tract on Ireland in 1678, but like his work on England, it was not published until some years after his death (Dublin, 1719). Hyde's work on the Irish rebellion was published in only one volume, but the inventory of Col. Baylor III's estate refers to two Clarendon volumes. Perhaps the second volume was Hyde's *An Historical View of the Affairs of Ireland* (London, 1731), which John Baylor IV or his father may have had bound in matching bindings with Hyde's *History of the Rebellion and Civil Wars in Ireland* so that they appeared as a set. IL.[30]

Jenkinson, Charles (created Earl of Liverpool in 1796) [1727-1808]. *Jenkinson's Discourse* [*A Discourse on the Conduct of the Government of Great-Britain, in Respect to the Neutral Nations, During the Present War*]. (London, 1758). BLB.

Johnson, Samuel [1709-84]. *Johnson's Dictionary* [*A Dictionary of the English Language*]. The first edition of Johnson's *Dictionary*, which he began in 1746, was released in London on April 15, 1755, in a two-volume, large folio edition of 2,000 copies. A second folio edition followed in 1755-56 and an octavo edition (abstracted from the folio edition) in 1760. Two Dublin octavo editions (both abstracted from the folio edition) appeared in 1758 and 1764. The third, corrected edition, in folio, was published in London in 1765. VG.

Juvenal (Decimus Iunius Iuvenalis) [fl. 1st to 2d cent. AD]. [no titles specified]. IL.[31]

[Langhorne, John] [1735-79]. *Effusions of Friendship & Fancy* [*The

Effusions of Friendship and Fancy]. 2 vols. London, 1763. VG.

Latin books. 19 vols. [no titles specified]. IL.

Lee, Richard Henry [1732-94]. *RHL Pamphlet* [unidentified pamphlet]. Lee's pamphlet, which was probably about the Stamp Act, was published by the *Virginia Gazette* in 1765, but no copies survive. VG.

Lesage, Alain-René [1668-1747]. *Gil Blas &c* [*Histoire de Gil Blas de Santillane*]. 4 vols. Paris, 1715-35. An abridged English version appeared in 1732 under the title *The History and Adventures of Gil Blas of Santillane* (London). Tobias Smollett, who later drew heavily upon the novel (particularly in his *Roderick Random*), translated the work in full; his translation was published under the title *The Adventures of Gil Blas of Santillane: A New Translation from the Best French Edition,* 4 vols. (London, 1749). BL.[32]

Lily (Lilye), William [ca. 1468-1522]. *Lily's Grammar* [*A Short Introduction of Grammar*]. Lily, an English classical scholar and the first headmaster of St. Paul's School, London, published what is generally considered to be the first edition of his *Grammar*, a textbook of Latin grammar, in 1540. Lily's grammar was the standard text in England for more than two and one-half centuries afterwards, and it was the usual treatise purchased by the colonial American gentry for the instruction of their children in Latin. BLB and ILL.

Littleton, Adam [1627-94]. *Littleton's Dictionary* [*Linguae Latinae liber dictionarius quadripartitus; A Latin Dictionary in Four Parts...*]. Dr. Littleton's famed Latin-English dictionary first appeared in 1673 in London and in a revised edition in 1678 (2 vols., London). (A number of booksellers persist, erroneously, in referring to the 1678 edition as the first edition.) Subsequent editions were published up to 1735, after which it was superseded by Robert Ainsworth's Latin-English Dictionary, *Thesaurus linguae Latinae compendiarius...* (London, 1736). IL.

Livy (Titus Livius or Titi Livi) [ca. 59 BC-17 AD]. [no title specified] [probably *History of Rome* or *Ab Urbe Condita*]. 5 vols. IL.[33]

London Magazine [*London Magazine, or Gentleman's Monthly Intelligencer*]. *London Magazine* was founded in London in 1732 as an alternative to the Tory-oriented *Gentleman's Magazine*, and its first iteration was published through 1784. 10 vols. (various dates, bound and gilt). IL.

Lyttelton, George, first Baron Lyttelton (usually referred to as Lord Lyttelton) [1709-73]. *Life of Henry 11th* [*The History (of the) Life of King Henry the Second...*]. Following a twenty-year effort, Lord Lyttelton published the first edition of this work in 1767-71, 4 vols. (London). Additional volumes were added in subsequent editions. The Baylors owned four volumes of what presumably was the first edition. Lyttelton's book, though no longer considered authoritative, was owned by a number of colonial gentry, including Thomas Jefferson. IL.[34]

Malebranche, Nicolas [1638-1715]. *Philosophy* [probably *De la recherche de la vérité...*]. 2 vols. Paris, 1674-75. BL.[35]

Malpighi, Marcellus (Marcello) [1628-94]. [no title specified] [possibly *Anatome plantarum*, *Opera omnia*, or *Opera posthuma*]. In addition to the numerous monographs and dissertations Malpighi published in Europe during his lifetime, the Royal Society of England, of which he was a fellow, published his work on plant circulation, *Anatome plantarum*, in London in 1675. In 1686-87, the Royal Society published a two-volume compendium of Malpighi's work under the title *Opera omnia, seu, Thesaurus locupletissimus botanico-medico-anatomicus...* (which was followed by other editions published in Leyden and Amsterdam). After Malpighi's death, his *Opera posthuma figuris aeneis illustrata quibus praefix est ejusdem vita a seipso scripta* appeared in London in 1697 (2 vols.), and subsequently in Leyden, Amsterdam, and Venice. The Baylors likely owned one of the *Opera omnia* or *Opera posthuma* editions. BL.[36]

Martyr, Justin (St. Justin of Caesarea) [ca. 100-ca. 165 AD]. [no title specified]. A number of editions of Martyr's early Christian writings were published in London in the seventeenth and eighteenth centuries, including those edited by John Biddle (1615-1662) and Henry Dowell (1641-1711). An English translation of Martyr's *Dialogue with Trypho*, ed. and trans. by William Jackson, was published in Oxford in 1755 under the title *Justin Martyr's Dialogue with Trypho the Jew*. A Greek-Latin edition of Martyr's *Apologiae*, published in Cambridge, England, in 1768, might have been picked up by John Baylor IV while he was attending university there on the recommendation of his don, William Bond, who later became a vicar. IL.[37]

Mascaron, Jules [1634-1703]. *Funeral Orations* [*Oraisons funèbres*]. The first edition of Mascaron's *Oraisons* appeared in 1666. A select collection of his funeral orations was published in 1704 as *Recueil des oraisons funèbres prononcées par messire Jules Mascaron...* (Paris). A more definitive French edition was published in Paris in 1740 under the title *Recueil des oraisons funèbres*. BL.

Massillon (Masillon), Jean Baptiste [1663-1742]. *Sermons* [*Sermons de M. Massillon*]. The first edition of Massillon's collected sermons was published posthumously in 1745 by his nephew, Abbé Joseph Massillon, under the title *Sermons de M. Massillon* (9 vols., Paris). Numerous editions followed throughout the eighteenth century in French and English. BP.

[Mears, John] [1695?-1767]. *Forms of Devotion for the Use of Families: With a Preface Recommending the Practice of Family Religion*. (London, 1758). BLB.

Ménage, Gilles [1613-92]. *Philology* and *Miscellanies in Prose Verse* [probably *Dictionnaire étymologique* and *Menagiana, ou bons mots, rencontres agréables, pensées judicieuses...*]. Ménage, who was perhaps the greatest linguistic scholar of his generation, published his *Dictionnaire étymologique* in 1670 (which was a revised edition of a French etymology he had published in 1650), as well as several other works of etymology and linguistic scholarship during his lifetime. After his death, his associates published a collection of his aphorisms and writings, *Menagiana* (Paris and Amsterdam, 1693), which went through several revisions and editions, the best of which was *Menagiana, ou, les bons mots et remarques critiques, historiques, morales, et d'erudition de M. Meange...*, 4 vols. (Amsterdam, 1762), which was also most likely the edition owned by John Baylor IV. BL.

Mézeray, François Eudes de [1610-83]. *History of France* (Abridged) [*Histoire de France depuis Faramond jusqu'au règne de Louis le Juste*]. Mézeray, appointed as royal historiographer to Louis XIV, published his renowned *Histoire de France* from 1643 to 1651 (3 vols., Paris). BL.

Mills, John [d. 1784]. *Husbandry* [*A New and Complete system of Practical Husbandry*]. The first edition of Mills' important treatise was published in London (5 vols., 1762-65). The Baylors owned all five volumes. IL.

Molière [Jean Baptiste Poquelin] [1622-73]. *Comedies*. Paris. Molière's plays were published individually in his lifetime, and numerous editions of his comedies were published in the eighteenth century in French and English. The first edition of his collected plays in English was published in London in 1714 by Bernard Lintott (trans. John Ozell), as *Works of Monsieur de Molière in Six Volumes*. BL.

Montagu, Lady Mary Wortley [1689-1762]. *Lady Montagu's Letters* [*Letters of the Right Honourable Lady M—ry W— M—e...*]. 3 vols. London, 1763. VG.[38]

Monthly Review. The Monthly Review; or Literary Journal. Published in London from 1749 through 1844. 11 vols. (various dates, 1750s-1760s). BLB and IL.

Moréri, Louis [1643-80]. *Hist. Dictionary* [*Le grand Dictionnaire historique, ou le mélange curieux de l'histoire sacrée et profane*]. The first edition of Moréri's *Dictionnaire historique* was published in Lyon in 1674. An expanded second edition, to which Moréri reportedly "applied himself with an assiduity that injured his constitution" and which lead to his death, appeared in 1681. Numerous French editions, largely revised and expanded by others, continued to appear throughout the eighteenth century. The first English edition, an amalgam of Moréri's work and that of many others, was published under the title *The Great Historical, Geographical and Poetical Dictionary; Being a Curious Miscellany of Sacred and Profane History....* 2 vols. (London, 1694). BL.[39]

Muratori, Lodovico Antonio [1672-1750]. *History of Antiquities* [*Antiquitates italicae medii revi*]. An Italian priest, classical scholar, and archivist, Muratori published his six-volume *Antiquitates italicae medii revi...* in Milan (1738-42). BL.

Ovid (Publius Ovidius Naso) [43 BC-17 AD]. *Ovid Metamorphosis* [*Metamorphoses*]. Sadly, no information survives about whether this book was a Latin version or an English translation. An English translation popular in Virginia throughout the colonial period was written by George Sandys (1578-1644), who worked on his translation while serving as resident treasurer of the Virginia Company at Jamestown, beginning in 1621. Sandys' translation was entitled *Ovid's Metamorphosis Englished by G[eorge] S[andys]* (London, 1626). IL.[40]

Pascal, Blaise [1623-1662]. *Thoughts Upon Religion, etc.* [*Pensées de M. Pascal sur la religion et sur quelques autres sujets*]. The first edition, known as the Port-Royal edition, was published by Pascal's nephew in Paris in 1670, and was followed by a subsequent Port-Royal edition in 1678 and an Amsterdam edition in 1684. BL.

Perkins, William [1558-1602]. *Parkins Works* [probably *The Works of that Famous and Worthie Minister of Christ in the Vniversitie of Cambridge, M.W. Perkins...*]. A one-volume collection of Rev.

Perkins' sermons was published in the year following his death (Cambridge, Eng., 1603). A second and third volume were added in subsequent editions published through 1635. 2 vols. IL.[41]

Pichon, Thomas [1700-81]. *History of Cape Breton* [*Genuine Letters and Memoirs, relating to the natural, civil, and commercial history of ... Cape Breton...*]. Pichon, a French polymath, British spy, and secretary to the governor of Cape Breton, published his *History* in London in 1760. IL.[42]

Pufendorf, Samuel, Baron von [1632-94]. *Upper Saxony Jurisprudence & History* [possibly *De statu imperii Germanici liber unus*]. This seventeenth-century German natural law philosopher and jurist's most famous work is *De jure naturae et gentium* (*On the Law of Nature and Nations*) (London, 1672), a treatise on international law that was translated into English by Basil Kennet and published under the title *Of the Law of Nature and Nations in London* in 1717. Though Pufendorf was born in Saxony, he is not know to have written a separate tract on Saxony jurisprudence. John Baylor IV may have had a copy of Pufendorf's *De statu imperii Germanici liber unus* (*On the Present State of Germany*), which was published in Latin under the pseudonym Severinus de Monzambano (Geneva, 1667). The first English edition appeared in 1690 (London) under the title *The Present State of Germany....* BL.

Rabelais, François [ca. 1494-1553]. *Works* [no titles specified]. Rabelais, a French monk, classics scholar and author of numerous works, is best known for his prose fictional work, *La vie de Gargantua et de Pantagruel*, which appeared in a series of four books from 1532 to 1551 (Paris). Select versions of his collected works appeared in frequent editions in the seventeenth and eighteenth centuries in French and English. 4 vols. IL.

Racine, Jean Baptiste [1639-99]. *Tragedies* [no titles specified]. Racine, a French poet and playwright, published his individual tragic plays during his lifetime. Compiled editions of his works, including his tragic plays, began to appear about sixty years after his death in numerous French and English versions. BL.

Rapin-Thoyras, Paul de [1661-1725]. *History of England* [*Histoire d'Angleterre...*]. Rapin's work was first published in French in The Hague in 1724-27 (10 vols.). Nicholas Tindal (1687-1774) translated Rapin's work into English and continued its coverage from the Glorious Revolution to the accession of George II in a revised fifteen-volume edition published in London (1725-31). Only two volumes are indicated on Col. Baylor III's estate inventory, but since John Baylor IV mentions the work on his list of French authors, it seems likely he purchased a French-language edition in Paris. BL and IL.

Raynal, Guillaume-Thomas (usually referred to as Abbé Raynal) [1713-96]. *History of the Indies* [*Histoire Philosophique et politique des établissements et du commerce des Européens dans le deux Indes*]. Often referred to as *Histoire de deux Indes*, the first French edition was published in Paris in 1771 (though dated 1770) in nine volumes. The first English edition was published in London as *Philosophical and Political History of the British Settlements and Trade in North America: From the French of Abbe Raynal* (4 vols., 1776). Numerous French and English editions were published through the end of the eighteenth century up to the 1820s. BL.[43]

Réaumur, René Antoine Ferchault de [1683-1757]. *Natural History of Insects* [*Mémoires pour servir a l'histoire des insectes*]. A French scientist and entomologist, Réaumur is best known for his monumental work, *Mémoires pour servir a l'histoire des insectes*, 6 vols. (Amsterdam, 1734-42). BL.

Reeves, John. *Farriery* [*The Art of Farriery both in Theory and Practice Containing the Causes, Symptoms, and Cure of all Diseases Incident to Horses...*]. Reeves's *Art of Farriery* was first published in London in 1758 and went through four editions, the last of which was published in 1778. The Baylors owned the first edition. BLB and IL.

Reynolds, Edward [1599-1676]. *Reynolds on the soul of man* [*A*

Treatise of the Passions and Faculties of the Soul of Man]. Reynolds, the Bishop of Norwich, first published his *Treatise* in London in 1640. IL.

Robertson, William [1721-93]. *History of Scotland* [*The History of Scotland, During the Reigns of Queen Mary and of King James VI...*]. Robertson's *History of Scotland* was first published in 1758-59 (2 vols., London). Colonel Baylor III purchased the fifth edition (London, 1762) from the *Virginia Gazette* in 1764. VG and IL.

Rohault, Jacques [1620-75]. *Physics* [*Traité de physique*]. The first edition was published in Paris in 1671 (2 vols. in 1). British alderman and philosopher Samuel Clarke translated Rohault's book into Latin, adding extensive notes reflecting his Newtonian perspective, and published his version in London in 1697. Clarke's translation appeared in four London editions, the final and best of which was published in 1718. Clarke's brother, Dr. John Clarke, author of *Clarke's Cordery* (see above), translated the work into English, which he published in London in 1723 (2 vols.). BL.

Rollin, Charles [1661-1741]. *Belles Lettres* and *History* [*De la manière d'enseigner et d'étudier les belles lettres* and *Histoire ancienne des Egyptiens, des Carthaginois, des Assyriens, des Babyloniens, des Mèdes et des Perses, des Macédoniens, des Grecs*]. Rollin published his four-volume book on the teaching and study of belles lettres, usually referred to as *Traité des études*, from 1726 to 1732 (Paris), and his more famous, though less original, *Histoire ancienne des Egyptiens...* in thirteen volumes from 1730 to 1738 (Paris). Numerous editions of Rollin's *Histoire* followed in both English and French. BL.

Rousseau, Jean-Jacques [1670-1741]. *Odes, Epistles, Epigrams, Comedies* and *Letters* [possibly *Oeuvres diverses*]. Selected collections of Rousseau's works were published during his lifetime in 1712 (Solothurn, Switzerland) and in 1723 (2 vols., London) under the title *Oeuvres diverses....* Following his death, numerous editions of his collected works were published in French and English. BL.

_____. *Rousseau's Eloisa* [*Eloisa; or, a series of original letters*]. Rousseau's *Eloisa*, called *Julie, ou la nouvelle Héloïse* in French, was first published in a four-volume edition in Paris in 1761 and in London the same year (4 vols.). Numerous editions in French and English followed. VG.

_____. *Rousseau's Emilius & Sophia* (VG) and *On Education* (IL) [*Emilius and Sophia: or, a New System of Education*]. Rousseau's novel, *Émile, ou De l'éducation*, containing his radical theories of education was first published in a two-volume edition in Paris in 1762. William Kenrick's (1730-79) four-volume English translation was published the same year in London, and subsequent English editions were published throughout the 1760s in London, Edinburgh, and Dublin. 2 vols. VG and IL.[44]

Sale, George et al. *Universal History* [*An Universal History, from the Earliest Account of Time...*]. The first twenty-one volumes were published in London from 1747 to 1754. Forty-four subsequent volumes were published under the title, *The Modern Part of An Universal History, From the Earliest Account of Time...* (London, 1759-66). John Baylor IV owned fifty-five volumes of the series. BLB and IL.

Salmon, Thomas [1679-1767]. *Modern History* [*Modern History; or, The Present State of all Nations...*]. 32 vols. London, 1725-39. BLB.

_____. *Universal Traveller* [*Universal Traveller: or, a Compleat Description of the Several Nations of the World...*]. 2 vols. London, 1752-53. VG and IL.

Saurin, Jacques (also known as Rev. James Saurin) [1677-1730]. *Sermons, Tracts, &c* [probably *Sermons sur divers textes de l'Escriture Sainte*]. 10 vols. (The Hague, 1708-49). Saurin's sermons were published posthumously in numerous French and English editions well into the nineteenth century. BL.[45]

Secondat, Charles-Louis de, Baron de La Brède et de Montesquieu (usually referred to as Montesquieu) [1689-1755]. *Spirit of the Laws, Grandeur and Delusions of the Romans,* and *Persian Letters,* &c [*De l'esprit des lois, Considérations sur les causes de la grandeur des Romains et de leur décadence,* and *Lettres persanes*]. Montesquieu was primarily known in colonial America for his *De l'esprit des lois* (*The Spirit of the Laws*), which he first published, anonymously, in 1748 (2 vols., Geneva). His *Lettres persanes* (*Persian Letters*), an epistolary satire that established his literary fame, was also published anonymously in 1721 (Amsterdam), though his authorship quickly became an open secret. He published his *Considérations sur les causes de la grandeur des Romains et de leur décadence* (*Considerations on the Causes of Greatness of the Romans and of their Decline*) in 1734 (Amsterdam). VG and BL.[46]

Sévigné, Marquise de (née Marie de Rabutin-Chantal) (usually referred to as Madame de Sévigné) [1626-96]. *Letters* [*Lettres de Marie Rabutin-Chantal*...]. An unauthorized edition of twenty-eight of Madame de Sévigné's letters appeared in 1725 (n.p. [Paris]) as *Lettres chosiers de Mme la marquise de Sévigné à Mme Grignan sa fille qui contiennent beaucoup de particularitiés de l'histoire de Louis XIV.* With the assistance of editor Chevalier de Perrin, Sévigné's granddaughter published an official version in 1734-37 (6 vols., Paris) BP.

Shakespeare, William [1564-1616]. [no titles specified]. 7 vols. IL.[47]

[Smith, William] [1727-1803]. *Bouquet's Expeditions* [*An Historical Account of the Expedition Against the Ohio Indians in the year MDCCLXIV*...]. Henry Bouquet (1719-65), a Swiss soldier of fortune, became an officer in the British army and defeated American Indian tribes in western Pennsylvania and the Ohio Valley against considerable odds during the French and Indian War. Smith's *Historical Account,* which he published anonymously in Philadelphia in 1765 and in London the following year, recounts the story of Bouquet's final campaign against the Shawnee, Seneca, and Delaware Indians in 1764. IL.

Smollett, Tobias [1721-71]. *Continuation* [*Continuation of the Complete History of England*]. 5 vols. London, 1760-65. Smollett's *Continuation* was a chronological extension of his *The Complete History of England, Deduced from the Descent of Julius Caeasar, to the Treaty of Aix la Chapelle, 1748*, 4 vols. (1757-58, London). A second edition of Smollett's *Complete History*, which was originally published in quarto, was issued in eleven octavo volumes in 1758-59 (London). The second edition of the *Complete History*, along with the first four volumes of the *Continuation*, was offered as a fifteen-volume set at the *Virginia Gazette*. IL.[48]

[_____]. *Roderick Random* [*The Adventures of Roderick Random*]. Smollett published his two-volume novel in London in 1748. Colonel Baylor III purchased the sixth edition (London, 1763) from the *Virginia Gazette* in 1764. VG.

Society of Gentlemen. *Dictionary on husbandry* [*The Complete Farmer, or, a General dictionary of husbandry...*]. More than one book appeared in the eighteenth century with the phrase *Dictionary of Husbandry* in its title, but the most likely candidate is *The Complete Farmer*, first published in London in 1766 and popular in Britain and colonial America. IL.

Stackhouse, Thomas [1677–1752]. *Stackhouse on Christianity* [*New History of the Holy Bible from the Beginning of the World to the Establishment of Christianity*]. 2 vols. London, 1737. IL.[49]

Sterne, Laurence [1713-68]. *Tristram Shandy* [*The Life and Opinions of Tristram Shandy, Gentleman*]. Sterne published the first two volumes of his novel in 1759 (London), and completed the subsequent seven volumes of *Tristram* by 1766. Only two volumes in the series were accounted for in the inventory of Col. Baylor III's estate, which were likely those in the first installment. IL.

Stith, Buckner [1722-91]. *Treatise on Tobacco* [exact title unknown]. Buckner Stith, a Brunswick County, Virginia, planter, paid £32 to Joseph Royle, publisher of the *Virginia Gazette*, to print a thousand copies of his pamphlet on tobacco, which was advertised in the *Gazette* as *Buckner Stith's Opinion on the Cultivation of Tobacco* (July 6, 1764). No copies of the pamphlet remain extant. VG.[50]

Swift, Jonathan [1667-1745]. *Swift's work* [no titles specified]. Swift was such a prolific writer that speculation regarding which titles the Baylors owned is hazardous, but presumably their collection included the works for which Swift is best known, including *Gulliver's Travels* and *A Modest Proposal*. 3 vols. IL.

Trapassi, Pietro Antonio Domenico (known by pseudonym Metastasio) [1698-1782]. *Dramatic Pieces &c* [possibly *Dissertazione su le Poesie drammatiche del sig. Abate Pietro Metastasio* or *Opere di Pietro Metastasio*]. A popular five-volume collection of Metastasio's works was produced during his lifetime by his collaborator and sometime enemy, Ranieri de' Calzabigi, in 1755 under the title *Dissertazione su le Poesie drammatiche del sig. Abate Pietro Metastasio* (Paris). The best eighteenth-century edition of his works is *Opere di Pietro Metastasio*, 12 vols. (Paris, 1780-82). BL.

Trenchard, John [1662-1723]. *Cato Major* [*Cato's Letters; or, Essays on Liberty, Civil and Religious, and Other Important Subjects*]. Under the pseudonym Cato (i.e., Cato the Younger [95-46 BC], the ancient Roman champion of civil liberties), John Trenchard and Thomas Gordon (d. 1750) jointly wrote 144 essays on liberty and republican principles that were published in the *London Journal* from 1720 to 1723. Beginning in 1723, their collected essays were published in London in book form, under the title *Cato's Letters*, in a number of editions. Colonel Baylor III purchased the four-volume fifth edition from the *Virginia Gazette* in 1754. VG.[51]

Unknown. Colonel Baylor III's estate inventory list mentions "37 books half worn," which appear on the list subsequent to the reference to "19 Latin Books." Given their condition and apparent placement next to the Latin books, they may have been Greco-Roman classic books for Col. Baylor III's children.

Venegas, Miguel [1680-1764]. *History of Calefonia* [*A Natural and Civil History of California*]. Venegas, a Mexican Jesuit priest, wrote his manuscript for the *Civil History* in the 1730s, which was extensively edited by a fellow Jesuit, Andrés Marcos Burriel, and finally published in Madrid in 1757 and in a popular English translation two years later, entitled *A Natural and Civil History of California: containing an accurate description of that country...*, 2 vols. (London, 1759). IL.

Vertot, Réné-Aubert, Sieur de [1655-1735]. *Revolutions of Rome, Portugal, Sweden, &c* [*Histoire des révolutions arrivés dans le government de la République Romaine, Histoire des Révolutions de Portugal,* and *Histoire des révolutions de Suède*]. Abbé de Vertot anonymously published his first work, *Histoire de la conjuration de Portugal* (Paris, 1689), which was republished under Vertot's name and under the title *Histoire des Révolutions de Portugal* in Paris in 1711 and in Amsterdam the following year. In 1695, he published *Histoire des révolutions de Suède...*, 2 vols. in 1 (Paris), followed by *Histoire des révolutions ... de la République Romaine* in 1719 (Paris). Each of these works was subsequently republished in numerous French and English editions throughout the eighteenth and early nineteenth centuries. BL.

Virgil (Publius Vergilius Maro or Vergilius) [70 BC-19 BC]. [no titles specified] [*Aeneid, Eclogues* or *Georgics*]. Virgil's works, in English or Latin, were considered essential among literate people in colonial America who could afford even only a few books. IL.

Virginia Gazette. *Interleaved Almanack* [*The Virginia Almanack for the Year of Our Lord God 1765*]. [1764]. VG.

Virginia law books, 3 vols. [no titles specified]. IL.

Vitruvius, Marcus Pollio [ca. 90-20 BC]. *The Architecture of M. Vitruvius Pollio; Translated from the Original Latin by W. Newton, architect* [not listed in BL or IL]. William Newton's *Vitruvius*, which appeared in 1771 (London), was the first published English translation of Books I-V of Vitruvius' *De architectura libri decem* (*Ten Books of Architecture*). In the year following Newton's death, James Newton, his brother and executor, arranged for a reissue of *Vitruvius* in a two-volume folio edition (London, 1791), which included a translation of all ten of Vitruvius' books on architecture, along with forty-six plates (many prepared by James Newton). William Newton's talents as an architect may have exceed his abilities as a translator of classical Latin. Joseph Gwilt, who translated Vitruvius' treatise in 1826, commented that Newton's translation "exhibits such a mixture of ignorance of the language of the original in translation of the text, with so much intelligence in some of the notes, that it is difficult to believe they are from the same hand." More recent scholarship, however, indicates this assessment is unduly critical. VHS.[52]

Voltaire (*nom de plume* of François-Marie Arouet) [1694-1778]. *Poems, Dramatic Pieces, Poetry, History, Literature* [no titles specified; probably an edition of collected works]. Voltaire's prolific works were published in innumerable editions, in French and English, throughout his lifetime and afterwards through today. BL and IL.[53]

_____. *Voltaire's Candidus* [*Candidus: or, The Optimist*]. Voltaire published his satirical novel, *Candide, ou l'Optimisme*, in Paris in 1759. Several English translations of Candide appeared in London and Edinburgh the same year, including William Rider's (1723-85) work under the title *Candidus; or The Optimist*. VG.

Walpole, Horace [1717-97]. *Noble Authors* [*A Catalogue of the Royal and Noble Authors of England, with lists of their works…*]. Walpole's *Catalogue* was first published in London in 1758 (2 vols.), followed by a corrected second edition during the same year and subsequent editions thereafter. IL.

Young, Edward [1683-1765]. *Young's Works* [*The Works of the Author of Night-Thoughts*]. Numerous editions of Young's collected poems appeared during his life and afterwards. Colonel Baylor III bought a four-volume London edition (either 1757 or 1762) from the *Virginia Gazette* in 1764. VG and IL.

Source Abbreviations

APS Proceedings	*Proceedings of the American Philosophical Society,* Philadelphia
BLB	John Baylor Letterbook, 1757-1765, VHS.
BP	Baylor Family Papers (Accession No. 2257), UVASC
CWM	College of William and Mary, Williamsburg, Va.
CWSC	Special Collections, John D. Rockefeller Jr. Library, Colonial Williamsburg Foundation, Williamsburg, Va.
DN	William B. Clark et al., eds., *Naval Documents of the American Revolution*, 11 vols. to date (Washington, D.C., 1964—)
DR	*Daingerfield v. Rootes*, Superior Court of Chancery for Richmond District, Fredericksburg, Va. (1809-23)
LOC	Library of Congress, Washington, D.C.

LVA   Library of Virginia, Richmond

MHM   Maryland Historical Magazine

MHS   Maryland Historical Society,
                             Baltimore

NP   John Norton and Sons Papers, 1750-
                             1902, CWSC.

TJP   Julian P. Boyd et al., eds., *The
                             Papers of Thomas Jefferson*, 33 vols.
                             to date (Princeton, N.J., 1950—)

UKNA   National Archives, Kew, England

UVASC   Albert and Shirley Small Special
                             Collections Library, University of
                             Virginia, Charlottesville

VG   *Virginia Gazette*

VHS   Virginia Historical Society,
                             Richmond

VMHB   *Virginia Magazine of History and
                             Biography*

WMQ   *William & Mary Quarterly*

Notes

Preface & Acknowledgements

1. Though most historians acknowledge that the Virginia gentry degenerated politically and economically after the Revolution, surprisingly little serious research has been conducted on the postwar fate of particular gentry families other than a few notables such as Thomas Jefferson, William Byrd III, and the Nelsons of York County. Part of the problem may stem from Jackson Turner Main's important study, "The One Hundred," *WMQ*, 3rd ser., 11 (July 1954): 354-84. Main culled Virginia real and personal property tax lists for 1787-88 to assemble a tentative list of the state's one hundred wealthiest individuals based on their ownership of land, slaves, and domestic farm animals (John Baylor IV is listed as owning 13,161 acres of land and 159 slaves). But personal net worth is determined from two components, assets and liabilities, and Main's study considered only the former. Most of the Virginia gentry identified by Main were heavily indebted to British merchants who, despite their vigorous postwar collection efforts, were unable to obtain court judgments until the U.S. Supreme Court finally cleared the path in 1796 in *Ware v. Hylton*, 3 U.S. 199 (discussed in the final chapter). Many were also ruined by the deep economic depression that followed the Revolution and that persisted longer in Virginia than in New England or the Mid-Atlantic states. Thus, beginning in the late 1790s and continuing through the first two decades of the nineteenth century, a number of Main's one hundred lost all or most of their holdings to British and American creditors, including the Armisteads, the Baylors, the Beverleys, the Braxtons, some of the Carters, the Carys, the Lees, the McCartys, the Pages, and the Randolphs. By not accounting for these postwar developments, Main's study tends to create the false impression that the Virginia gentry, as a whole, survived the Revolution intact—the opposite of what actually happened. (In Main's defense, many of the records needed to accomplish a more complete study of the gentry

in the postwar period, especially British Treasury records and federal court records in Virginia, had not been adequately catalogued and microfilmed and thus were not readily available in 1954.) The reality is that the Revolution and its aftermath devastated the Virginia gentry more widely and deeply than scholars have generally realized.

2. *The Education of Henry Adams: An Autobiography* (Boston, 1918), 56-58.

3. Louis B. Wright, *The First Gentlemen of Virginia: Intellectual Qualities of the Early Colonial Ruling Class* (San Marino, Calif., 1940), 1, 349.

4. Louis B. Wright, "Richard Lee II: A Belated Elizabethan in Virginia," *Huntington Library Quarterly* 1 (Oct. 1938): 1-35; "Letter of Col. Nathaniel Burwell" [Nathaniel Burwell to James Burwell, June 13, 1718], *WMQ*, 1st ser., 7 (July 1898): 43-44. On the Byrd diary, see Louis B. Wright and Marion Tinling, eds., *The Secret Diary of William Byrd of Westover, 1709-1712* (Richmond, Va., 1941). For other examples of books that began to attack the myth during this period, see Louis Morton, *Robert Carter of Nomini Hall: A Virginia Tobacco Planter of the Eighteenth Century* (Williamsburg, Va., 1941); Hunter D. Farish, ed., *Journal and Letters of Philip Vickers Fithian, 1773-1774: A Plantation Tutor of the Old Dominion* (Williamsburg, Va., 1943); Burton J. Hendrick, *The Lees of Virginia: Biography of a Family* (Boston, 1935).

5. Julie H. Williams, *The Significance of the Printed Word in Early America* (Westport, Conn., and London, 1999), 52. Examples of the Virginia gentry's private literature abound. See, for example, J. A. Leo Lemay, ed., *Robert Bolling Woos Anne Miller: Love and Courtship in Colonial Virginia, 1760*; Jack P. Greene, ed., *The Diary of Colonel Landon Carter*, 2 vols. (Charlottesville, Va., 1965); Richard B. Davis, "The Colonial Virginia Satirist: Mid-Eighteenth Century Commentaries on Politics, Religion, and Society," *Transactions of the American Philosophical Society*, New Ser., 57 (1967): 1-74.

6. Kevin J. Hayes, *The Road to Monticello: The Life and Mind of Thomas Jefferson* (New York, 2008), 327. On relations between the gentry and nongentry in Virginia and colonial America, see Gordon S. Wood, *The*

Radicalism of the American Revolution (New York, 1991), chaps. 1-5; Jack P. Greene, "Society, Ideology and Politics: An Analysis of the Political Culture of Mid-Eighteenth Century Virginia," in *Negotiated Authorities: Essays in Colonial Political and Constitutional History* (Charlottesville, Va., and London, 1994), 259-318. A "deferential society" has been defined as one "consisting of an elite and a nonelite, in which the nonelite regard the elite, without too much resentment, as being of a superior status and culture to their own, and consider elite leadership in political matters to be something normal and natural." (J. G. A. Pocock, "The Classical Theory of Deference," *American Historical Review* 81 [June 1976]: 516.) A growing number of scholars believe, however, that the concept of deference "may have become too slippery to be very useful in helping us understand social and political relations in the eighteenth-century world." (Richard R. Beeman, "The Varieties of Deference in Eighteenth-Century America," *Early American Studies* 3 [Fall 2005]: 313.) Others have called for complete burial of the concept. See John K. Alexander, "Reflections on Political Deference in Early America: Let's Meet at the Graveside," ibid., 383-401. It is unreasonable to expect deference, as a historiographic construct, to have a one-size-fits-all applicability to early America. As Richard Beeman points out, the American colonies, despite their common language and shared legal traditions and culture, were "extraordinarily disconnected from one another, displaying among themselves and within themselves significant varieties of political behavior." (Beeman, *The Varieties of Political Experience in Eighteenth-Century America* [Philadelphia, 2004], 2.) Nevertheless, deference, however shaken by backcountry politics, nascent evangelical movements, and rising republicanism, remains a critically important concept in understanding colonial Virginia. On public virtue and the Virginia gentry, see Jack P. Greene, "The Concept of Virtue in Late Colonial British America," in *Imperatives, Behaviors and Identities: Essays in Early American Cultural History* (Charlottesville, Va., and London, 1992), 208-35.

7.   [Thomas Anburey], *Travels through the Interior Parts of America*, 2 vols. (London 1789), 2:345-46. Anburey plagiarized and liberally borrowed portions of his book from Rev. Andrew Burnaby and others. But his observations and experiences, including this one, appear for the most part to be genuine. That the Virginia gentry did not produce literature intended primarily for the nongentry does not mean the gentry, as a class, regarded the nongentry with hostility or disdain.

In reviewing William Wirt's draft biography of Patrick Henry, St. George Tucker (1752-1827) sought to correct Wirt's "exaggeration" and romanticized misapprehensions regarding the pre-Revolutionary Virginia gentry. To be sure, "[t]he rich rode in Coaches, or Chariots, or on fine horses," Tucker acknowledged, "but they never failed to pull off their hats to a poor man whom they met, & generally, appear'd to me to shake hands with every man in a Court-yard, or a Churchyard.... [A]s far as I could judge, the planter who own'd half a dozen negroes, felt himself perfectly upon a level with his rich neighbor that own'd a hundred." The Virginia gentry were, Tucker contended, "a race of harmless aristocrats" utterly lacking in mean-spiritedness toward nongentry whites. (St. George Tucker to William Wirt, Sept. 25, 1815, in "William Wirt's Life of Patrick Henry," *WMQ*, 1st ser., 22 [April 1914]: 252-53.) Tucker was born in Bermuda to a respectable merchant family and came to Virginia in 1772 (the same year Wirt was born) to attend law school at the College of William and Mary. As an educated outsider and successful lawyer who married into and interacted with the Virginia gentry, Tucker was in an ideal position to observe and assess them. On Wirt's literary constructions of the Virginia gentry, see William R. Taylor, "William Wirt and the Legend of the Old South," *WMQ*, 3rd ser., 4 (Oct. 1957): 477-93.

8. Richard Beale Davis, *A Colonial Southern Bookshelf: Reading in the Eighteenth Century* (Athens, Ga., 1979), 11. Davis's most important contributions to Southern intellectual history are his *Intellectual Life in the Colonial South, 1585-1763*, 3 vols. (Knoxville, Tenn., 1978) and *Intellectual Life in Jefferson's Virginia, 1790-1830* (Knoxville, Tenn., 1964). See also Richard B. Davis, ed., *Literature and Society in Early Virginia, 1608-1840* (Baton Rouge, La., 1973). For a bibliography of Davis's writings through 1977, see J.A. Leo Lemay, ed., *Essays in Early Virginia Literature Honoring Richard Beale Davis* (New York, 1977), vii-xii. The regional bias toward Virginia and the South among many historians lingers, but in somewhat more subtle iterations. Edmund S. Morgan, for example, wrote an odd study of what he called the "Puritan Ethic," by which he meant a particular set of values shared by American patriots in the 1760s and 1770s, such as industry, resourcefulness, and thrift. (Edmund S. Morgan, "The Puritan Ethic and the American Revolution," *WMQ*, 3rd ser., 24 [Jan. 1967]: 3-43.) Emphasizing that "Puritan Ethic" was merely "an appropriate short-hand term," Morgan disclaimed any regional monopoly on these values, and, as if to throw a bone to the Wright-

Davis set, he nominated Richard Henry Lee of Virginia and Henry Laurens of South Carolina as honorary embodiments of the ethic. But, as historian C. Vann Woodward wondered, "[T]here is *something* about the name that does raise questions." (C. Vann Woodward, "The Southern Ethic in a Puritan World," *WMQ*, 3rd ser., 25 [July 1968]: 350.) Among other things, if Morgan really believed that these values were widely held throughout America, why didn't he simply call them the "*American* Ethic"?

Chapter 1

1. None of the persons named "John Baylor" in this book is known to have used numeric suffixes as part of their names. Numeric suffixes are given here merely to help distinguish them from one another. On Baylor's background and family, see "The Baylor Family," *VMHB* 6 (Oct. 1898): 197-99; Patricia Latford, "The Baylor Family in America: John Baylor, Book II" (unpublished manuscript, 2007). Researchers should be wary of *Baylor's History of the Baylors* (privately printed, 1914), by Orval W. Baylor and Henry B. Baylor, as this work is full of errors and dubious suppositions. For a history of Gonville and Caius College, see Christopher Brooke, *A History of Gonville and Caius College* (Suffolk, Eng., 1985).

2. Robert Carter to Messrs. [Micajah and Richard] Perry, Sept. 27, 1720, in Louis B. Wright, ed., *Letters of Robert Carter, 1720-1727: The Commercial Interests of a Virginia Gentleman* (San Marino, Calif., 1940), 54. On John Baylor II's importation of slaves, see Baylor Ledgers, 1719-1755, 3 vols., BP; Walter Minchinton, Celia King, and Peter Waite, eds., *Virginia Slave Trade Statistics 1698-1775* (Richmond, Va., 1984), 43-49; Walter Minchinton, ed., "The Virginia Letters of Isaac Hobhouse, Merchant of Bristol," *VMHB* 66 (Oct. 1958): 278-301. After long neglect, the literature on the trans-Atlantic slave trade has significantly expanded in recent years. See, for example, James A. Rawley, with Stephen D. Behrendt, *The Transatlantic Slave Trade: A History*, rev. ed. (Lincoln, Neb., 2005); Herbert S. Klein, *The Atlantic Slave Trade* (New York, 1999); Hugh Thomas, *The Slave Trade: The Story of the Atlantic Slave Trade, 1440-1870* (New York, 1997); Douglas B. Chambers, "The Transatlantic Slave Trade to Virginia in Comparative Historical Perspective, 1698-1778," in *Afro-Virginian History and Culture*, ed. John Saillant (New York, 1999), 3-28. David

Eltis's *The Trans-Atlantic Slave Trade: A Database on CD-ROM* (Cambridge, Eng., 1999) has been expanded into a free online edition at: www.slavevoyages.org.

3. H. F. Cary, ed., *The Poetical Works of Alexander Pope* (London, 1859), 109. For a history of the town of Newmarket and its race course, see Rebecca Cassidy, *The Sport of Kings: Kinship, Class and Thoroughbred Breeding in Newmarket* (Cambridge, Eng., 2002); R. C. Lyle, *Royal Newmarket* (London, 1945); John P. Hore, *The History of Newmarket, and the Annals of the Turf,* 3 vols. (London, 1886). Regarding Baylor's land grants, see Grants, July 6, 1726, from Lt. Gov. Hugh Drysdale to John Baylor, for 3,360 acres and 8,400 acres, respectively (Mss 11:1 B3445:1; Mss 11:1 B3445:2), VHS.

4. César de Saussure, *A Foreign View of England in the Reigns of George I & George II*, trans. Madame Van Muyden (New York and London, 1902), 288; Dennis Le Marchant, *Memoir of John Charles, Viscount Althorp, Third Earl Spencer* (London, 1876), 74.

5. Daniel Defoe, *A Tour Through the Whole Island of Great Britain*, 3 vols. (London, 1724-26), 1:117; Hugh Jones, *The Present State of Virginia*, ed. Richard L. Morton (1724; Chapel Hill, N.C., 1956). In addition to his aversion to gaming, Defoe scorned newfangled forms of wealth creation, especially trading in company stocks. See, for example, [Daniel Defoe], *The Free-Holders Plea Against Stock-Jobbing Elections of Parliament Men* (London, 1701); idem, *The Anatomy of Exchange-Alley: or, A New System of Stock-Jobbing* (London, 1719). On the gaming dice at Jamestown, see www.apva.org/ngex/c2dice.html. On gambling among the colonial Virginia gentry, see T. H. Breen, "Horses and Gentlemen: The Cultural Significance of Gambling Among the Gentry of Virginia," *WMQ*, 3rd ser., 34 (April 1977): 239-57.

6. One source indicates there were twenty-eight "horse matches run" at Newmarket in the fall of 1718. (J.B. Muir, *Ye Olde New-Markitt Calendar of Matches, Results, and Programs from 1619 to 1719* [London, 1892], 52.)

7. For Baylor's legislative service, see Cynthia Miller Leonard, comp., *The General Assembly of Virginia, July 30, 1619-January 11, 1978:*

A Bicentennial Register of Members (Richmond, Va., 1978), 78-82, 86-93. In an important study, Jack P. Greene analyzed the roles and influence of 630 members of the House of Burgesses between 1720 and 1776 and concluded that the body was dominated by about 110 members during that period (and Baylor was not among them). See Jack P. Greene, "Foundations of Political Power in the Virginia House of Burgesses, 1720-1776," *WMQ*, 3rd ser., 16 (Oct. 1959): 485-506.

8. Jack P. Greene, *Political Life in Eighteenth-Century Virginia* (Williamsburg, Va., 1986), 14. Regarding the quotidian influence of county courts, one historian has suggested that county-level government and Williamsburg constituted "[t]wo nearly separate political worlds" and that matters in the "provincial world of Williamsburg and London rarely concerned or influenced them [local residents], but the activities of the parish vestry and county court did." (John G. Kolp, *Gentlemen and Freeholders: Electoral Politics in Colonial Virginia* [Baltimore and London, 1998], 191, 195.)

9. On the county courts and "gentlemen justices" in colonial Virginia, see A. G. Roeber, *Faithful Magistrates and Republican Lawyers: Creators of Virginia Legal Culture, 1680-1810* (Chapel Hill, N.C., 1981), chaps. 2-4; David J. Mays, *Edmund Pendleton, 1721-1803: A Biography*, 2 vols. (Cambridge, Mass., 1952), chap. 4; Charles S. Sydnor, *Gentlemen Freeholders: Political Practices in Washington's Virginia* (Chapel Hill, N.C., 1952), chap. 6. Regarding the trial and execution of Tom, Col. Baylor's slave, see Douglas B. Chambers, *Murder at Montpelier: Igbo Africans in Virginia* (Jackson, Miss., 2005), 125.

10. Sydnor, *Gentlemen Freeholders*, 64; T. E. Campbell, *Colonial Caroline: A History of Caroline County, Virginia* (Richmond, Va., 1954), 346-47. Although the majority of Virginia's county justices before the Revolution were not lawyers, they had—in addition to their experience and common sense—some guidance. Often at least one (and preferably two) of the justices was an attorney, such as Edmund Pendleton in Caroline County. These attorney-justices were designated "Quorum" justices by the governor, and at least one of them was required to be present for most judicial actions. Moreover, the justices had access to an excellent handbook: George Webb's *Office and Authority of a Justice of the Peace* (Williamsburg, Va., 1736), which was the first Anglo-American legal treatise. Modeled on William

Nelson's book of the same name for English justices (London, 1704), Webb's 364-page guide combined English law, Virginia statutes, and local practices ("customs of the country") in a practical, easy-to-understand format complete with forms and procedural instructions intended for busy Virginia planters. Webb, who had been asked by Lt. Gov. William Gooch to write the book, understood his task and his audience perfectly. In a preface he explained that he "avoided all References to Laws and Law Books" because "[t]he far greatest Part of our Inhabitants are unfurnish'd with those Books, or diverted from Reading them, by the necessary Affairs of their Plantations, and the innocent Pleasures of a Country Life." (Ibid., ix.) Webb's book remained in print at the *Virginia Gazette* through the early 1750s. On justice of the peace manuals in colonial America, see John A. Conley, "Doing It by the Book: Justice of the Peace Manuals and English Law in Eighteenth Century America," *Journal of Legal History* 6 (Dec. 1985): 257-98.

11. John Smith, *A Map of Virginia* (Oxford, 1612), in Philip L. Barbour, ed., *The Complete Works of Captain John Smith (1580-1631)*, 3 vols. (Chapel Hill, N.C., and London), 1:143 (emphasis added); William Strachey, *The Historie of Travell into Virginia Britania*, ed. Louis B. Wright and Virginia Freund, Hakluyt Society, 2nd Ser., Vol. CIII (London, 1953), 32. In contrast to Smith's and Strachey's initial reactions to America, William Bradford (1590-1657) saw the continent as "a hideous and desolate wilderness, full of wild beasts and wild men.... The whole country, full of woods and thickets, represented a savage hue." (William Bradford, "Of Plymouth Plantation," in *American Literature: The Makers and the Making, Book A, Beginnings to 1826* [New York, 1973], 20-21.) The extreme concentration of land ownership in Britain survived well into the nineteenth and early twentieth centuries. As late as 1860, for example, one-quarter of the land in England and Wales was owned by 710 individuals, and nearly three-quarters of all the land in Britain was held by fewer than 5,000 people. See David Cannadine, *The Decline and Fall of the British Aristocracy* (New York and London, 1990), 55.

12. Douglas S. Freeman, *George Washington: A Biography*, 7 vols. (1948-57), 1:6. On Fitzhugh, see Richard B. Davis, ed., *William Fitzhugh and His Chesapeake World, 1676-1701* (Chapel Hill, N.C., 1963), 3-48. On Fairfax, see Stuart E. Brown, Jr., *Virginia Baron: The Story of Thomas 6th Lord Fairfax* (Berryville, Va., 1965). For Byrd's land

accumulations, see William Byrd Title Book, 1637-1734 (Mss 5:9 B9965:1), VHS, which was published in part in Rebecca Johnston, "William Byrd Title Book," *VMHB* 47 (1939): 191-217, 285-314; 48 (1940): 31-56, 107-29, 222-37, 328-40; 49 (1941): 37-50, 174-80, 269-78, 354-63; 50 (1942): 169-79, 238-63. The history of the Northern Neck proprietary to 1745 (when its western boundaries were finally settled) is recounted in exhaustive but splendid detail in Freeman, *George Washington*, 1:447-525. Surprisingly, there is no scholarly biography of Robert "King" Carter. See Katharine L. Brown, *Robert "King" Carter: Builder of Christ Church* (Staunton, Va., 2001); Clifford Dowdey, *The Virginia Dynasties: The Emergence of "King" Carter and the Golden Age* (Boston and Toronto, 1969); Carl F. Cannon, Jr., "Robert ('King') Carter of 'Corotoman'" (MA thesis, Duke University, 1956).

13. According to one study of the Virginia Council, divvying up large land grants "was the most divisive factor in councilor politics in the late 1740s and throughout the 1750s." (James L. Anderson, "The Governors Councils of Colonial America: A Study of Pennsylvania and Virginia, 1660-1776" [PhD diss., University of Virginia, 1967], 240). Regarding general land ownership patterns in Virginia in 1700, see Warren M. Billings, John E. Selby, Thad W. Tate, *Colonial Virginia: A History* (White Plains, N.Y., 1986), 122-23. The land grants (other than those in the Northern Neck) are listed in H. R. McIlwaine et al., eds., *Executive Journals of the Council of Colonial Virginia, 1680–1775*, 6 vols. (Richmond, Va., 1925–66), and are analyzed (with emphasis on the gentry) in Manning C. Voorhis, "The Land Grant Policy of Colonial Virginia, 1607-1774" (PhD diss., University of Virginia, 1940), esp. appendix I. For a more recent discussion of the Virginia gentry's landgrab, see Anthony S. Parent, Jr., *Foul Means: The Formation of a Slave Society in Virginia, 1660-1740* (Chapel Hill, N.C., and London, 2003), chap. 2. For the form and technical details of the grants, see Fairfax Harrison, *Virginia Land Grants: A Study of Conveyancing in Relation to Colonial Politics* (privately printed, 1925).

14. Harry J. Carman, ed., *American Husbandry* (1775; New York, 1939), 164. Though for many years the authorship of *American Husbandry* had been attributed to Arthur Young, Carman presents a solid case (pp. xxxix-lxi) that its probable author was Dr. John Mitchell (1711-68) of Urbanna, Va. For a biographical sketch of Dr. Mitchell, see Whitfield J. Bell, Jr., *Patriot-Improvers: Biographical Sketches of Members of the*

American Philosophical Society, Volume 1, 1743-1768 (Philadelphia, 1997), 138-48. On soil depletion at Chesapeake tobacco plantations, see Allan Kulikoff, *Tobacco and Slaves: The Development of Southern Cultures in the Chesapeake, 1680-1800* (Chapel Hill, N.C., and London, 1986), 47-51. Robert "King" Carter's will has been published in *VMHB* 5 (May 1898): 408-28, 6 (July 1898): 1-32. On partible inheritance of land among the Virginia gentry, see Daniel B. Smith, *Inside the Great House: Planter Family Life in Eighteenth-Century Chesapeake Society* (Ithaca, N.Y., and London, 1980), 242-48.

15. Regarding the Loyal Company, see Archibald Henderson, "Dr. Thomas Walker and the Loyal Company of Virginia," *Proceedings of the American Antiquarian Society* 41 (1931): 77-178. On Baylor's involvement in the Ohio Company, see Lois Mulkearn, ed., *George Mercer Papers Relating to the Ohio Company of Virginia* (Pittsburgh, Pa., 1954), 250, 292.

16. George Washington to William Crawford, Sept. 17, 1767, in W. W. Abbot et al., eds., *The Papers of George Washington, Colonial Series*, 10 vols. (Charlottesville, Va., 1983-95), 8:28. On Baylor's membership in the Mississippi Company, see Minutes of General Meeting of Mississippi Company, Dec. 16, 1767, in Clarence E. Carter, "Documents Relating to the Mississippi Land Company, 1763-1769," *American Historical Review* 16 (Jan. 1911): 318. On the Proclamation of 1763 and Virginia land companies, see Eugene M. Del Papa, "The Royal Proclamation of 1763: Its Effect Upon Virginia Land Companies," *VMHB* 83 (Oct. 1975): 406-11. For an extensive and fascinating treatment of the numerous competing land companies in colonial America, see Charles Royster, *The Fabulous History of the Dismal Swamp Company: A Story of George Washington's Times* (New York, 1999).

17. John Baylor to George Washington, June 20, 1757, in W. W. Abbot et al., eds., *Papers of George Washington, Colonial Series*, 4:242-43. Christopher Gist (1706-59), a frontiersman and surveyor, was one of the earliest Europeans to explore the Ohio Valley. He acted as a guide for George Washington and served under him in the first armed confrontation of the French and Indian War, the Battle of Fort Necessity (1754). See Kenneth P. Bailey, *Christopher Gist: Colonial Frontiersman, Explorer, and Indian Agent*, (Hamden, Conn., 1976). On Baylor's protest, see Campbell, *Colonial Caroline*, 183.

18. For Baylor's militia service under Washington, see Abbot et al., eds., *Papers of George Washington, Colonial Series*, 3:111, 129; John Baylor to George Washington, June 7, 1756, ibid., 3:199 (in which Baylor thanks Washington for the opportunity to serve and promises to "pursue every necessary Step" to have deserters captured and sent to Washington). Not surprisingly, the same men who held political sway in the counties and in Williamsburg also generally composed the top ranks in the state militia. See Richard R. Beeman, *The Old Dominion and the New Nation* (Lexington, Ky., 1972), 106-7.

19. Charles I to Governor and Council of Virginia, Nov. [?], 1627, in W. Noel Sainsbury et al., eds., *Calendar of State Papers, Colonial Series, 1574-1660* (London, 1860), 86. For a discussion of the tobacco trade between Virginia and England (including Charles I's attitude toward the weed), see Neville Williams, "England's Tobacco Trade in the Reign of Charles I," *VMHB* 65 (Oct. 1957): 403-49.

20. Regarding the Virginia plantation system and British tobacco merchants, see Kulikoff, *Tobacco and Slaves*; T. H. Breen *Tobacco Culture: The Mentality of the Great Tidewater Planters on the Eve of Revolution* (Princeton, 1985). See also James H. Soltow, *The Economic Role of Williamsburg* (Williamsburg, Va., 1965); Arthur P. Middleton, *Tobacco Coast: A Maritime History of the Chesapeake Bay in the Colonial Era* (Newport News, Va., 1953), chap. 4.

21. A bill of exchange worked much like a modern check. A planter who owed a debt in pounds sterling to a British creditor or who wished to acquire goods or credit locally in the colonies from someone who desired credit in pounds sterling would draw a bill of exchange upon the British merchant with whom the planter maintained a tobacco consignment account and present the bill as payment for the debt or goods. A bill of exchange was often endorsed and traded multiple times before it was finally redeemed. On the use of bills of exchange in the American colonies, see John J. McCusker, *Money and Exchange in Europe and America, 1600-1775: A Handbook* (Chapel Hill, N.C., 1978), 19-22. A problem related to the prohibition of exporting British pounds was the extreme scarcity of specie in the colonies, especially Virginia. See, for example, Leslie V. Brock, *The Currency of the American Colonies 1700-1764: A Study in Colonial Finance and Imperial Relations* (New York, 1975), 465-527. The inadequate money supply in Virginia, coupled with the Navigation Acts, which

required that all American-grown tobacco be sent to Britain in British ships and which actively discouraged domestic manufacturing, made the planters' thralldom to their British consignment agents and their addiction to British merchandise increasingly worse through the colonial period.

22. George Washington to George Mason, April 5, 1769 (in which Washington describes the gentry as those who wish to live "genteely and hospitably"), in Abbot et al., eds., *Papers of George Washington, Colonial Series*, 8:179; John Baylor III to Flowerdewe and Norton, Sept. 16, 1760, BLB; Robert Beverley to [John Bland], Dec. 27, 1762, in Robert Beverley Letterbook, 1761-93, LOC. It is interesting to contrast Beverley's orders from London with those of his more frugal father, William Beverley (1696-1756). Whereas the younger Beverley wanted dinnerware of "the most fashionable sort," his father asked for a "set of cheap blew and White China." (William Beverley to Micajah Perry, July 12, 1737, in Worthington C. Ford., ed., "Letters of William Beverley," *WMQ*, 4 [April 1895]: 225.)

23. Jones, *Present State of Virginia*, 84; William Gooch to Thomas Gooch, Dec. 28, 1727, Letters of William Gooch, 1727-1751 (typescript), VHS; James Blair, *Our Saviour's Divine Sermon on the Mount*, 2nd ed., 2 vols. (London, 1740), 1:127. For numerous examples of the merchandise order lists of Virginia planters, see NP. Regarding the twin gentry ethos of gentility and hospitality among the Chesapeake colonial elite, see Michal J. Rozbicki, *The Complete Colonial Gentleman: Cultural Legitimacy in Plantation America* (Charlottesville, Va., and London, 1998), chap. 5 and passim.

24. On the consumer revolution in colonial America, see T. H. Breen, "'Baubles of Britain': The American and Consumer Revolutions of the Eighteenth Century," *Past and Present* 119 (May 1988): 73-104; idem, "An Empire of Goods: The Anglicization of Colonial America, 1690-1776," *Journal of British Studies* 25 (Oct. 1986): 467-99. Breen has expanded his theories in "Baubles of Britain" regarding the politicization of consumer goods during the run-up to the American Revolution in *The Marketplace of Revolution: How Consumer Politics Shaped American Independence* (New York, 2004). On the importation of glassware, see John J. MacCusker and Russell R. Menard, *The Economy of British America, 1607-1789* (Chapel Hill, N.C., 1991), 284.

25. Andrew Burnaby, *Travels Through the Middle Settlements in North-America* (London, 1775), 41; "Journal of a French Traveller in the Colonies, 1765," *American Historical Review* 26 (July 1921): 743; Francis Fauquier to the Board of Trade, Nov. 3, 1762, in George Reese, ed., *The Official Papers of Francis Fauquier, Lieutenant Governor of Virginia, 1758-1768*, 3 vols. (Charlottesville, Va., 1983), 2:818. By the 1760s, a growing chorus of clerics and laity cautioned against the planters' excessive consumption and extravagant lifestyles. See Jack P. Greene, "A Mirror of Virtue for a Declining Land: John Camm's Funeral Sermon for William Nelson," in *Essays in Early Virginia Literature*, ed. J. A. Leo Lemay, 185. For a brief but useful overview of the Virginia tobacco planters' cycle of consumption and debt, see Bruce H. Mann, *Republic of Debtors: Bankruptcy in the Age of American Independence* (Cambridge, Mass., and London, 2002), 131-38.

Chapter 2

1. Will of John Baylor, IV, Oct. 30, 1807, in *DR*; Kevin J. Hayes, *The Library of William Byrd of Westover* (Madison, Wis., 1997), ix, 96. For a catalogue of the books sold by Jefferson to the LOC, see E. Millicent Sowerby, *Catalogue of the Library of Thomas Jefferson*, 5 vols. (Washington, D.C., 1952-59). For a discussion of the limitations of Sowerby's effort, see Douglas L. Wilson, "Sowerby Revisited: The Unfinished Catalogue of Thomas Jefferson's Library," *WMQ*, 3rd ser., 41 (Oct. 1984): 651-28. On the story of Jefferson's transaction with the Library of Congress, see Dumas Malone, *Jefferson and His Time*, vol. 6, *The Sage of Monticello* (Boston, 1981), 169-184. For a brief overview of Jefferson and his books, see also Douglas L. Wilson, *Jefferson's Books* (Chapel Hill, N.C., 1996). For an extended treatment of Jefferson as bookman, see Hayes, *Road to Monticello*.

2. George K. Smart, "Private Libraries in Virginia," *American Literature* 19 (Mar. 1938): 24-52, 33. Smart's study was preceded by John M. Patterson's "Private Libraries in Virginia in the Eighteenth Century" (MA thesis, University of Virginia, 1936), but Patterson's work pales in comparison.

3. The Gunston Hall probate inventory also includes selected inventories from Anne Arundel County and Annapolis, in Maryland, and in Virginia,

Norfolk and Fredericksburg, along with James City, Elizabeth City, Lancaster, Surrey, Richmond, Frederick, Charles City, Spotsylvania, Middlesex, Westmoreland, and York counties. Gunston Hall divided the probate estates into ascending groups of material wealth—Old-Fashioned; Decent; Aspiring; and Elite—using categories and their respective criteria borrowed from Barbara G. Carson's work, *Ambitious Appetites: Dining, Behavior, and Patterns of Consumption in Federal Washington* (Washington, D.C., 1990). (Lois Green Carr and Lorena Walsh pioneered the use of probate inventories as a means of assessing living standards in the Chesapeake. See Lois Green Carr and Lorena S. Walsh, "Inventories and the Analysis of Wealth and Consumption Patterns in St. Mary's County, Maryland, 1658-1777," *Historical Methods*, 13 [Spring 1980]: 81-104; idem, "The Standard of Living in the Colonial Chesapeake," *WMQ*, 3rd ser., 45 [Jan. 1988]: 135-59.)

Carson's taxonomy, which Gunston Hall adopted *in toto*, determines levels of affluence based on the type and quantity of household dining utensils. While such a methodology is certainly helpful in analyzing personal wealth and consumption patterns, especially in assessing gentility (or one's pretensions to it), employing it as the sole means of classifying socioeconomic status is deeply flawed. First, during the consumer revolution that began in the mid-eighteenth century and peaked just before the Revolution, aspirants to the Virginia gentry increasingly acquired household goods, such as furniture, china, and silverware, in quantities and quality that ultimately became virtually indistinguishable from those of the "real" gentry. Archeological excavations in Fairfax County, Va., for example, indicate "remarkable similarities" between domestic material culture in gentry households and those of near-wealthy pretenders so that, "from an archeological standpoint, social aspirants … pass for gentlemen." (Andrew S. Veech, "Signatures of Gentility: Assessing Status Archeologically in Mid-Eighteenth-Century Fairfax County, Virginia" [PhD diss., Brown University, 1998], 8.) Carr and Walsh reached a similar conclusion: "[T]able knives and forks and fine earthenware, the social props for genteel dining, were confined to the rich at first, but by the 1770s were considered desirable and affordable by some well down on the economic scale." (Carr and Walsh, "Standard of Living in the Colonial Chesapeake," 138.) This phenomenon was part of the growing refinement of colonial America, as items that were previously regarded as luxury goods exclusively for the rich trickled down to the middling classes. See Richard L. Bushman, *The Refinement of*

America: Persons, Houses, Cities (New York, 1992), 77.

Second, and more fundamentally, the Carson classification ignores land and slaves, the principal sources of the gentry's wealth. Landon Carter Jr. (1738-1801), son of Landon Carter of Sabine Hall (1710-1778), is ranked merely as "Aspiring," a genus at which both father and son would have been justifiably appalled. According to his inventory, Landon Carter Jr. had a personal estate worth more than £30,000, one of the very largest among the entire 325 inventories. Daniel French (1723-1771), builder of Pohick Church in Fairfax County, Va., where he served as a vestryman along with his intimate friend George Washington, is also relegated to "Aspiring" status. In addition to his personal estate of £6,963 (including sixty slaves), French owned some four thousand acres of desirable land in three Virginia counties when he died. There is no doubt that French was a well-established member of Virginia's gentry elite, but Gunston Hall's classification demotes him to the level of a social-climbing wannabe simply because his table service did not measure up. (On French, see David M. French, "The Daniel French Families and Their Lands," *Yearbook: The Historical Society of Fairfax County* 23 [1991-92]: 27-44.) Both Carter and French, and presumably others in the Gunston Hall list, illustrate that there is not necessarily a correlation between extensive wealth (i.e., in lands and slaves, as it was measured by the gentry) and household luxury goods. One study of 43 colonial-era mansions and large houses in Virginia's Northern Neck concluded that among the wealthy "the drive to acquire luxurious goods and the motivation to build an elegant house were not closely linked in colonial Virginia." (Camille Wells, "Social and Economic Aspects of Eighteenth-Century Housing on the Northern Neck in Virginia" [PhD diss., CWM, 1994], 158.)

Finally, the estates of the richest Virginians were often probated in the General Court in Richmond, the records of which were destroyed during the Civil War, and any Virginian whose personal assets exceeded his debts could dictate in his will that inventory and appraisement were not required, as was the case with Robert Carter of Nomini Hall, who owned one of the largest libraries in colonial Virginia. Regarding the limitations of using personal property inventories in Virginia, see Harold B. Gill Jr. and George M. Curtis, III, "Virginia's Colonial Probate Policies and the Preconditions for Economic History," *VMHB* 87 (Jan. 1979): 68-73.

4.   Joe W. Kraus, "Private Libraries in Colonial America," *Journal of Library History* 9 (1974): 31-53, 33. Gunston Hall Plantation's

inventory is available online at www.gunstonhall.org/probate/inventory.htm. For an extensive list of Virginia estates indicating widespread book ownership among the lesser Virginia gentry, see "Books in Colonial Virginia," *VMHB* 3 (Jan. 1900): 299-303; ibid., *VMBH*, 10 (April 1903): 389-405.

5. Henry Cabot Lodge, *George Washington*, 2 vols. (Boston and New York, 1889), 1:23; Carl Bridenbaugh, *Myths and Realities: Societies of the Colonial South* (Baton Rouge, La., 1952), 40. Richard Beale Davis's study of private libraries, "Books, Libraries, Reading, and Printing," is in his *Intellectual Life in the Colonial South, 1585-1763*, 3 vols. (Knoxville, Tenn., 1978), 2:491-526. See also Wright, *First Gentleman of Virginia*. It is truly difficult to understand how Carl Bridenbaugh concluded that the Virginia gentry lacked a strong book and literary culture given the wealth of materials that had been published or readily available to scholars when he wrote his *Myths and Realities*. See, for example, the pre-1952 sources listed in David Gillespie and Michael H. Harris, "A Bibliography of Virginia Library History," *Journal of Library History* 6 (1971): 72-90.

6. François de La Rochefoucauld-Liancourt, *Travels Through the United States of North America...*, 2 vols. (London, 1799), 2:112. On the importation of British books into colonial America, see James Raven, "The Importation of Books in the Eighteenth Century," in *A History of the Book in America*, vol. 1, *The Colonial Book in the Atlantic World*, ed. Hugh Amory and David D. Hall (Cambridge, Eng., 2000), 186. For the nonimportation resolutions, see *Virginia Gazette* (Purdie & Dixon), May 25, 1769; The Association Entered Into ... By the House of Burgesses... (Broadside), June 22, 1770 [Williamsburg, Va.]. The 1770 resolutions added another luxury favorite of the Virginia gentry—horses—to the list of banned imports, but still did not include books or periodicals. Regarding the bookplates, see Charles Alan Dexter, *American Book-Plates: A Guide to their Study with Examples* (New York and London, 1894), passim.

7. Cynthia Z. Stiverson and Gregory A. Stiverson, "The Colonial Retail Book Trade: Availability and Affordability of Reading Material in Mid-Eighteenth-Century Virginia," in *Printing and Society in Early America*, ed. William L. Joyce et al. (Worcester, Mass., 1983), 169-71; Gregory A. Stiverson and Cynthia Z. Stiverson, "Books Both Useful and Entertaining: A Study of Books Purchased and Reading Habits

of Virginians in the Eighteenth Century," Colonial Williamsburg Foundation Research Report 25 (unpublished manuscript, 1977), 182-185. See also John E. Molnar, "Publication and Retail Book Advertisements in the *Virginia Gazette*, 1736-1780" (PhD diss., University of Michigan, 1978), which provides a bibliographic analysis of all books and imprints offered for sale in extant copies of the *Virginia Gazette* from 1736 to 1780.

For purposes of this study, books need to be distinguished from other print media. Recent scholarship has demonstrated that, contrary to a long-established historiography seemingly overawed by the importation of the first American printing press in Massachusetts as early as 1639, almost a century before one appeared in Virginia, colonial Virginia in fact had a well-established print culture. Aside from the ubiquitous Bible, which was present even in the poorest households, Virginia's print culture among the nonelite was based largely on items published and disseminated by the *Virginia Gazette*, whose various proprietors (sometimes cooperatively, other times competitively) operated what today would be regarded as a highly integrated and synergistic enterprise. The *Gazette* was the colony's official printer of laws, legislative journals, and other public documents. In addition to its newspaper, which had a weekly run of 1,000-1,500 copies at mid-century, the *Gazette* office annually published 3,000-5,000 copies of the *Virginia Almanack*, which was available at retail for only seven and a half pence. Moreover, the *Gazette* regularly churned out a high volume of pamphlets, broadsides, and other print materials. It also ran a profitable post office and retained post riders and other independent contractors who distributed and sold *Gazette* materials throughout Virginia. Subscribers and readers, in turn, are known to have commonly passed around their copies of *Gazette* materials, thus multiplying the *Gazette*'s readership far beyond the number of items printed. See Roger P. Mellen, "A Culture of Dissidence: The Emergence of Liberty of the Press in Pre-Revolutionary Virginia" (PhD diss., George Mason University, 2007); David A. Rawson, "'Guardians of Their Own Liberty': A Contextual History of Print Culture in Virginia Society, 1750 to 1820" (PhD diss., CWM, 1998); Susan Stromei Berg, "Agent of Change or Trusted Servant: The Eighteenth-Century Williamsburg Press" (MA thesis, CWM, 1993).

8. Irving Brant, *James Madison*, 6 vols. (Indianapolis, Ind., and New York, 1941-61), 1:56; Alexander Brown, *The Cabells and Their Kin* (Boston and New York, 1895), 89-91.

9. Lowell H. Harrison, "A Virginian Moves to Kentucky, 1793," *WMQ*, 3rd ser., 15 (April 1958): 208-9. John Hook (1746-1808), a Scottish merchant backed by his partner, David Ross of Petersburg, Va., perhaps the richest man in Virginia in the 1770s, ordered about sixty titles from Britain for sale in his retail store in rustic New London, Va. Although about half the titles were devotional tracts, his order included works by Daniel Defoe, Henry Fielding, Tobias Smollett, Plutarch, and even Samuel Johnson's *Dictionary*. (Shipping Invoices, 1772, John Hook Papers, 1737-1889, Rare Book, Manuscript, and Special Collections Library, Duke University, Durham, N.C.; reprinted in Ann S. Martin, *Buying Into the World of Goods: Early Consumers in Backcountry Virginia* [Baltimore, 2008], 86-88.) It is not clear how well these books sold, but in any case Hook's collection was not typical of backcountry merchants. Far more typical was the store inventory of Scottish merchant John Glassford in Colchester, Va. In 1759 Glassford's store sold 111 books, almost all of them religious (including 20 Bibles, 40 prayer books, and 11 Psalters). (Colchester Store Ledger, 1759-60, John Glassford and Company Records, LOC.)

    Similarly, in Orange County, N.C., almost all the 586 titles sold at William Johnston and Richard Bennehan's store from 1769 to 1777 consisted of religious books. See Elizabeth Cometti, "Some Early Best Sellers in Piedmont North Carolina," *Journal of Southern History* 16 (Aug. 1950): 324-37. When Messrs. Johnston and Bennehan attempted to broaden their stock list in 1773 by adding novels such as *Tristram Shandy, Peregrine Pickle, Roderick Random, Gil Blas, Tom Jones*, and *Paradise Lost*, their effort failed miserably. All the novels went unsold, though the merchants' devotional titles continued to sell well until the Revolution. "The people of Orange County," noted Cometti, "would not be corrupted by profane literature." (Ibid., 330-31.) On North Carolina print culture, see also Patrick M. Valentine, "Libraries and Print Culture in Early North Carolina," *North Carolina Historical Review* 3 (July 2005): 293-325.

10. Douglas Adair, ed., "The Autobiography of the Reverend Devereux Jarratt, 1732-1763," *WMQ*, 3rd ser., 9 (July 1952): 366, 373-74, 377, 381, 388. On the social origins of Anglican clergy in Virginia, see Joan Gunderson, *The Anglican Ministry in Virginia, 1723-1766: A Study in Social Class* (New York and London, 1989).

11. Joseph F. Kett and Patricia A. McClung, "Book Culture in Post-Revolutionary Virginia," *Proceedings of the American Antiquarian*

Society 94 (April 1984): 109, 137, table 4.2. The situation in England appears to have been similar, at least in the early eighteenth century. In a sample of probate inventories from eight geographic locales in England for the year 1725, 56 percent of the inventories of London residents owned books, while only 13 percent of the estates of those who lived in villages or rural areas owned books. See Lorna Weatherill, "The Meaning of Consumer Behaviour in Late Seventeenth- and Early Eighteenth-Century England," in *Consumption and the World of Goods*, ed. John Brewer and Roy Porter (London and New York, 1983), 220, table 10.4.

12. John Pory to [Sir Dudley Carleton], Sept. 30, 1619, in Susan Myra Kingsbury, ed., *The Records of the Virginia Company of London*, 4 vols. (Washington, D.C., 1906-35), 3:222; William Fitzhugh to Nicholas Hayward, Jan. 30, 1687, in Richard B. Davis, ed., *William Fitzhugh and His Chesapeake World, 1676-1701*, 203. Before the founding of any English settlement in America, Richard Hakluyt (1552-1616), who had the most important literary influence upon English colonization in the late sixteenth century, recommended books as an essential article for English colonists to take with them. In particular, books about discoveries in the East and West Indies would "kepe men occupied from worse cogitations, and ... raise their myndes to courage and highe enterprizes." (Richard Hakluyt, *A Particuler Discourse Concerninge...* [1584], in David B. Quinn and Alison M. Quinn, eds., *Discourse of Western Planting* [London, 1993], 127.) Capt. John Smith mentioned the presence of books among the first adventurers at Jamestown. See, e.g., John Smith, *The General History of Virginia...* (London, 1624), in Barbour, ed., *Complete Works of Captain John Smith*, 2:80. In 1618, the Virginia Company authorized a new college at Henrico for the education of Virginians and Native Americans. Several benefactors had donated money and books for the school—which would have formed the first institutional library in America—but the Indian massacre of March 1622, followed by the Crown's revocation of the Company's charter two years later, stopped the project. See Robert H. Land, "Henrico and its College," *WMQ*, 2nd ser., 18 (Oct. 1938): 453-98; John M. Jennings, *The Library of the College of William and Mary in Virginia, 1693-1793* (Charlottesville, Va., 1968), 1-5. On Pory and books in early Virginia, see William S. Powell, "Books in the Virginia Colony before 1624," *WMQ*, 3rd ser., 5 (April, 1948): 177-84. For the books exported in 1697/8 by Perry, Lane & Co., see Jacob M. Price, *Perry of London* (Cambridge, Mass.,

1992), 108.

13. Robert Beverley to Samuel Athawes, Nov. 18, 1763, in Robert Beverley Letterbook, 1761-93, LOC; William Byrd II to Mrs. Armiger, June 25, 1729, in Marion Tinling, ed., *The Correspondence of the Three William Byrds of Westover, Virginia, 1684-1776*, 2 vols. (Charlottesville, Va., 1977), 1:413. Books were also an important component of the gentry's social authority in colonial Virginia. See Rhys Isaac, "Books and the Social Authority of Learning: The Case of Mid-Eighteenth Century Virginia," in *Printing and Society*, 228-49. Regarding the Horatian ideal in eighteenth-century Virginia, see William M.S. Rasmussen and Robert S. Tilton, *Old Virginia: The Pursuit of a Pastoral Ideal* (Charlottesville, Va., 2003).

14. Jessica Kross, "Mansions, Men, Women, and the Creation of Multiple Publics in Eighteenth-Century British North-America," *Journal of Social History* 33 (Winter 1999): 385; J. Lewis Peyton, *History of Augusta County, Virginia* (Staunton, Va., 1882), 334.

15. Charles M. Andrews, *Colonial Folkways: A Chronicle of American Life in the Reign of the Georges* (New Haven, Conn., Toronto, and London, 1916), 156. On the dissemination of knowledge and information among the Virginia gentry, see Richard D. Brown, *Knowledge Is Power: The Diffusion of Information in Early America, 1700-1865* (New York and Oxford, 1989), 54-55. For Pole's library catalogue, see *VMHB* 17 (July 1909): 147-50. For an example of formal pleas for the return of books, see the repeated requests of Peyton Randolph's executors for the return of his books: *VG* (Purdie), Jan. 12, 1776 (twice repeated); *VG* (Dixon and Hunter), Jan. 13, 1776 (twice repeated). Apparently, many books were never returned despite the executor's plea for "common honesty." (*VG* [Purdie and Dixon], Aug. 29, 1771.)

16. [William Wirt], *The Letters of the British Spy* (Richmond, Va., 1805), 88-89. On Wirt and his library, see Davis, *Intellectual Life*, 103-104. On the decline of the Virginia gentry in the post-Revolutionary period, see Herbert E. Sloan, *Principal and Interest: Thomas Jefferson and the Problem of Debt* (Charlottesville, Va., and London, 1995), 14-22. Regarding the shift in political power from the planter aristocracy to lawyers, see Anthony F. Upton, "The Road to Power in Virginia in the Early Nineteenth Century," *VMHB* 62 (July 1954): 259-80. See

also E. Lee Shepard, "Lawyers Look at Themselves: Professional Consciousness and the Virginia Bar, 1770-1850," *American Journal of Legal History* 25 (Jan. 1981): 1-23. On Tocqueville's observations about American lawyers, see Alexis de Tocqueville, *Democracy in America*, ed. J. P. Mayer, trans. George Lawrence, 2 vols. (1835; New York, 1969), 1:chap. 8.

17. John Adams to Benjamin Rush, March 19, 1812, in Gordon S. Wood, *Revolutionary Characters: What Made the Founders Different* (New York, 2006), 33; Paul K. Longmore, *The Invention of George Washington* (Berkeley and Los Angeles, Calif., 1988), 214; George Washington to David Humphreys, July 25, 1785, in W. W. Abbot et al., eds., *The Papers of George Washington: Confederation Series*, 6 vols. (Charlottesville, Va., 1992-97), 3:149. Dr. Nicholas Flood (d. 1776) of Richmond Co., Va., owned more than nine hundred volumes of mostly history, biography, and classical literature, as well as 288 medical books. (Inventory of Dr. Nicholas Flood, Feb. 8, 1777, Richmond Co., Va., Will Book 7 [1767-87], 239-70.)

18. Inventory of John Parke Custis, Feb. 20, 1782, Fairfax Co., Va., Will Book D (1772-83), 274-88; Inventory of Dr. John Stewart, Aug. 22, 1797, Prince Georges Co., Md., Inventories 1796-1800, 186-89. Regarding the library of Daniel Parke Custis, see "Catalogue of the Library of Daniel Parke Custis," *VMHB* 17 (Oct. 1909): 404-12. On Washington's library, see Frances L. Carroll and Mary Meacham, *The Library at Mount Vernon* (Pittsburgh, Pa., 1977), 86. Washington's library is sometimes erroneously described as having had 800-900 titles rather than volumes. See, for example, Richard B. Davis, *Intellectual Life in Jefferson's Virginia*, 1790-1830 (Chapel Hill, N.C., 1964), 89.

19. Rhys Isaac, *Landon Carter's Uneasy Kingdom: Revolution and Rebellion on a Virginia Plantation* (Oxford and New York, 2004), 85-86; Wright, *First Gentlemen of Virginia*, 249; Katherine T. Read, "The Library of Robert Carter of Nomini Hall" (MA thesis, CWM, 1970) (*N.B.:* covers only Carter's titles listed by Fithian); Wilson Miles Cary, *Sally Cary: A Long Hidden Romance of Washington's Life* (privately printed, 1916), 81-104; C. Malcolm Watkins, *The Cultural History of Marlborough* (Washington, D.C., 1968), 42-43, 191-208. The usual size given for Robert Carter's library is approximately fifteen hundred volumes (consisting of those counted by Fithian at Nomini Hall in 1773-74 and about 458 titles that Carter kept at his Williamsburg

house). But, as historian and librarian John R. Barden has pointed out, Carter continued to buy large quantities of books until his death in 1804. Barden estimates Carter's total library at around three thousand volumes. See John R. Barden, "Reflections of a Singular Mind: The Library of Robert Carter of Nominy Hall," *VMHB* 96 (Jan. 1988): 83-94. The precise size of Mercer's library is uncertain. In an estate sale advertisement, his son and executor reported that he located "more than 1200" volumes, but that "upwards of 400 volumes" had been previously borrowed and not returned. (*VG* [Rind], Dec. 15, 1768.) According to one bibliographer, the actual count may have been as high as eighteen hundred volumes, but that number may include books Mercer held for sale as a merchant. See Bennie Brown, "The Ownership of Architectural Books in Colonial Virginia," in *American Architects and Their Books to 1848*, ed. James F. O'Gorman and Kenneth Hafertepe (Amherst, Mass., 2001), 24. For a catalogue of the Sabine Hall library just prior to its donation to the University of Virginia in 1979, see Carol E. Curtis, "The Library of Landon Carter of Sabine Hall, 1710-1778" (MA thesis, CWM, 1981). For other important Virginia private libraries, see William J. Simpson Jr., "A Comparison of the Libraries of Seven Colonial Virginians, 1754-1789," *Journal of Library History* 9 (1974): 54-65. At 850 volumes (384 titles), Lady Jean Skipwith (1748-1826) of Prestwould in Mecklenburg County, Va., assembled by far the largest library owned by a woman in colonial and post-Revolutionary Virginia. See Mildred K. Abraham, "The Library of Lady Jean Skipwith: A Book Collection from the Age of Jefferson," *VMHB* 91 (July 1983): 296-347.

20. Estate Inventory of Richard Henry Lee, Aug. 1, 1794 (typescript), Jesse Ball DuPont Memorial Library, Stratford, Va. For a biography of Richard Henry Lee, see J. Kent McGaughy, *Richard Henry Lee of Virginia: A Portrait of an American Revolutionary* (Lanham, Md., 2004).

21. For a comprehensive list and description of lost and destroyed Virginia county records, see "Lost Records Localities: Counties and Cities With Missing Records," n.d. [2008], LVA. On the Richmond evacuation and fire, see Nelson Lankford, *Richmond Burning: The Last Days of the Confederate Capital* (New York, 2002).

22. Regarding the fact that there were insufficient surviving records from the colonial period to fill the first volume of the *Calendar of Virginia*

State Papers, see Edward F. Heite, "Redcoats, Yankees and Pie Plates: Conquering Armies and Other Misfortunes Have Destroyed Much of Virginia 's Heritage," *Virginia Cavalcade* 27 (Spring 1968): 12-17.

23. *VG* (Purdie and Dixon), June 8, 1769; ibid., Nov. 12, 1767; "Libraries in Colonial Virginia," *WMQ*, 1st ser., 4 (Jan. 1896): 156; Inventory of Philip Ludwell Lee, March 20, 1776, Westmoreland Co., Va., Inventory Book 6 (1771-83), 173-176; Inventory of Peyton Randolph, Jan. 5, 1776, York Co., Va., Wills & Inventories Book 22 (1771-83), 337-41; Thomas Jefferson to William W. Hening, Sept. 3, 1820, Thomas Jefferson Papers, LOC. In addition to the foregoing items, the *Virginia Gazette* abounds with references to estate sales of "large and valuable" libraries. The Lee family library at Stratford Hall remained with the mansion when it was sold in 1822 to William Clarke Somerville (1790-1826), according to Ethel M. Armes, *Stratford Hall: The Great House of the Lees* (Richmond, Va., 1936), 461. Anticipating a political appointment (John Quincy Adams appointed him Minister to Sweden, but Somerville died in France en route), Somerville offered to sell the Stratford library of "three or four thousand volumes" to Thomas Jefferson for the University of Virginia library. "The books are generally of the best London and Paris Editions, in folio, Quarto, & Octavo—many of them old and rare works and they form altogether," he wrote, "the best private Library I have seen in this country." (William C. Somerville to Thomas Jefferson, Jan. 3, 1825 [typescript], Jesse Ball duPont Memorial Library, Stratford, Va.) In reply, Jefferson informed Somerville that funds for the university had yet to be appropriated by the Virginia legislature and that when they were made available it would be up to the university's board of visitors to determine how they would be spent. (Thomas Jefferson to William C. Somerville, Jan. 17, 1825 [typescript], Jesse Ball duPont Memorial Library, Stratford, Va.)

24. Robert A. Lancaster, Jr., *Historic Virginia Homes and Churches* (Philadelphia and London, 1915), 350. On Chatham, see Ralph Happel, *Chatham: The Life of a House* (Philadelphia, 1984). Fitzhugh had about 125 books at his Alexandria home when he died there in 1809. See Inventory of William Fitzhugh, Dec. 30, 1809, Alexandria, Va., Orphans Court, Will Book C, 319-21. See also Lee A. Wallace, Jr., "Report on the Disposition of Books and Other Personal Property in the Estates of: Richard Henry Lee, General and Mrs. Henry Lee, Charles and Ann Butler Carter, William and Ann Randolph Fitzhugh,

Mr. and Mrs. George Washington Parke Custis" (unpublished typescript, 1980), VHS.

25. *Maryland Gazette*, July 7, 1773. On colonial Maryland private libraries, see Joseph T. Wheeler, "Books Owned by Marylanders, 1700-1776," *MHM* 35 (1940): 337-53; idem, "Reading Interests of the Professional Classes in Colonial Maryland," *MHM* 36 (1941): 281-302; "Reading Interests of Maryland Planters," *MHM* 37 (1942): 26-41 and 291-310. One scholar notes that Wheeler's statistical "methodology is questionable," but he fails to explain why. See Carl E. Garrigus, Jr., "The Reading Habits of Maryland's Planter Gentry," *MHM* 92 (Spring 1997): 37-53. On Lloyd's library, see Edwin Wolf, 2nd, "The Library of Edward Lloyd IV of Wye House," *Winterthur Portfolio* 5 (1969): 87-121.

26. Worthington C. Ford, ed., *Diary of Cotton Mather*, 2 vols. (1911; New York, 1957), 1:77, 548. Cotton Mather's library was an amalgamation of books he acquired as well as those he inherited from his father and other family members. Regarding the size of the Mather family library, see Colonial Society of Massachusetts, *Transactions, 1915-1916*, 18 (Boston, 1917): 408 (which unequivocally states that his library "must have totaled about 4,000 volumes" at his death); Julius H. Tuttle, *The Libraries of the Mathers* (Worcester, Mass., 1910), 27-30 (which is less certain on the point but suggests that he died with more than 3,000 volumes). Tuttle also cites a letter from Samuel Mather, Cotton Mather's grandson, which states that his father, who was also named Samuel, owned a library of "7000 or 8000 Volumes of the most curious and chosen Authors, and a prodigious number of valuable Manuscripts, which had been collected by my Ancestors for five Generations." (Ibid., 33.) If this statement is accurate, the elder Samuel Mather would have had the probable distinction of owning the largest private library in colonial America. On Logan and his library, see Edwin Wolf 2nd, *The Library of James Logan of Philadelphia* (Philadelphia, 1974). On Franklin's library, see Edwin Wolf 2nd and Kevin J. Hayes, *The Library of Benjamin Franklin* (Philadelphia, 2006).

Chapter 3

1. John Baylor III to Flowerdewe and Norton, Jan. 18, 1759, BLB;

Invoice to Robert Cary & Co., May, 1, 1759," in Abbot, ed. *Papers of George Washington, Colonial Series*, 6:317-18. Some of Washington's biographers have erroneously concluded that his request for a "small piece in Octavo—call'd a New System of Agriculture, or a Speedy-Way to grow Rich" referred to *The Horse-Hoeing Husbandry* (London, 1733) by Jethro Tull (1674-1741). See, for example, Paul L. Haworth, *George Washington: Farmer* (Indianapolis, Ind., 1915), 73; Richard N. Smith, *Patriarch: George Washington and the New American Nation* (Boston and New York, 1993), 67.

2. Invoice to Robert Cary & Co., May 1, 1759, in Abbot, ed., *Papers of George Washington, Colonial Series*, 6:318 (see also George Washington to Richard Washington, April 5, 1778, in ibid., 5:111-13); George Washington to John Didsbury, Nov. 30, 1759, in ibid., 6:374; Forms of Writing, and the Rules of Civility and Decent Behavior in Company and Conversation, ante 1747, in ibid., 1:1-4. Didsbury shod several others of the Virginia gentry, who were probably aping Baylor and Washington as well as each other. See Bills from John Didsbury, June 24, 1772, July 1, 1772, Aug. 10, 1772, NP. Such was Didsbury's reputation in Virginia that cobblers who had apprenticed under him were prone to boast about it in their advertisements. See, for example, *VG* (Dixon), Nov. 18, 1775; *VG* (Purdie), June 28, 1776. British retailer Catherine Rathell, whose Williamsburg shop carried only "the very best & most fashionable goods," carried an off-the-rack line of Didsbury's "neatest shoes, pumps and slippers." (*VG* [Rind], April 13, 1769.) Washington ordered shoes from Didsbury until at least 1773.

3. Charles S. Carey, ed., *Letters Written by Lord Chesterfield to His Son*, 2 vols (London, 1872), 2:345; Robert Carter to Micajah Perry Sr. and Micajah Perry Jr., March 25, 1721, in Robert Carter Letter Book, 1720-21 (typescript by Edmund Berkeley Jr.), Huntington Library, San Marino, Calif.; John Baylor III to [Robert] Cary & Co., Sept. 7, 1761, BLB; John Baylor III to John Didsbury, Aug. 16, 1763, ibid. For an interesting study of gout among the elite throughout history, see Roy S. Porter and G. S. Rousseau, *Gout: The Patrician Malady* (New Haven, Conn., and London, 1998).

4. Richard Beale Davis, *A Colonial Southern Bookshelf: Reading in the Eighteenth Century* (Athens, Ga., 1979), 19; *Monthly Review; or Literary Journal* (London) (hereafter cited as *MR*) (Dec. 1758), 603; *MR* (June 1759), 477. On the *Monthly Review*, see Wilbur T.

Albrecht, "Monthly Review," in *British Literary Magazines: The Augustan Age and the Age of Johnson, 1689–1788*, ed. Alvin Sullivan (Westport, Conn., 1983), 231–37; Edwin N. Oakes, "Ralph Griffiths and the 'Monthly Review'" (PhD diss., Columbia University, 1961). Regarding the *Monthly Review* in the context of British eighteenth-century periodicals, see Barbara M. Benedict, "Readers, Writers, Reviewers, and the Professionalization of Literature," in *The Cambridge Companion to English Literature, 1740-1830*, ed. Thomas Keymer and John Mee (Cambridge, Eng., 2004), 3-23. On early British periodicals generally, see Walter Graham, *English Literary Periodicals* (New York, 1930). For an alphabetical list of British newspapers and periodicals published during the American colonial period, see Ronald S. Crane and F. B. Kaye, *A Census of British Newspapers and Periodicals, 1620-1800* (Chapel Hill, N.C., 1927).

5.   William Nelson to John Norton, Sept. 6, 1766, Aug. 14, 1767, Sept. 4, 1769, in Letterbook, 1766-75, of William Nelson and Thomas Nelson Jr., LVA; Robert Carter Nicholas to John Norton, May 20, 1768, in Frances Norton Mason, ed., *John Norton and Sons: Merchants of London and Virginia*, 2nd ed. (Newton Abbot, Devon, Eng., 1968), 52. Regarding Nelson's business activities and wealth, see Emory G. Evans, "The Rise and Decline of the Virginia Aristocracy in the Eighteenth Century: The Nelsons," in *The Old Dominion: Essays for Thomas Perkins Abernathy*, ed. Darrett B. Rutman (Charlottesville, Va. 1964), 72-73. For a brief discussion of Nelson's library (as it existed under his grandson William Nelson Jr.), see Emory G. Evans, *Inventory of the Library of William Nelson, Jr., of Yorktown, Virginia* (Williamsburg, Va., 1972). Nelson mentioned in his letter to Norton that the book he called *Art of Drawing Without a Master* was printed by Carington Bowles (1724-93); hence, Bernard Lens's *For the Curious Young Gentlemen and Ladies...* may be the unidentified *Art of Drawing* referred to in Janice G. Schimmelman, "Books on Drawing and Painting Techniques Available in Eighteenth-Century American Libraries and Bookstores," *Winterthur Portfolio* 19 (Summer-Autumn 1984): 193-94.

6.   Hunter D. Farish, ed., *Journal and Letters of Philip V. Fithian* (Williamsburg, Va., 1943), 48; Robert Carter to Edward Hunt and Sons, June 5, 1767, Robert Carter Letterbook, 1764-68, CWSC; idem, April 7, 1770, Robert Carter Letterbook, 1770-73, CWSC.

7. John Page to John Norton, Oct. 11, 1771, Mason, ed., *John Norton and Sons*, 199-200; "Memoir of Colonel John Page of Rosewell," in *The Virginia Historical Register III*, ed. William Maxwell, 145 (Richmond, Va. 1850), 151; Thomas Jefferson to John Page, Feb. 21, 1770, in *TJP*, 1:35. Regarding Page and his scientific pursuits, see T. B. McCord Jr., "John Page of Rosewell: Reason, Religion, and Republican Government from the Perspective of a Virginia Planter, 1743-1808" (PhD diss., American University, 1990), 35-39. Astronomy appears to have been a popular pastime in colonial Virginia. No less than nine astronomy titles were advertised for sale in the *Virginia Gazette*, and a surprising number of estate inventories mention astronomy books. See Molnar, "Publication and Retail Book Advertisements," 243. On William Small, see Martin R. Clagett, "William Small, 1734-1775: Teacher, Mentor, Scientist" (PhD diss., Virginia Commonwealth University, 2003).

8. Henry Fitzhugh to John Stewart and Campbell, June 6, 1770, Henry Fitzhugh Papers, 1746-89, Rare Book, Manuscript, and Special Collections Library, Duke University, Durham, N.C.

9. Robert Beverley to Samuel Athawes, July 16, 1771, in Robert Beverley Letterbook, 1761-93, LOC.

10. Peter J. Parker, "The Philadelphia Printer: A Study of Eighteenth-Century Businessmen," *Business History Review* 40 (Spring 1966): 31; John Baylor III to John Norton & Sons, Aug. 14, 1765, BP.

11. Virginia Gazette Daybooks, 1750-52 and 1764-66, University of Virginia (microfilm edition) (hereafter cited as *Daybooks*). The *Daybooks* did not record cash purchasers by name, but most book buyers, including Baylor, usually bought on store credit. In their "Books Both Useful and Entertaining" the Stiversons catalogued all known titles offered by the *Gazette* and thoughtfully analyzed the *Daybooks*. The Stiversons' manuscript is an essential resource for any study of books in colonial Virginia. For a discussion of the comparative cost of books purchased through London agents versus the *Gazette* retail store, see Stiverson and Stiverson, "Colonial Retail Book Trade," 170-71.

12. *MR* (June 1759): 497-501; *MR* (Dec. 1758): 552-53.

13. Donald Greene, "Samuel Johnson, Journalist," in *Newsletters to Newspapers: Eighteenth-Century Journalism: Papers Presented at a Bicentennial Symposium, at West Virginia University, Morgantown, West Virginia, March 31-April 2, 1976*, ed. Donovan H. Bond and W. Reynolds McLeod (Morgantown, W.Va., 1977), 89. For a history of *Gentleman's Magazine* from its inception until Edward Cave's death in 1754, see C. Lennart Carlson, *The First Magazine: A History of the Gentleman's Magazine...* (Providence, R.I., 1938). Some of the most important pieces appearing in *Gentleman's Magazine* during Cave's editorship have been assembled by E. A. Reitan in *The Best of Gentleman's Magazine, 1731-1754* (Lewiston, N.Y., 1987). With the title he gave his periodical, Cave invented the term *magazine* in its modern, literary sense. Prior to 1731, *magazine* meant only an arsenal or arms storehouse, but the popularity of Cave's journal soon led other British publications to accept and imitate his use of the term. Under the definition of *magazine* in his *Dictionary of the English Language* (1755), Samuel Johnson noted: "Of late this word has signified a miscellaneous pamphlet, from a periodical miscellany named the *Gentleman's Magazine*, by Edward Cave."

14. *The Works of Vicesimus Knox, D.D.*, 7 vols. (London, 1824), 1:6, 144. For the Library Company's order, see Board of Directors of Library Co. of Phila. to Thomas Hutchinson, Bookseller, March 31, 1732, Library Company of Philadelphia. Edwin Wolf 2nd speculated that, based on their "signs of use," *The Spectator*, *The Tatler*, and the *Guardian*, another British periodical, were the most popular of the Library Company's entire collection in the eighteenth century. (*A Catalogue of Books Belonging to the Library Company of Philadelphia*, introd. by Edwin Wolf 2nd, facsimile ed. [Philadelphia, 1956], x.) According to its official history, the Library Company of Philadelphia "flourished because it adopted a purchasing policy responsive to the needs of its intellectually alert, economically ambitious, but non-elite membership." (Edwin Wolf 2nd et al., *At the Instance of Benjamin Franklin: A Brief History of the Library Company of Philadelphia*, rev. ed. [Philadelphia, 1995], 4.) On the history of *The Tatler*, see Richmond P. Bond, The Tatler: *The Making of a Literary Journal* (Cambridge, Mass., 1971). For a history and critical analysis of *The Spectator*, see Michael Ketcham, *Transparent Designs: Reading, Performance and Form in the Spectator Papers* (Athens, Ga., 1985). For modern reprints of *The Tatler* and *The Spectator*, including an introduction and editorial notes, see Donald F. Bond, ed., *The Spectator*, 5 vols.

(Oxford, 1987); idem., *The Tatler*, 3 vols. (Oxford, 1987).

15. Davis, *Colonial Southern Bookshelf,* 114; Walter B. Edgar, "The Libraries of Colonial South Carolina" (PhD diss., University of South Carolina, 1969), 22; Inventory of Maj. William Walker, July 1763, Stafford Co., Va., Liber O (1748-67), 525; Inventory of Traverse Cooke, Dec. 11, 1759, Stafford Co., Va., Liber O (1748-67), 369; Inventory of Nathaniel Chapman, Feb. 3, 1762, Charles Co., Md., Inventories Book (1753-66), 316; Martin, *Buying into the World of Goods,* 86. On the *Spectator* in Maryland, see Garrigus, Jr., "Reading Habits of Maryland's Planter Gentry," 50-51. For the two inventories that mention *Gentleman's Magazine,* see Inventory of James Nevison, June 11, 1760, Charles Co., Md., Inventories Book (1753-66), 227; Inventory of George Washington, Aug. 20, 1810, Fairfax Co., Va., Loose Papers (copy) (*N.B.*: original filed copy is lost; contemporary duplicate is in Washington Papers, Mount Vernon Ladies Association, Mount Vernon, Va.). Regarding Byrd's subscription to *Gentleman's Magazine,* see Hayes, *Library of William Byrd,* 461, 521. Several Gunston Hall sample inventories mention "bound magazines," "London magazines," or the like, making specific identification impossible. Robert Carter of Nomini Hall, who had spent two years in London at the Inns of Court, read both *The Spectator* and *Gentleman's Magazine.* Farish, ed., *Philip V. Fithian,* 93.

16. "Sketch of the Early Life of James Boswell, Written by Himself for Jean Jacques Rousseau, 5 December 1764," in Frederick A. Pottle, *James Boswell: The Earlier Years: 1740-1769* (New York and Toronto, 1966), 2; Donald Greene, ed., *Samuel Johnson: The Major Works* (Oxford and New York, 1984), 649; James Madison to Richard D. Cutts, Jan. 4, 1829, in William C. Rives, *History of the Life and Times of James Madison,* 3 vols. (Boston, 1859-68), 1:25. Regarding the influence of *The Spectator* on Franklin, see Janette Seaton Lewis, "'A Turn of Thinking': The Long Shadow of *The Spectator* on Franklin's *Autobiography*," *Early American Literature* 13 (Winter 1978), 268-77. On politeness, see Lawrence E. Klein, "Politeness and the Interpretation of the British Eighteenth Century," *Historical Journal* 45 (2002): 869-898; idem, "Politeness for Plebs: Consumption and Social Identity in Early Eighteenth-Century England," in *The Consumption of Culture, 1600-1800: Image, Object, Text,* ed. Ann Bermingham and John Brewer (New York and London, 1995), 362-82. Regarding politeness in the context of *The Spectator* and the culture of Georgian Britain,

see John Brewer, *The Pleasures of the Imagination* (New York, 1997), 99-108.

17. Robert Skipwith to Thomas Jefferson, July 17, 1771, in *TJP*, 1:75; Thomas Jefferson to Robert Skipwith, Aug. 3, 1771, ibid., 1:79. On the idiosyncrasies of Jefferson's list of recommended books for Robert Skipwith, see Douglas L. Wilson, "Thomas Jefferson's Library and the Skipwith List," *Harvard Library Bulletin*, new ser., 3 (Winter 1992-93): 56-72. For the Northumberland Co. study, see W. Preston Haynie, *Northumberland County Bookshelf, or A Parcel of Old Books, 1650-1852* (Westminster, Md., 1994), passim.

18. On Noel, see Garrat Noel, *A Catalogue of Books...* (New York, 1762), 7. On Bell, see *Robert Bell's Sales Catalogue*, June 15, 1773 (Philadelphia), 21-22.

19. Benjamin Franklin to William Strahan, Nov. 27, 1755, in Leonard W. Labaree et al., eds., *The Papers of Benjamin Franklin*, 38 vols. to date (New Haven, Conn., and London, 1959—), 6:277-78. On Franklin's friendship with Strahan, see J. A. Cochrane, *Dr. Johnson's Printer: The Life of William Strahan* (Cambridge, Mass., 1964), chap. 8.

20. John Baylor III to John Norton & Sons, Aug. 14, 1765, BLB; Brown, *Knowledge Is Power*, 45. For a list of Thomas Lewis's books, see Inventory of the Estate of Thomas Lewis, ca. 1790, Lewis Family Papers, 1749-1920, VHS. On trans-Atlantic communication during the pre-Revolutionary era, see Michael Kraus, *The Atlantic Civilization: Eighteenth-Century Origins* (Ithaca, N.Y., 1949), 23-43; Ian K. Steele, *The English Atlantic, 1675-1740: An Exploration of Communication and Community* (New York and Oxford, 1986). Regarding excerpts from British magazines in the *Virginia Gazette*, see Robert M. Myers, "The Old Dominion Looks to London: A Study of English Literary Influences upon the Virginia Gazette (1736-1766)," *VMHB* 54 (July 1946): 195-217.

21. On *Gentleman's Magazine* as an arbiter of gentility in Georgian Britain, see E. A. Reitan, "The Eighteenth-Century Gentleman: Evidence from the *Gentleman's Magazine*, 1731-54," *Political Studies at Central Missouri State University* 11 (1983): 22-34.

22. *MR* (Dec. 1758), 542-49.

23. John Baylor III to Cary & Co., Sept. 14, 1762, Aug. 16, 1763, BLB.

24. Keith S. Furrows, "An Analysis of the *Gentleman's Magazine*, An Eighteenth-Century Periodical" (MA thesis, California State University, 2003), chap. 4. On the expansion of coverage of America in the years before the Revolution, see Michael Kraus, "Literary Relations Between Europe and America in the Eighteenth Century," *WMQ*, 3rd ser., 3 (July 1944): 215-16.

25. For the text of the Two-Penny Act, see William Waller Hening, ed., *The Statutes at Large; Being a Collection of all the Laws of Virginia...*, 13 vols. (Richmond, Va., 1809-23), 7:240.

26. For the petition to the Board of Trade, see Memorial of the Clergy of Virginia to the Board of Trade, C.O. 5/1329, ff. 119-20. Regarding the appeals to the Privy Council, see Joseph H. Smith, *Appeals to the Privy Council from the American Plantations* (New York, 1950), 615-21. On the Parson's Cause generally, see Richard L. Morton, *Colonial Virginia*, 2 vols. (Chapel Hill, N.C., 1960), 2:751-819. Regarding the legal and constitutional issues in the Parson's Cause, see Arthur P. Scott, "The Constitutional Aspects of the Parson's Cause," *Political Science Quarterly* 31 (Dec. 1916): 558-77. On the Parson's Cause in the larger context of conflicts between the gentry and the Anglican Church in Virginia, see Rhys Isaac, "Religion and Authority: Problems of the Anglican Establishment in Virginia in the Era of the Great Awakening and the Parsons' Cause" *WMQ*, 3rd ser., 30 (Jan. 1973): 3-36; idem, *The Transformation of Virginia* (Chapel Hill, N.C., 1982), chap. 7.

27. Thomas Jefferson to William Wirt, Aug. 14, 1814, in Paul Leicester Ford, ed., *The Works of Thomas Jefferson*, Federal Edition, 12 vols. (New York and London, 1904-5), 11:402; Rev. [William] Kay to Bishop of London, June 14, 1752, in William S. Perry, ed., *Historical Collections Relating to the American Colonial Church*, 5 vols. (Hartford, Conn., 1870-78): 1:389; Thomas Sherlock to Board of Trade, June 14, 1759, in ibid., 1:461-463; [Landon Carter], *A Letter to the Right Reverend Father in God, the Lord B——p of L——n* (Williamsburg, Va., 1759), 43. For a useful discussion of the pamphlet war, see Glenn C. Smith, "The Parsons' Cause, 1755-65," *Tyler's Quarterly Historical*

and Genealogical Magazine 21 (1939-40): 140-71, 291-306.

28. Lyman H. Butterfield, ed., *The Diary and Autobiography of John Adams*, 4 vols. (Cambridge, Mass., 1961), 2:120; Bernard Bailyn, ed., *Pamphlets of the American Revolution, 1750-1766* (Cambridge, Mass., 1965), 293; Richard Bland, *A Letter to the Clergy of Virginia...* (1760), 3, 13. Bland cited the Ciceronian maxim, "*Salus populi est suprema lex*" ("The welfare of the people is the supreme law"), which became a frequent battle cry among the American intelligentsia in the years preceding the Revolution. See Peter N. Miller, *Defining the Common Good: Empire, Religion, and Philosophy in Eighteenth-Century Britain* (Cambridge, Eng., 1994), 80. On Bland, see Clinton Rossiter, "Richard Bland: The Whig in America," *WMQ*, 3rd ser., 10 (Jan. 1953): 33-79.

29. Joseph Royle to Rev. John Camm, Aug. 1, 1763, Aug. 5, 1763, in Camm, *A Single and Distinct View*, 47-48.

30. Camm, *A Single and Distinct View*, 4-10.

31. Bailyn, *Pamphlets*, 297; *Daybooks*, f. 67; Stiverson and Stiverson, "Books Useful and Entertaining," 137.

32. [Richard Bland], *The Colonel Dismounted: or the Rector Vindicated* (Williamsburg, Va., 1764), 22. For a bibliography of the Carter-Camm-Bland pamphlets, see William Clayton-Torrence, *A Trial Bibliography of Colonial Virginia (1754-1776)*, Special Report of the Virginia State Library (Richmond, Va., 1910). See also Homer Dale Kemp, "The Pre-Revolutionary Virginia Polemical Essay: The Pistole Fee and the Two-Penny Acts" (PhD diss., University of Tennessee, 1972). Though he fully recognized the extent to which Bland and Carter "expressed many of the same ideas that soon appeared in more genuine Revolutionary disputes," historian Thad Tate argued that in the end the Parson's Cause was "[a]t most ... contributory rather than decisive to the advent of the Revolution in Virginia." (Thad W. Tate, "The Coming of the Revolution in Virginia: Britain's Challenge to Virginia's Ruling Class, 1763-1776," *WMQ*, 3rd ser., 19 [July 1962], 332.)

33. Edmund S. Morgan, *The Stamp Act Crisis: Prologue to Revolution*

(Chapel Hill, N.C., 1953), 96.

34. Francis Fauquier to Board of Trade, June 5, 1765, in Reese, ed., *Official Papers of Francis Fauquier,* 3:1250; John Pendleton Kennedy, ed., *Journals of the House of Burgesses of Virginia, 1761-1765* (Richmond, Va., 1907), 360.

35. E. J. Miller, "The Virginia Legislature and the Stamp Act," *WMQ* 1st ser., 21 (April 1913): 238; Morgan, *Stamp Act Crisis,* 97.

36. Greene, ed., *Diary of Colonel Landon Carter,* 2:1046. Regarding Carter's growing disenchantment with Britain, see ibid., 1:28-48. There is no definitive treatment of neutrality or passive loyalism among the Virginia gentry. The best source remains Keith B. Berwick, "Loyalties in Crisis: A Study of the Attitudes of Virginians in the Revolution" (PhD diss., University of Chicago, 1959). See also James L. Anderson, "The Virginia Councillors and the American Revolution," *VMHB* 82 (Jan. 1974); Isaac S. Harrell, *Loyalism in Virginia: Chapters in the Economic History of the Revolution* (Durham, N.C., 1926). Nor has any study been made of neutrality or loyalism among eighteenth-century Virginians educated in Britain.

37. John Baylor III to John Norton, Sept. 18, 1764, in Mason, *John Norton and Sons,* 11; Brant, *James Madison,* 1:60; Ralph Ketcham, *James Madison: A Biography* (Charlottesville, Va., 1990), 19-21; Account Book of Donald Robertson, 1758-75 (Mss 5:3 R5456:1), VHS. Selected portions of Robertson's account book have been transcribed and published in *VMHB* in the following volumes and pages: 33 (April 1925): 194-98; (July 1925): 288-92; 34 (April 1926): 14-148, (July 1926): 232-36; 35 (Jan. 1927): 55-56.

38. John Baylor III to Cary & Co., Sept. 6, 1760, BLB; *Daybooks,* ff. 22, 64, 131. Regarding the Baylor daughters at Croyden, see J. Hall Pleasants, "Genealogy: The Gorsuch and Lovelace Families," *VMHB* 25 (Oct. 1917): 247. On the education of young women in the colonial and post-Revolutionary periods, see Linda K. Kerber, *Women of the Republic: Intellect & Ideology in Revolutionary America* (Chapel Hill, N.C., 1980), 193-200; Catherine Clinton, "Equally Their Due: The Education of the Planter Daughter in the Early Republic," *Journal of the Early Republic* 2 (Spring 1982): 39-40. See also Thomas Woody, *A*

History of Women's Education in the United States, 2 vols. (New York, 1974); Christie Ann Farnham, *The Education of the Southern Belle: Higher Education and Student Socialization in the Antebellum South* (New York, 1994).

39. *VG*, April 11, 1755, April 18, 1755; Stiverson and Stiverson, "Books Useful and Entertaining," 319; *MR* (April 1755), 292-324; *Gentleman's Magazine* (April 1755), 149-151; *London Magazine* (April 1755), 193-200. Chesterfield's letters first appeared in Robert Dodsley's London periodical, *The World*, on Nov. 28, 1764 and Dec. 5, 1764. Chesterfield was supposed to have been Johnson's patron during the grueling seven-year effort to create the *Dictionary*, but Chesterfield's support, financial and otherwise, was virtually nonexistent, a fact that led Johnson to castigate him following publication of the letters in *The World*. See Henry Hitchings, *Defining the World: The Extraordinary Story of Dr. Johnson's Dictionary* (New York, 2005), 181-86. For a bibliography of Johnson's *Dictionary* and his other works, see J. D. Fleeman, *A Bibliography of the Works of Samuel Johnson: Treating His Published Works from the Beginning to 1984* (New York and Oxford, 2000). On the history of the *Dictionary*'s publication, see Allen H. Reddick, *The Making of Johnson's Dictionary, 1746-1773*, rev ed. (Cambridge, Eng., 1996). Peter Presley Thornton's books are in Inventory of Peter Presley Thornton, Nov. 14, 1780, Northumberland Co., Va., Record Book 11, 57-60. For William Cabell's extensive book list, see List of Books Belonging to the Estate of William Cabell, n.d. [ca. 1798], Cabell Family Papers, 1693-1913, 1743-1823 (Mss. 65 C12), Special Collections, Earl Gregg Swem Library, CWM.

40. John Baylor to George Washington, June 20, 1757, in Abbot, ed., *Papers of George Washington, Colonial Series*, 4:242.

41. *Gentleman's Magazine* (April 1739), 200.

42. George Braxton to John Lidderdale, Sept. 21, 1761, in Frederick Horner, *The History of the Blair, Banister, and Braxton Families* (Philadelphia, 1898), 146-47. The "race Books" mentioned by Braxton were almost certainly Heber's *Historical List*. On the importation of thoroughbreds into colonial America, see John Hervey, *Racing in America, 1665-1865*, 2 vols. (privately printed, 1944), 1:61, 281-90. Though scarce and expensive (only 800 copies were printed for members of the New

York-based Jockey Club) and not without errors, Hervey's *Racing in America* remains the best overall source for the history of American thoroughbred horses and racing during the colonial period. See also Francis B. Culver, *Blooded Horses of Colonial Days* (privately printed, 1922). On *Bulle Rock*, see Fairfax Harrison, *The Equine F.F.Vs.: A Study of the Evidence for the English Horses Imported into Virginia Before the Revolution* (privately printed, 1928), 52-54.

43. Burnaby, *Travels*, 24; Johann D. Schoepf, *Travels in the Confederation, 1783-1784*, ed. and trans. Alfred J. Morrison (Philadelphia, 1911), 65; [Lord Adam Gordon], "Journal of an Officer in the West Indies Who Traveled over a Part of the West Indies, and of North America," in *Travels in the American Colonies*, ed. Newton D. Mereness (New York, 1916), 405.

44. John Baylor III to John Backhouse, Aug. 3, 1761, BLB; Samuel Lyde to John Baylor III, Oct. 25, 1754, BP. The groom selected by Samuel Lyde had worked for "several Noblemen," including Sir Edward O'Brien (1705-65), one of the greatest turfmen in eighteenth-century Ireland who once bet his castle on a horse (and won). For a list of the known thoroughbreds imported by Baylor and other Virginians, see Hervey, *Racing in America*, 281-90. The cost of a live-in tutor in mid-eighteenth-century Virginia was about £30 a year. See Jackson T. Main, *The Social Structure of Revolutionary America* (Princeton, 1965), 243. For Baylor's losses at horse racing, see John Baylor Ledgers, 1732-55, BP. Baylor occasionally entered his horses in Virginia races in the 1760s, but with little improvement in results. In the fall of 1767, for example, the *Virginia Gazette* reported that William Byrd III had won a £100 purse when his horse, *Valiant Tryall*, beat Baylor's horse, *Britannicus*, "with great ease." (*VG* [Purdie and Dixon], Oct. 29, 1767.) Notwithstanding Baylor's horse breeding and racing, it is not at all true, as one historian claims, that Baylor's horse-breeding activities were so pervasive that he was a "tobacco planter merely in name." (Kenneth Cohen, "Well Calculated for the Farmer: Thoroughbreds in the Early National Chesapeake, 1790-1850," *VMHB* 115 [Oct. 2007]: 376.) Barring bad weather or other disaster, Baylor annually produced about fifty hogsheads at each of his plantations in Caroline and Orange counties. Any planter who produced 100 hogsheads of tobacco annually was a major planter.

45. Harrison, *The Equine F.F.Vs*, 100. On *Fearnought*'s 1761 record, see

Reginald Heber, ed., *An Historical List of Horse-Matches Run; and of Plates and Prizes Run for in Great Britain and Ireland, in the Year 1761* (London, 1762), xxxiv.

46. The bill of sale for *Fearnought* was in the possession of Dr. John R. Baylor (1822-1897) (Col. Baylor III's great-grandson), but its present whereabouts are unknown. See W. G. Stannard, "Racing in Colonial Virginia," *VMHB* 2 (Jan. 1895): 301. According to a nineteenth-century source, *Fearnought* cost £289. (Patrick N. Edgar, *The American Race-Turf Register, Sportsman's Herald, and General Stud Book*, 2 vols. [New York, 1833], 1:33). But Edgar was mistaken; £289 was the amount for which *Fearnought* was appraised in Col. Baylor's estate in 1772, by which time the horse was past his prime.

47. John Baylor to John Backhouse, July 18, 1764; BLB; Edgar, *American Race-Turf Register*, 1:33; Edwin M. Betts, ed., *Thomas Jefferson's Farm Book* (Chapel Hill, N.C., and London, 2001), 92. On *Fearnought*, see also Hervey, *Racing in America*, 76-80; Culver, *Blooded Horses of Colonial Days*, 100-1, 104-5; Harrison, *Equine F.F.Vs.*, 98-105; idem, *Early American Turf Stock, 1730-1830*, 2 vols. (privately printed, 1935), 2:116-19. On *Big Brown*'s connections to *Fearnought*, see Thomas Katheder, "Belmont Favorite Big Brown's Virginia Legacy," *Fauquier Times-Democrat* (Warrenton, Va.), June 4, 2008. After Baylor's death, an estate sale notice claimed he had no less than "fifty choice blooded horses." (*VG* [Purdie and Dixon], Oct. 1, 1772.) During the same week that Capt. Quinney delivered *Fearnought* he made the rounds at other large Virginia plantations along the Rappahannock River to drop off goods and pick up tobacco, including a stop at Col. Landon Carter's Sabine Hall. See Greene, *Diary of Col Landon Carter*, 1:270.

48. The 1760s marked the beginning of financial ruin for the majority of Virginia's large planters (not just the relative few who have been studied), a fact that seems to have escaped the notice of most scholars of the period. On the London economic crises in the 1760s, see Joseph A. Ernst, "The Political Economy of the Chesapeake Colonies, 1760-1775: A Study in Comparative History," in *The Economy of Early America: The Revolutionary Period, 1763-1790*, ed. Ronald Hoffman et al. (Charlottesville, Va., 1988), 196-205. Regarding the successive droughts in Virginia during the 1760s, see, for example, Greene, *Diary of Col. Landon Carter*, 1:293 (in which Landon Carter complains in

his diary, "This is my 7th drye year."); Richard Corbin to Capel and Osgood Hanbury, Feb. 15, 1767, Richard Corbin Letterbook, 1758-68, CWSC (in which Corbin claimed, "Less tobacco has not been made since 1758.") On increasing taxes in Virginia during the 1760s, see Alvin Rabushka, *Taxation in Colonial America* (Princeton, N.J., and Oxford, 2008), chaps. 23 and 28; Robert A. Becker, *Revolution, Reform, and the Politics of American Taxation, 1763-1783* (Baton Rouge, La., 1980), 78-79.

On the smallpox outbreak and economic conditions in Caroline Co., see T. E. Campbell, *Colonial Caroline*, 180. Smallpox epidemics raged throughout America in 1764. See, for example, Colonial Society of Massachusetts, *Medicine in Colonial Massachusetts, 1620-1820* (Boston, 1980), 74 (Boston); John R. Quinan, *Medical Annals of Baltimore from 1608 to December 1880* (Baltimore, 1884) (Maryland); William W. Abbot, *The Royal Governors of Georgia, 1754-1775* (Chapel Hill, N.C., 1959), 102 (Savannah, Ga.); Robert H. Jackson, *From Savages to Subjects: Missions in the History of the American Southwest* (Armonk, N.Y., and London, 2000), 98 (Native Americans in present-day Texas); Colin G. Calloway, *The Scratch of a Pen: 1763 and the Transformation of North America* (New York, 2006), 45 (Native Americans in Great Lakes and Ohio Valley regions). As Boston became "one great hospital" due to the 1764 outbreak, John Adams had himself inoculated against the disease. See David McCullough, *John Adams* (New York, 2001), 56.

49. John Baylor III to John Backhouse, July 18, 1764, July 28, 1769, BLB.

50. *James Ritchie & Co. v. Baylor*, in Caroline Co., Va., Order Book (1765-67), 320, 427.

51. For the story of Robinson scandal, see Mays, *Edmund Pendleton*, chap. 11; Joseph A. Ernst, "The Robinson Scandal Redivivus: Money, Debts, and Politics in Revolutionary Virginia," *VMHB* 77 (April 1969): 146-73. For the list of Robinson's borrowers, see Mays, *Edmund Pendleton*, appendix II.

52. For the Norton list of debtors, see List of Foreign Debtors to John Norton & Sons, July 31, 1770, NP.

53. John Baylor III to John Backhouse, July 28, 1769, BLB. For a discussion of Virginia's boycott of British goods, see Woody Holton, *Forced Founders: Indians, Debtors, Slaves, and the Making of the American Revolution in Virginia* (Chapel Hill, N.C., and London, 1999), 77-105.

54. Will of John Baylor III, Feb. 19, 1770, in *VMHB* 24 (1916): 367-73; *VG* (Purdie and Dixon), March 25, 1773.

Chapter 4

1. Philip V. Fithian to John Peck, Aug. 12, 1774, in Farish, ed., *Journal and Letters*, 161; Jay B. Hubbell and Douglas Adair, "Robert Munford's 'The Candidates,'" *WMQ*, 3rd ser., 5 (April 1948): 223. Although Munford's play is a satiric farce, Munford, a member of the Virginia gentry who was educated in Britain, was not poking fun at how colonial Virginians looked at formal education. Robert Munford and Col. Baylor III had a connection that appeared in Munford's *The Candidates*. Robert Munford (ca. 1737-1784), first elected to the House of Burgesses in 1765, supported Patrick Henry's Stamp Act resolutions in opposition to Col. Baylor and the Tidewater elite (discussed in the previous chapter). In *The Candidates*, one of the voters, Captain Paunch, dismisses Mr. Smallhopes, a candidate for office, and satirically remarks that he (Paunch) would "as soon send to New-Market, for a burgess." (Robert Munford, *A Collection of Plays and Poems* [Petersburg, Va., 1798], 19.) Munford may have had the English Newmarket in mind, but he was probably referring to Col. Baylor's Newmarket. See Rodney M. Baine, *Robert Munford: America's First Comic Dramatist* (Athens, Ga., 1967), 61.

2. On Rev. Boucher, including his relationship with the Dulanys and Washington, see Anne Y. Zimmer, *Jonathan Boucher: Loyalist in Exile* (Detroit, Mich., 1978), esp. chaps. 4 and 5.

3. Robert I. Wilberforce and Samuel Wilberforce, *The Life of Wilberforce*, 5 vols. (London, 1838), 1:4-5. Almost all secondary sources that mention John Baylor IV's education at Putney claim he was sent there at age twelve; in fact, he was about sixteen. (Among other confirmations of this fact, a 1770 letter from Baylor's mother, Frances, mentions his "nearly 5 years absence" from Virginia. Frances W. Baylor to John Baylor IV,

May 25, 1770, in Ellen C. B. Baylor Commonplace Book, 1752-1906, VHS.) Moreover, a number of secondary sources erroneously state that Wilberforce and Baylor were classmates at Cambridge. Wilberforce matriculated at St. John's College at Cambridge in 1776, four years after Baylor had left Cambridge for good.

4. Robert Carter to Lewis Burwell, Aug. 22, 1727, Robert Carter Letterbook, 1727-28, UVASC. Regarding Baylor's admittance to Cambridge, see John Venn et al., comps., *Biographical History of Gonville and Caius College, 1349-1897*, 7 vols. (Cambridge, Eng., 1897-1978), 2:89. Regarding American colonial students in Britain, see William L. Sachse, *The Colonial American in Britain* (Madison, Wis., 1956), 47-69. One scholar counted 117 Virginians who matriculated at Oxford, Cambridge, Edinburgh, the Inns of Court, and other universities and schools in Britain during the period 1658-1798. See Virginia R. Hornsby, "The Higher Education of Virginians in Colonial Days," (MA thesis, CWM, 1936). See also Mary N. Stanard, *Colonial Virginia and its Customs* (Philadelphia and London, 1917), 287-294. For a list of Americans who matriculated at Oxford and Cambridge universities during the colonial period, see Willard Connely, "Colonial Americans in Oxford and Cambridge," *American Oxonian* 29 (1942): 75-77. Though reasonably accurate as far as it goes, Connely's list is not complete (it includes John Baylor IV, for example, but does not include his father or grandfather, who were known to have attended Cambridge). On Americans at the Inns of Court, see Alfred Jones, *American Members of the Inns of Court* (London, 1924); C.E.A. Bedwell, "American Middle Templars," *American Historical Review* 25 (July 1920): 680-89.

5. John Baylor IV to John Backhouse, July 14, 1772 (Mss 2 B3445a1), VHS.

6. John Frere to John Hatley Norton, April 1, 1768, NP; Frances W. Baylor to John Baylor IV, May 25, 1770, in Ellen C. B. Baylor Commonplace Book, 1752-1906, VHS (emphasis in original).

7. John Norton to John Hatley Norton, April 21, 1770, Feb. 24, 1772, NP. On the firm of John Norton & Sons, see Jacob M. Price, "Who Was John Norton?: A Note on the Historical Character of Some Eighteenth-Century London Virginia Firms," *WMQ*, 3rd ser., 19 (July

1962): 400-407; Samuel M. Rosenblatt, "The Significance of Credit in the Tobacco Consignment Trade: A Study of John Norton and Sons, 1768-1775," *WMQ*, 3rd ser., 19 (July 1962): 389-93 and Rosenblatt's introduction in Mason, ed., *John Norton and Sons*.

8. For the petition to dock the entail on Baylor lands, see Petition of John Baylor et al., May 18, 1774, in John Pendleton Kennedy, ed., *Journal of the House of Burgesses of Virginia, 1773-1776* (Richmond, Va., 1905), 109. Not quite three years after his father's death, Baylor advertised the sale of 3,000 acres at Newmarket of "well timbered land," including "two plantations, in good repair with proper and convenient edifices for farming, or making tobacco." (*VG* [Purdie], March 10, 1775.)

9. Susanna Norton Turner to John Hatley Norton, June 28, 1772, NP. In Greek mythology, Comus, a follower of Dionysus, was associated with nocturnal excess and revelry. However, Turner's mention of "Comus' Cup" in her letter was likely inspired by George Colman's *Comus: A Masque* (London, 1772), which was a popular adaptation of John Milton's *A Maske Presented at Ludlow Castle* (1634). In Milton's version, as in Colman's, Comus attempts, unsuccessfully, to debauch an ingénue by having her drink from his magical cup.

10. Burton J. Hendrick, *The Lees of Virginia* (Boston, 1935), 146; Edmund Jennings Jr. to Arthur Lee, [n.d., ca. Dec. 1767], Letterbook, 1753-69, Jennings Family Papers 1737-1837, VHS. More than a few elite Virginians who were sent to Britain for their education found themselves "floating in limbo," as historian Kenneth Lockridge put it, between their being rejected in England for being mere provincials and their feeling alienated and disaffected in Virginia. (Kenneth A. Lockridge, *The Diary, and Life, of William Byrd II of Virginia, 1674-1744* [Chapel Hill, N.C., and London, 1987], 155-58.) Though Arthur Lee, a radical Whig, had spent much of his time back in Virginia composing political screeds attacking what he perceived as British tyranny, at the same time he desperately wanted to return to London, where, according to his biographer, he could "learn the nature of metropolitan radicalism and the inner politics of the British empire" while "bask[ing] in the pleasures offered by Georgian society." (Louis W. Potts, *Arthur Lee: A Virtuous Revolutionary* [Baton Rouge, La., and London, 1981], 54.) Regarding the experiences of American colonial students in London, see Julie M. Flavell, "'The School for

Modesty and Humility': Colonial American Youths in London and their Parents, 1755-1775," *Historical Journal* 42 (No. 2, 1999): 377-403. For a review and analysis of the letters and journals of some 1,000 Americans who visited Great Britain in the mid-eighteenth century, see Susan L. Lively, "Going Home: Americans in Britain, 1740-1776" (PhD diss., Harvard University, 1996).

11. William Lee to Samuel Thorp, June 6, 1785, in "Some Notes on Green Spring," *VMHB* 38 (Jan. 1930): 46.

12. Peter Ackroyd, *London: The Biography* (London, 2000), 305; John Dickinson to Mary C. Dickinson, Jan. 19, 1754, in H. Trevor Colbourn, ed., "A Pennsylvania Farmer at the Court of King George: John Dickinson's London Letters, 1754-56," *Pennsylvania Magazine of History and Biography* 86 (July 1962): 253; John Dickinson to Samuel Dickinson, May 25, 1754, Aug. 15, 1754, in ibid., 269, 278.

13. M. Dorothy George, "London and the Life of the Town," in *Johnson's England: An Account of the Life & Manners of His Age*, ed. Arthur S. Turberville, rev. ed., 2 vols. (Oxford, 1967), 1:166-68. On eighteenth-century London, see Roy Porter, *London: A Social History* (London, 1994); Richard B. Schwartz, *Daily Life in Johnson's London* (Madison, Wis., 1983); M. Dorothy George, *London Life in the Eighteenth Century* (New York, 1965).

14. William Bond to John Baylor IV, July 15, 1773, BP. Bond subsequently became a rector at Wheatacre, Norfolk. His obituary is in *Gentleman's Magazine* (June 1832): 569-70. On Washington's attendance at Baylor's ball, see Donald Jackson and Dorothy Twohig, eds., *The Diaries of George Washington*, 6 vols. (Charlottesville, Va., and London, 1976-79), 3:141. Baylor also had a two-night visit with Washington at Mount Vernon in April 1773. Ibid., 3:171.

15. On George W. Baylor's service to Washington, see Arthur F. Lefkowitz, *George Washington's Indispensable Men: The 32 Aides-de-Camp Who Helped Win American Independence* (Mechanicsburg, Pa., 2003), passim. A few details of Baylor's trans-Atlantic journey and peregrinations about Britain and France are in Memorandum Book of John Baylor IV, Oct. 1775-March 1778, BP. See also John Norton to George W. Fairfax, Jan. 6, 1776, in Edward D. Neill, *The Fairfaxes of*

England and America in the Seventeenth and Eighteenth Centuries...
(Albany, N.Y., 1868), 170-71 (mentioning that Baylor had written
Norton to advise him of his arrival in Scotland by Jan. 1776). Baylor's
son John V stated that the reason his father went to Britain in 1775
was "to calm by his presence the fears of many heavy British creditors
against the estate of his late father." (Memorial of John Baylor V, Sept.
5, 1853, BP.) Indeed, Baylor's inherited debts were heavy, but at that
time he seems to have had little realization of just how oppressive and
serious they were.

Chapter 5

1. Arthur Lee to Committee of Secret Correspondence, Feb. 18, 1777, in
    Francis Wharton, ed., *The Revolutionary Diplomatic Correspondence
    of the United States*, 6 vols. (Washington, D.C., 1889), 2:273.
    Regarding the American diplomatic initiatives in France, see Jonathan
    R. Dull's *A Diplomatic History of the American Revolution* (New
    Haven, Conn., and London, 1985), 57-96, and "Franklin the Diplomat:
    The French Mission," *Transactions of the American Philosophical
    Society* 72 (1982), 1-76. For a recent study that focuses on Franklin's
    role as the de facto head of the delegation, see Stacy Schiff, *A Great
    Improvisation: Franklin, France, and the Birth of America* (New York,
    2005), 7-125. On the French tobacco monopoly and its role in the
    American negotiations for assistance, see Jacob M. Price, *France and
    the Chesapeake: A History of the French Tobacco Monopoly, 1674-
    1791, and of Its Relationship to the British and American Tobacco
    Trades*, 2 vols. (Ann Arbor, Mich., 1973), 2:700-17.

2. William Lee to Arthur Lee, Aug. 14, 1777, in Worthington C. Ford,
    Letters of William Lee, 3 vols. (New York, 1891), 1:219.

3. John Baylor IV to George Baylor, Sept. 27, 1777, BP. The subject
    of Baylor's recommendation was Karl Philip Rudolf von Bonstetten
    (1738-1824), a former Prussian army officer. Following Baylor's letter
    of introduction, Bonstetten traveled to Charleston, S.C., seeking an
    officer's commission in George Washington's Contiental Army. The
    Commander-in-Chief had already been inundated with unsolicited
    offers from idle European aristocratic military officers and had
    discovered that many of them were far more trouble than they were
    worth. "I do most devoutly wish," Washington confided in an *entres*

nous missive to Gouverneur Morris, "that we had not a single foreigner among us, except the Marquis de Lafayette." (George Washington to Gouverneur Morris, July 24, 1778, in John C. Fitzpatrick, ed., *Writings of George Washington*, 39 vols. [Washington, D.C., 1931-44], 12:227-28.) Bonstetten appealed to Henry Laurens, President of the Continental Congress, but Laurens, doing his best to politely rebuff him, informed him that "there are many valuable Characters of different Nations ... unemployed" in America's war of independence. (Henry Laurens to Baron de Bonstetten, May 3, 1778, in Paul H. Smith, ed., *Letters of Delegates to Congress*, 1774-1789, 26 vols. [Washington, D.C., 1976-2000], 9:575.) The pestiferous Bonstetten persisted in his efforts until the Continental Congress officially notified him in November 1779 that his services were not needed. In a letter he wrote some years afterwards, he falsely claimed service under Washington as a brevet lieutenant colonel. In 1781 he became an officer in the Swiss DeMeuron Regiment, a mercenary force raised by France to protect the Dutch East India Company in Cape Town, South Africa. Bonstetten should not be confused with his Swiss cousin, Charles Victor de Bonstetten (1745-1832), a once-famous European literary figure and intellectual. (I am indebted to Dr. Beat Immenhauser, Bern, Switzerland, for information regarding Baron von Bonstetten.)

4. Lund Washington to George Washington, Feb. 8, 1776, in Philander D. Chase et al., eds., *The Papers of George Washington, Revolutionary War Series*, 16 vols. to date (Charlottesville, Va., 1985—), 3:271; *The Journal of Nicholas Cresswell*, 1774-77 (New York, 1924), 173-74. On people stealing salt, see Michael A. McDonnell, *The Politics of War: Race, Class, and Conflict in Revolutionary Virginia* (Chapel Hill, N.C., 2007), 151-52. On the scarcity problem generally, see Francis C. Huntley, "Salt: A Study in Colonial Economy" (MA thesis, University of California, Berkeley, 1948); Larry G. Bowam, "The Scarcity of Salt in Virginia During the American Revolution," *VMHB* 77 (Oct. 1969): 464-72. On the *Koulikan's* cargo, see *Geo. III v. Thamas Kouli Kan* (1778), High Court of Admiralty, Prize Court (HCA 32/462/2/1-118), UKNA.

5. Silas Deane to [_] Setoref, Sept. 19, 1777, in *The Deane Papers, Collections of the New York Historical Society*, 5 vols. (New York, 1887-91), 2:138; Benjamin Franklin to Silas Deane, June 10, 1777, ibid., 2:70.

6. George III to Lord North, April 6, [1777], in Benjamin F. Stevens, ed., *B.F. Stevens's Facsimiles of Manuscripts in European Archives Relating to America, 1773-1783*, 25 vols. (London, 1889-98) (hereafter cited as *BFS*), No. 249; Lord North to the Earl of Sandwich, Dec. 1, 1777, in G. R. Barnes and J. H. Owen, eds., *The Private Papers of John, Earl of Sandwich, First Lord of the Admiralty, 1771-1782*, 4 vols. (London, 1932-38), 1:255-56. On the advance intelligence regarding the *Koulikan*, see [Joseph Hynson] to [Lt. Col. Edward Smith], Nov. 25, 1777, in *BFS*, No. 309. Regarding British espionage in France during this period, see Samuel F. Bemis, "British Secret Service and the French-American Alliance," *American Historical Review* 29 (April 1924): 474-95; John P. Vaillancourt, "Edward Bancroft (@ Edwd. Edwards), Estimable Spy," *Studies in Intelligence* (Winter 1961): A53-A67 (CIA journal article, declassified in 1993). For studies of French covert aid to America, both by former U.S. intelligence officers, see Kenneth A. Daigler, "American Covert Action in the Revolutionary War," *Intelligencer: Journal of U.S. Intelligence Studies* 15 (Fall/Winter 2006-7): 39-46; James M. Potts, *French Covert Aid in the American Revolution* (New York and Lincoln, Neb., 2005).

7. John Lloyd to Henry Laurens, Feb. 6, 1778, in David R. Chestnutt et al., eds., *The Papers of Henry Laurens*, 16 vols. (Columbia, S.C., 1968-2002), 11:416. Regarding British tobacco imports during the Revolution, see Price, *France and the Chesapeake*, 682-83. On British naval superiority in the Atlantic and its disruption of the American economy, see Richard Buel Jr., *In Irons: Britain's Naval Supremacy and the American Revolutionary Economy* (New Haven, Conn., and London, 1998).

8. *Lloyd's Evening Post, and British Chronicle* (London), Jan. 23-26, 1778. On Hynson's presence on board the *Hector*, see Report of Jacques Donatien Leray de Chaumont, April 18, 1778, in *BFS*, No. 810. For the details of the capture of the *Koulikan*, see Henry [Henri] Grand to Rodolphe-Ferdinand Grand, Jan. 29, 1778, intercepted copy (in French) in SP 78/306, f. 244, UKNA; Journal of the H.M.S. *Hector* (Capt. John Hamilton), Adm. 51/466, UKNA. Another copy of Grand's letter, from the Archives Du Ministère Des Affaires Estrangères, Paris, along with an English translation, is reprinted in *DN*, 11:937-43.

9. John Baylor IV to Lord North, February 5, 1778, BP; John Adams to Horatio Gates, March 23, 1776 in Smith, ed., *Letters of Delegates to*

Congress, 1774-89, 3:432. For the Prohibitory Act, see 16 Geo. III c. 5.

10. Henry [Henri] Grand to Rodolphe-Ferdinand Grand, Jan. 29, 1778, SP 78/306, f. 244, UKNA (reprinted in *DN*, 11:937-43); Marquis de Noailles to Henri Grand, March 3, 1778, intercepted copy (in French) in SP 78/306, f. 311, UKNA. On Noailles's protest and demand for compensation, see Marquis de Noailles to Lord Weymouth, Feb. 24, 1778 [misprinted as 1777], in *DN*, 8:607-8 (in which Noailles asserted Britain had violated a "triple foundation" of international law, treaties, and "Peace and good Relations"). Noailles was probably right. According to the international maritime doctrine of "free ships, free goods," a widely accepted principle that had been enshrined in a number of eighteenth-century treaties (including Anglo-French treaties), neutral ships could trade with a belligerent nation as long as the trade was not conducted through a blockaded port and did not include "contraband." Though in theory this principle seemed straightforward, in practice it led to many disputes, particularly over what constituted contraband. See John B. Moore, "Contraband of War," *APS Proceedings* 51 (Jan. 1912): 18-49. See also Pitman B. Potter, *The Freedom of the Seas in History, Law, and Politics* (New York, 1924), chap. VII.

11. Silas Deane to Henry Grand, Nov. 27, 1777, in *The Deane Papers*, 2:255; Silas Deane to Benjamin Harrison, Nov. 26, 1777, ibid., 2:243.

12. Silas Deane to Peter [Pierre] Landais, Sept. 5, 1777, ibid., 2:123. See also Lord Stormont's Letter to Lord Weymouth, May 21, 1777, in which Stormont describes the French practice of "double Commissions," whereby a French vessel, laden with goods useful to the American rebels, has an ostensible itinerary in the French West Indies and a secret destination at an American port. (SP 78/302, ff. 261-62, UKNA; reprinted in *DN*, 855-56.)

13. Affidavit of George Binsteed and Charles Allan, Feb. 1, 1778, in *Geo III v. Thamas Kouli Kan*.

14. Deposition of Alexander Boyd, Feb. 13, 1778, *Geo. III v. Thamas Kouli Kan*. Regarding the seizure of the *Freeman*, see *Geo. III v. Freeman*,

High Court of Admiralty, Prize Court (HCA 32/335/11/1-27), UKNA. See also George C. Rogers Jr., *The History of Georgetown County, South Carolina* (Spartanburg, S.C., 1990), 118-19. On Boyd's claim of escape, see Silas Deane to Capt. Boyd, Sept. 10, 1777, *Deane Papers*, 2:133. For Boyd's declaration on Jan. 11, 1778, see Lords Commissioners of the Admiralty to George Harris, [Jan. 31, 1778], SP 42/52, ff. 56-57, UKNA (reprinted in *DN*, 11:947). On Lord North's legislative efforts regarding captured Americans, see Sheldon S. Cohen, *Yankee Sailors in British Gaols: Prisoners of War at Forton and Mill, 1777-1783* (Newark, N.J., and London, 1995), 25-29. Prior to the act suspending habeas corpus for American rebels, Lord Chief Justice Mansfield, in a fascinating conceptual precursor to the U.S. prison facility at Guantanamo, proposed holding captured Americans offshore in floating jails to keep them just beyond the jurisdictional reach of the British constitution. See ibid., 27.

15. [Joseph Hynson] to [Lt. Col. Edward Smith], Nov. 25, 1777, in *BFS*, No. 309; Lord Stormont to Lord Weymouth, Dec. 3, 1777, ibid., No. 1752 (reprinted in *DN*, 8:1063-64).

16. Henri Grand to John Baylor, March 28, [1778], BP.

17. Louis Teissier to Rodolphe-Ferdinand Grand, Feb. 10, 1778, Correspondance Politique, Angleterre, vol. 528, f. 294, Archives Du Ministère Des Affaires Estrangères, Paris.

18. Deposition of John Baylor, March 28, 1778, *Geo. III v. Thamas Kouli Kan*. Among the unanswered questions regarding Baylor's French episode is whether Baylor was supposed to assist in the procurement of Virginia tobacco—including tobacco from Newmarket—for the *Koulikan*'s return voyage to France. In light of Boyd's statement that the *Koulikan* was supposed to stop at Virginia for tobacco before sailing back to France and the fact that British officials knew that Baylor was a major tobacco planter, it is puzzling that Baylor's inquisitors never asked him about tobacco.

Through financier Robert Morris, a member of the Secret Committee of Correspondence, Silas Deane had commercial ties with Norton and Beale, a Williamsburg, Va.-based partnership controlled by Baylor's cousin, John H. Norton, but no record survives that suggests Baylor's journey on the *Koulikan* was related to Deane's efforts. See, for example, Silas Deane to Norton and Beale, Sept. 10, 1777, in *The Deane Papers*, 2:136. (Regarding Deane's intertwined business dealings and his diplomatic duties, see Robert R. Crout, "The Diplomacy of Trade: The Influence of Commercial Considerations on French Involvement in the Angloamerican War of Independence, 1775-78" [PhD diss., University of Georgia, 1977].) It is possible that Baylor was nothing more than a mere passenger on the *Koulikan*, and that his status as a Virginia tobacco planter was of no consequence to Grand and his partners, but given the enormous risk presented by having an American on board a French ship officially bound for the French West Indies, it is highly unlikely. As John Lloyd pointed out, "The Owners of french Ships destined for America have for some time past been disinclined to take any Passengers ... from a fear of being searched by the British Cruizers." (John Lloyd to Henry Laurens, Feb. 6, 1778, in Chestnutt, ed., *Papers of Henry Laurens*, 11:415.)

In September 1781, Baylor, back at Newmarket, received a letter from an unidentified but well-informed Frenchman advising him that Comte de Grasse, the French admiral, had arrived at the mouth of the York River "with *twenty eight of the Line* besides Frigates and six thousand Land Troops on Board," and that the "particulars" of the information came from Marquis de Lafayette himself. "If I could have the satisfaction of seeing you just now," the Frenchman wrote cheerfully, "I think I could embrace you with as much cordiality as we did at Nantes on the news of the Burgoinade" [the defeat of British General Burgoyne at the Battle of Saratoga in Oct. 1777]. ([?] to John Baylor, Sept. [_], 1781, BP.)

19. Prince Hoare, *Memoirs of Granville Sharp, Esq.* (London, 1820), 124. For Sharp's lexicographic contribution, see Granville Sharp, *Remarks on the Uses of the Definitive Article in the Greek text of the New Testament* (Durham, Eng., 1798). On Lord Mansfield's decision, see *Somerset v. Stewart*, 20 How. St. Tr. 1 (1772), in Helen T. Catterall, ed., *Judicial Cases Concerning American Slavery and the Negro*, 5 vols. (Washington, D.C., 1926-37), 1:15. For an extensive discussion of the thorny legal issues presented by the *Somerset* case, see William M. Wiecek, "Somerset: Lord Mansfield and the Legitimacy of Slavery in the Anglo-American World," *University of Chicago Law Review* 42 (Autumn 1974): 86-146. Steven M. Wise's book, *Though the Heavens May Fall: The Landmark Trial that Led to the End of Human Slavery* (Cambridge, Mass., 2005), presents an engaging treatment of the case's background and aftermath, but overstates its influence in

bringing about the end of slavery in Britain.

20. Hoare, *Memoirs of Granville Sharp*, 195. For a biography of Lennox, see Alison G. Olson, *The Radical Duke: Career and Correspondence of Charles Lennox, Third Duke of Richmond* (Oxford, 1961). There is no modern biography of Granville Sharp.

Baylor's views about slavery, including his thoughts about its long-term viability in Virginia, are not known; however, evidence suggests that Baylor, and especially his wife, Frances, had serious misgivings about it. In August 1800 Frances Baylor wrote Virginia Gov. James Monroe, who had a reputation for insisting on due process in capital cases involving slaves, beseeching him to commute the death sentence of one Harry, a slave who had been convicted of rape and whose fate she had read about in a newspaper. "I had supposed," she remarked, "the Penitentiary House was erected for the confinement of all criminals; certainly it is not intended to preclude that most unhappy race of people from benefits which I blush to think has too long been withheld." She added, "'God is no respecter of persons'; the black and yellow are equally objects of his care with whites." (Frances Baylor to James Monroe, Aug. 31, 1800, in William P. Palmer et al., eds., *Calendar of Virginia State Papers and Other Manuscripts...*, 11 vols. [Richmond, Va., 1875-93], 9:135.) (Slave Harry was executed on Sept. 5, 1800, as scheduled.) Although Mrs. Baylor's quotation, "God is no respecter of persons," is from the Bible (Acts 10:34-35), she may have also intended to invoke Jupiter Hammon's work, *An Address to the Negroes of the State of New-York* (1787). Jupiter Hammon (1711-1806?), a New York-born slave, authored several pietistic Christian works, including his *Address*, which featured the biblical quote used by Mrs. Baylor prominently on its title page. Hammon's *Address* was published in New York in 1787 and reprinted in Philadelphia the same year, and it gained significant notoriety in slave emancipation and repatriation circles.

In October 1800 John Baylor IV and five fellow justices of the peace in Caroline County formally recommended to Gov. Monroe that Scipio, "a negro Slave the property of Paul Thilman" who had been convicted of "Conspiracy and insurrection" in connection with Gabriel's slave insurrection, be pardoned because he was a "young lad not above 18 or 19 years of age" who "appears to be very ignorant" and was drawn into the conspiracy by another slave. Monroe granted the pardon. (Petition of John Hoomes et al. to Gov. James Monroe, n.d. [Oct. 1800], pardoned [on reverse side] on Nov. 8, 1800, in

Palmer et al., eds., *Calendar of Virginia State Papers*, 9:166.) On Gabriel's revolt and the attitude of Virginia planters toward slavery at the time, see Douglas R. Egerton, *Gabriel's Rebellion: The Virginia Slave Conspiracies of 1800 and 1802* (Chapel Hill, N.C., and London, 1992).

21. For chilling accounts of Baylor's Massacre, see Adrian C. Leiby, *The Revolutionary War in the Hackensack Valley: The Jersey Dutch and the Neutral Ground, 1775-1783*, rev. ed. (New Brunswick, N.J., 1992), 165-72; James Thacher, *A Military Journal During the American Revolutionary War from 1775 to 1783* (Boston, 1823), 147-50. On the archeological excavation of the former tanning vats, see D. Bennett Mazur and Wayne M. Daniels, *The Massacre of Baylor's Dragoons* (Bergen County, N.J., Hist. Soc., n.d.). General Grey's biographer acknowledges that the savagery occurred but suggests, with no evidence to rebut the firsthand accounts of the American soldiers, that the brutality was exaggerated (only "a few Americans were unnecessarily slaughtered," he writes). See David Nelson, *Sir Charles Grey, First Earl Grey: Royal Soldier, Family Patriarch* (Madison, N.J., 1996), 68. Grey was later ennobled as the first Earl Grey for his military service. For a discussion of the ethics of Grey's tactics, see Armstrong Starkey, "Paoli to Stony Point: Military Ethics and Weaponry During the American Revolution," *Journal of Military History* (Jan. 1994): 7-27. See also Stephen Conway, "'The Great Mischief Complain'd of': Reflections on the Misconduct of British Soldiers in the Revolutionary War," *WMQ*, 3rd ser., (July 1990): 370-90; idem, "To Subdue America: British Army Officers and the Conduct of the Revolutionary War," *WMQ*, 3rd ser., (July 1986): 381-407.

22. Memorial of John Baylor V, Sept. 4, 1853, BP. On the role of St. Eustatius in the American Revolution, see J. Franklin Jameson, "St. Eustatius in the American Revolution," *American Historical Review* 8 (July 1903): 683-708. James Clay, a London merchant whom Baylor had met in St. Eustatius, dismissed the island as a "Barren Rock." (James Clay to John Baylor, July 25, 1779, Baylor Family Papers, Ms 59.1, CWSC.) In a post-script, Clay mentioned that "two vessels just arrived in York River from Nantz [Nantes] with brass ordnance &ec for the States." See also James Clay to James Withers, Aug. 10, 1779, NP.

23. Oct. 27. 1779, *Journal of the House of Delegates of Virginia, 1779*

(Williamsburg, Va., 1780), 31. For the testaments regarding Baylor's loyalty, see statement of George Baylor, Oct. 14, 1779, and statement of Edmund Pendleton, Oct. 13, 1779, in Box 1, BP.

Chapter 6

1. Colonel Baylor III's letterbooks, 1749-65 (Mss1 B3445 a 1-2), were first deposited at LVA by Baylor descendants in 1925, and then removed by one of them and given to VHS twenty years later. *Daingerfield v. Rootes* was part of a flood of internecine litigation brought by Baylor family members against their siblings and others in the post-Revolutionary period. The case was filed in the Superior Court of Chancery in Fredericksburg, Virginia (1809), in connection with a claim by one of John Baylor IV's sisters that she had never received the legacy due her from her father's estate. A few loose items from the destroyed probate records of Caroline County, including a copy of John Baylor IV's will (but not his estate inventory), survive in Caroline County, Va., Circuit Court. Records, 1741-1871, Robert Alonzo Brock Collection, Henry E. Huntington Library, San Marino, Calif.

2. Baylor's French-European author-book catalogue, along with some 2,000 other Baylor family items in the BP, was loaned to UVASC by Baylor descendants in 1946 and donated by them in 1954.

3. Gregory A. Johnson, a collections supervisor at UVASC, believes that the ink (which appears to be dye based rather than iron gall based) and the type and texture of the paper (which has no visible watermark) suggest the list may date from the 1830s (e-mail to author, Nov. 28, 2007). The list, which includes anachronistic elements such as the long "s" (ſ), less common in handwriting after the eighteenth century, is likely a later copy of the original.

4. "Memoir of Colonel John Page of Rosewell," 145.

5. Genevieve Yost, "The Reconstruction of the Library of Norborne Berkeley, Baron De Botetourt, Governor of Virginia, 1768-1770," *Papers of the Bibliographical Society of America* 36 (1942): 104.

6. Hendrick, *Lees of Virginia*, 31; Maude H. Woodfin, ed., *Another Secret*

Diary of William Byrd of Westover, 1739-1741 (Richmond, Va., 1942), 386-87; Farish, ed., *Journal and Letters*, 72; Richard B. Davis, *Francis Walker Gilmer* (Richmond, Va., 1937), 350; Rufus Rockwell Wilson, ed., *Burnaby's Travels Through North America* (New York, 1904), 53. Regarding Richard Lee II's classical learning, see Louis B. Wright, "Richard Lee II: A Belated Elizabethan in Virginia," *Huntington Library Quarterly* 1 (Oct. 1938): 1-35. For a list of his books, see "Libraries in Colonial Virginia," *WMQ*, 1st ser., 4 (April 1894): 247-49. James Logan was fluent in ancient Greek and, followed by Cotton Mather, probably owned more books in that language than anyone else in colonial America. In an 1827 address, J. Burton Harrison, whose Virginia-gentry forbears had been tutored by Scottish teachers, said that during most of the eighteenth century, "Scotch education ... consisted chiefly of Latin" and "[o]f Greek, there was but little taught in Scotland, and that, as it is now, rather superficially." A. J. Morrison, *The Beginnings of Public Education in Virginia, 1776-1860* (Richmond, Va., 1917), 51-52.

7.   Thomas Jefferson to Robert Skipwith, Aug. 3, 1771, in *TJP*, 1:76-81. Regarding titles by Greek authors listed in the *Virginia Gazette*, see Molnar, "Publication and Retail Book Advertisements," 264-67. Among inventoried private libraries in colonial South Carolina, the majority of Greco-Roman titles were in English translation. See Edgar, "Libraries of South Carolina," 32. On Latin and Greek titles published in colonial America, see Raoul N. Smith, "A Bibliography of Books on Language and Languages Printed in the United States through the Year 1800," *Historiographia Linguistica* 4 (1977): 207-43. According to an advertisement for the sale of his library, Dr. John Mitchell (the probable author of *American Husbandry*) owned a "Curious Collection of Books, in most Sciences, particularly Physic, Surgery, and Botany, in Greek, Latin, French, and English." (*VG*, April 17, 1746.)

8.   Thomas Jefferson to Peter Carr, Aug. 19, 1785, in *TJP*, 8:407; Thomas Jefferson to Bernard Moore, ca. 1768, copied in Thomas Jefferson to Gen. John Minor, Aug. 30, 1814, Special Collections, Biddle Law Library, University of Pennsylvania, Philadelphia; Thomas Jefferson to John Brazier, Aug. 24, 1819, in Andrew A. Lipscomb and Albert E. Bergh, eds., *The Writings of Jefferson*, 20 vols. (Washington, D.C., 1903-1904), 15:208. The original of Jefferson's letter to Bernard Moore is lost; its text survives because Jefferson reproduced his copy of it, along with some additions, in his subsequent letter to Gen. John

Minor, who sought Jefferson's advice regarding appropriate readings for his eldest son, John Minor, who intended to pursue legal studies. See Morris L. Cohen, "Thomas Jefferson Recommends a Course of Law Study," *University of Pennsylvania Law Review* 119 (April 1971): 823-44. Jefferson informed Gen. Minor that he wrote his letter to Bernard Moore "near 50. years ago," which would place it around 1767-69. Scholars and researchers have wrongly disputed Jefferson's recollection of when he wrote the Moore letter. Morris Cohen, for example, concluded that the Moore letter must have been written in "the early 1770's." Cohen and others, however, mistook Bernard Moore (b. ca. 1750), the recipient of Jefferson's letter, for the far more prominent Col. Bernard Moore (ca. 1716-1775) of Chelsea in King William Co., Va., who bore no known relation to the former Moore. Colonel Moore was more than fifty years old when Jefferson wrote his letter, while the younger Moore was about seventeen. On Jefferson and his Greek studies, see Carl J. Richard, *The Founders and the Classics: Greece, Rome, and the American Enlightenment* (Cambridge, Mass., and London, 1994), 26-30 (*N.B.*: Richard does not acknowledge Jefferson's exceptionalism regarding his fluency in ancient Greek).

9.   Helen D. Bullock, "A Dissertation on Education in the Form of a Letter from James Maury to Robert Jackson, July 17, 1762," *Papers of the Albemarle Historical Society* 2 (1941-42): 40-41, 43. Robert "King" Carter, who died three decades before Maury's letter, would have regarded the teacher's views as heretical. Carter expected his sons, whom he sent to England for their education, to become "Absolute Masters" of classical languages and insisted that they be taught with the "Old School books that We and Our forefathers learned." "It is not," he harrumphed, by "reading a few scraps in the Poets & other Classicks that makes boys understand the Scope & designe of the [ancient] Authors," but rather immersive studies in the languages. (Robert Carter to William Dawkins, Jan. 28, 1724, Robert Carter Letter Book, 1723-24, Carter Family Papers, VHS.)

10. Richard Ambler to Edward and John Ambler, May 20, 1749, in Lucille Griffith, ed., "English Education for Virginia Youth: Some Eighteenth-Century Ambler Family Letters," *VMHB* (Jan. 1961): 16.

11. William J. Ziobro, "Classical Education in Colonial America," in *Classical Antiquity and the Politics of America: From George Washington to George W. Bush*, ed. Michael Meckler (Waco, Texas,

2006), 17-18; "The Statutes of the College of William and Mary in Virginia," *WMQ*, 1st ser., 16 (April 1908): 246-47. On the College of William and Mary, see also Robert P. Thomson, "The Reform of the College of William and Mary, 1763-1780," *APS Proceedings* 115 (June 1971): 187-213.

12. Inventory of John Parke Custis, Feb. 20, 1782, Fairfax Co., Va., Will Book D (1772-1783), 274-88; Watkins, *Cultural History*, 200, 202; Kevin J. Hayes, *The Mind of a Patriot: Patrick Henry and the World of Ideas* (Charlottesville, Va., and London, 2008), 24, 69, appendix.

13. Bailyn, *Pamphlets of the American Revolution*, 21 (Bailyn was quoting Charles F. Mullet's "Classical Influences on the American Revolution," *Classical Journal* 35 [Nov. 1939]: 93); Richard, *Founders and the Classics*, 7-8. A related historiographical debate, sometimes called liberalism versus republicanism, has raged for decades over the relative influence of John Locke's political theories on American revolutionary thought compared to classical republican philosophy grounded in the writings of Aristotle and Polybius. See Eric Nelson, *The Greek Tradition in Republican Thought* (Cambridge, Eng., 2004), chap. 6. On classical education in colonial America, see (in addition to Richards' excellent *Founders and the Classics*) Richard M. Gummere, *The American Colonial Mind and the Classical Tradition* (Cambridge, Mass., 1963); idem, "The Heritage of the Classics in Colonial North America: An Essay on the Greco-Roman Tradition," *APS Proceedings* 99 (April, 1955): 68-78; Meyer Reinhold, *Classica Americana: The Greek and Roman Heritage in the United States* (Detroit, Mich., 1984). Led by proponents such as Benjamin Franklin and Benjamin Rush, a strong undercurrent developed in the years preceding the Revolution that questioned the usefulness of Greco-Roman studies and advocated a more utilitarian curriculum. See Meyer Reinhold, "The Quest for 'Useful Knowledge' in Eighteenth-Century America," *APS Proceedings* 119 (April 1975): 108-132; idem, "Opponents of Classical Learning in America During the Revolutionary Period," *APS Proceedings* 112 (August, 1968): 221-34. Regarding the Greco-Roman tradition in American intellectual history, see Caroline Winterer, *The Culture of Classicism: Ancient Greece and Rome in American Intellectual Life, 1780-1910* (Baltimore and London, 2002).

14. Inventory of Sarah Ball, Oct. 8, 1742, Lancaster Co., Va., Wills and Deeds Book No. 13 (1736-43), 290-93; Inventory of Sarah Jones,

June 15, 1720, Northumberland Co., Va., Record Book No. 1718-26, 116; Inventory of Sabine T. Marshall, March 18, 1768, Charles Co., Md., Inventories (1766-73), 182-89. For the study of Maryland probate inventories, see Garrigus Jr., "Reading Habits of Maryland's Planter Gentry," 41. For the Northumberland Co. analysis, see Haynie, *Northumberland County Bookshelf*, 5. The founding trustees and benefactors of Georgia apparently regarded the *Whole Duty of Man* as important as the Bible. In 1733 they sent 187 copies of *Whole Duty of Man* along with 186 copies of the Bible to the new colony. See Ross W. Beales and James N. Green, "Libraries and Their Users," in *A History of the Book*, ed. Hugh Amory and David D. Hall, 400.

15. On Stackhouse's alleged habit of writing at his pub, see William Page and P. H. Ditchfield, eds., *The Victoria History of the County of Berkshire*, 5 vols. (London, 1906-1927), 3:277-278.

16. For a biography of Smollett, see Lewis M. Knapp, *Tobias Smollett: Doctor of Men and Manners* (Princeton, N.J., 1949). Regarding Smollett and his contributions to the *Universal History*, see Louis L. Martz, "Tobias Smollett and the Universal History," *Modern Language Notes* 56 (Jan. 1941): 1-14. The preference for histories, biographies, and geographies was dominant elsewhere in colonial America and eighteenth-century Britain. During the period 1773-84, more than 45 percent of all borrowings from the subscription library in Bristol, England, were works of history, travel, or geography. See Brewer, *Pleasures of the Imagination*, 181. According to the 1741 catalogue of the Library Company of Philadelphia, 132 of its 375 titles fell into similar categories. See George Boudreau, "'Highly Valuable & Extensively Useful': Community and Readership Among the Eighteenth Century Middling Sort," *Pennsylvania History* 63 (July 1996): 317. The 1770 catalogue of the Charleston Library Society, a Charleston, S.C., subscription library, indicates that the same subjects composed 23 percent of all its titles. See James Raven, *London Booksellers and American Customers: Transatlantic Literary Community and the Charleston Library Society, 1748-1811* (Columbia, S.C., 2002), 185, fig. 2.

17. *Daybooks*, f. 22. On Robertson and his work, see Stewart J. Brown, ed., *William Robertson and the Expansion of Empire* (Cambridge, Eng., 1997).

18. Trevor Colbourn, *The Lamp of Experience: Whig History and the Intellectual Origins of the American Revolution*, rev. ed. (Indianapolis, Ind., 1998), 5, 7. For a useful bibliographical essay regarding the influence of classical and Whiggish historians in colonial America, see Forrest McDonald, "A Founding Father's Library," *Literature of Liberty* 1 (Jan.-Mar. 1978): 4-15. On the influence of Whiggish theories and thinking in the formation of the American republic, see Gordon S. Wood, *The Creation of the American Republic, 1776-1787* (Chapel Hill, N.C., and London, 1998), chap. 1 and passim.

19. Bailyn, *Pamphlets of the American Revolution*, 33; Thomas Jefferson to George Washington Lewis, Oct. 25, 1825, in Lipscomb and Bergh, eds., *Writings of Jefferson*, 16:125. On Jefferson's early exposure to Rapin, see Marie Kimball, *Jefferson: The Road to Glory, 1743-1776* (New York, 1943), 13.

20. David Hume to James Oswald, June 28, 1753, in John H. Burton, ed., *Life and Correspondence of David Hume*, 2 vols. (Edinburgh, 1846), 1:381; David Hume to Matthew Sharp, Feb. 25, 1754, ibid., 1:386; Ernest C. Mossner, *The Life of David Hume* (Edinburgh, 1954), 316.

21. Mossner, *Life of David Hume*, 318; Thomas Jefferson to John Norvell, June 11, 1807; in Ford, ed., *Works of Thomas Jefferson*, 10:452 (*N.B.*: Ford's transcription of this letter is erroneously dated June 14, 1807); Thomas Jefferson to William Duane, Aug. 12, 1810, in Lipscomb and Bergh, eds., *Writings of Jefferson*, 12:406. Regarding Jefferson's hostility towards Hume's *History of England*, see Douglas L. Wilson, "Jefferson vs. Hume," *WMQ*, 3rd ser., 46 (Jan. 1989): 49-70; H. Trevor Colbourn, "Thomas Jefferson's Use of the Past," *WMQ*, 3rd ser., 15 (Jan. 1958): 56-70. In one study of booksellers' lists and the catalogues of private and institutional libraries, Hume's *History* was easily more than twice as popular as Rapin's *History* during the late colonial and post-Revolutionary periods. See David Lundberg and Henry F. May, "The Enlightened Reader in America," *American Quarterly* 28 (Summer 1976): 262-93. For an impressive compendium of commentary about Hume's *History* and his political thinking in America up to the antebellum period, see Mark G. Spencer, ed., *Hume's Reception in Early America*, 2 vols. (Bristol, Eng., 2002). Jefferson similarly denounced William Blackstone's *Commentaries on the Laws of England* (1765-69), calling the work a "malign influence" that was responsible for the American legal profession's "slide into

toryism." (Thomas Jefferson to Judge John Tyler, June 17, 1812, in Lipscomb and Bergh, eds., *Writings of Jefferson,* 13:166; Thomas Jefferson to James Madison, Feb. 17, 1826, in Ford, ed., *Works of Thomas Jefferson*, 12:456). "Blackstone and Hume," Jefferson sniffed, "have made tories of all England, and are making tories of those young Americans whose native feelings of independence do not place them above the wily sophistries of a Hume or a Blackstone." (Thomas Jefferson to Horation G. Spafford, March 17, 1814, in Lipscomb and Bergh, eds., *Writings of Jefferson,* 13:120.)

22. On the *Letters of Junius* and authorship question, see Francesco Cordasco, *Junius and His Works: A History of the Letters of Junius and the Authorship Controversy* (Fairview, N.J., 1986); Alvar Ellegard, *Who Was Junius?* (Stockholm, 1962).

23. Memorial of John Baylor V, Sept. 4, 1853, BP; Robert A. Brock, ed., *The Official Records of Robert Dinwiddie*, 2 vols. (Richmond, Va., 1883-84), 2:104 n. Another Baylor descendant, George Baylor (1842-1902), confirms that John Baylor IV "for some reason … felt so deep an interest in the subject, style or authorship, as to transcribe them [Junius's letters] as they were published." (George Baylor, *Bull Run to Bull Run; or, Four Years in the Army of Northern Virginia* [Richmond, Va., 1900], 396.)

24. Forrest McDonald, foreword to Joseph Addison, *Cato: A Tragedy and Selected Essays*, ed. Christine D. Henderson and Mark E. Yellin (Indianapolis, Ind., 2004), viii. On Cato and Washington, see Margaret M. Forbes, "Addison's Cato and George Washington," *Classical Journal* 55 (Feb. 1960): 210-12. Regarding *Cato's* popularity in colonial America, see Fredric M. Litto, "Addison's *Cato* in the Colonies" *WMQ*, 3rd ser., 23 (July 1966): 431-49.

25. Alan B. Howes, ed., *Laurence Sterne: The Critical Heritage* (London, 1995) 63; Brooke Allen, "Laurence Sterne," *The New Criterion* 20 (Jan. 2002): 22-30. For a biography of Sterne, see Ian Campbell Ross, *Laurence Sterne: A Life* (Oxford and New York, 2002). Jefferson's passion for Sterne's novel was unusual because "Jefferson, unlike many of his fellow Virginians, was not fond of prose fiction." (William Peden, "Some Notes Concerning Thomas Jefferson's Libraries," *WMQ*, 3d ser., [July 1944]: 271 n.) An excerpt from Sterne's novel is

the only entry from prose fiction in Jefferson's literary commonplace book. See Douglas L. Wilson, ed., *Jefferson's Literary Commonplace Book* (Princeton, N.J., 1989), 11.

26. *TJP*, 6:196; Thomas Jefferson to Peter Carr, Aug. 10, 1787, ibid., 12:15. Regarding Jefferson and *Tristram Shandy*, see Andrew Burstein, *The Inner Jefferson: Portrait of a Grieving Optimist* (Charlottesville, Va., and London, 1995), chap. 2.

27. Hayes, *Mind of a Patriot*, 10. On Washington's familiarity with *Tristram Shandy*, see Douglas Southall Freeman, *George Washington: A Biography*, 6 vols. (New York, 1948-1954), 1:401 n.

28. Christopher Fox, ed., *The Cambridge Companion to Jonathan Swift* (Cambridge, Eng., 2003), 15; Richard Henry Lee to [Landon Carter], Feb. 2, 1766, in James C. Ballagh, ed., *The Letters of Richard Henry Lee*, 2 vols. (New York, 1911-14), 1:12-14. An earlier critic of Orrey's work noted that "the grudging praise and feeble estimate of Swift's genius shown in the 'Remarks' are mainly due to the poverty of Orrery's own mind." Leslie Stephen, ed., *Dictionary of National Biography*, 63 vols. (New York and London, 1882-1900), 6:111. Unable to obtain a license to publish an American edition of Churchill's *Poems*, Rivington craftily bought up 2,200 sheets of the third edition (London, 1766), added a new title page, which was dated 1768 but bore no printer's name or place of publication, and bound them in blue boards in two volumes along with his list of subscribers. See Leroy Hewlett, "James Rivington, Tory Printer," in *Books in America's Past: Essays Honoring Rudolph H. Gjelsness*, ed. David Kaser (Charlottesville, Va., 1966), 165-193. Landon Carter subscribed to Rivington's edition of Churchill's *Poems* and also owned the second edition published in London in 1765, which was apparently the one Lee wished to borrow. Colonel Baylor was not listed among Rivington's subscribers. For a biography of Churchill, see William C. Brown, *Charles Churchill: Poet, Rake and Rebel* (Lawrence, Kan., 1953). On Rivington, see Leroy Hewlett, "James Rivington, Loyalist Printer, Publisher, and Bookseller of the American Revolution, 1724-1802: A Biographical-Bibliographical Study" (PhD diss., University of Michigan, 1958).

29. Wilson, ed., *Jefferson's Commonplace Book*, 10, 100-105. For a biography of Young, see Harold B. Forster, *Edward Young: The Poet*

of 'Night Thoughts', 1683-1765 (Norfolk, Eng., 1988).

30. *Daybooks*, ff. 9, 22.

31. Thomas Jefferson to Robert Skipwith, August 3, 1771, in *TJP*, 1:76-81; [Lucinda Lee Orr], *Journal of a Young Lady of Virginia, 1782* [1787] (Baltimore, 1871), 12. At the time *Journal of a Young Lady* was first published in 1871, its authorship was unknown and it was incorrectly dated. It has since been confirmed as the diary of Lucinda Lee Orr written in 1787. See Hendrick, *Lees of Virginia*, 365 n. Other Virginia planters also ordered books intended for females readers in their household. Colonel Wilson Cary, for example, ordered his executors to "send to England" for Samuel Richardson's novels, *Sir Charles Grandison* (1753), *Pamela* (1740), and *Clarissa* (1748), "all lettered and bound in calf," for his granddaughter Sarah (Sally) Cary. (Fairfax Harrison, *The Virginia Carys: An Essay in Genealogy* [privately printed, 1919].) The literature on female reading habits in the eighteenth-century Chesapeake is scant but starting to grow. See Catherine Kerrison, *Claiming the Pen: Women and Intellectual Life in the Early American South* (Ithaca, N.Y., and London, 2006); Kevin J. Hayes, *A Colonial Woman's Bookshelf* (Knoxville, Tenn., 1996).

32. For an interesting discussion of the epistolary form among female writers, including Lady Montagu, see Amanda Gilro and W.M. Verhoeven, eds., *Epistolary Histories: Letters, Fiction, Culture* (Charlottesville, Va., and London, 2000).

33. Elizabeth C. Cook, *Literary Influences in Colonial Newspapers, 1704-1750* (New York, 1912) 193.

Chapter 7

1. Franklin B. Dexter, ed., *The Literary Diary of Ezra Stiles*, 2 vols. (New York, 1901), 2:296-297; Thomas Jefferson to Robert Skipwith, August 3, 1771, in *TJP*, 1:76-81. Regarding the reception of French books and language in colonial America, see Howard Mumford Jones, *America and French Culture, 1750-1848* (Chapel Hill, N.C., 1927), chap. 6; Paul M. Spurlin, "The Founding Fathers and the French Language," *Modern Language Journal* 60 (March 1976): 86-88; idem, *The French Enlightenment in America: Essays on the Times of*

the Founding Fathers (Athens, Ga., 1984), chap. 2.

2. Davis, *Colonial Southern Bookshelf*, 11; Inventory of Philip Thomas Lee, July 30, 1780, Charles Co., Md., Inventories (1785-91), 246-60; Inventory of Dr. Nicholas Flood, Feb. 8, 1777, Richmond Co., Va., Will Book 7 (1767-87), 239-70.

3. Regarding French books advertised in the *Virginia Gazette*, see Molnar, "Publication and Retail Book Advertisements," 268-70. See also Stiverson and Stiverson, "Books Both Useful and Entertaining," appendix. Thomas Jefferson, who assumed responsibility for the care and education of his nephew Peter Carr when the boy's father died prematurely, insisted he become proficient in French. "You are now, I expect, learning French," Jefferson wrote from Paris. "You must push this," Jefferson admonished, "because the books which will be put into your hands when you advance into Mathematics, Natural philosophy, Natural History, &c. will be mostly French, these sciences being better treated by the French than the English writers." (Thomas Jefferson to Peter Carr, Aug. 19, 1785, in *TJP*, 8:407.) Jefferson's views about the importance of learning French, however, were far from typical in eighteenth-century America.

4. H. E. Scudder, ed., *Recollections of Samuel Breck: With Passages From His Note-Books (1771-1862)*, (Philadelphia, 1877), 46-47; Marquis de Chastellux, *Travels in North America in the Years 1780, 1781 and 1782*, trans. and ed. Howard C. Rice, Jr., 2 vols. (Chapel Hill, N.C., 1963), 2:497-98; J. P. Brissot de Warville, *New Travels in the United States of America, 1788* trans. Mara S. Vamos, ed. Durand Echeverria (Cambridge, Mass., 1964), 394. Though a few French-language religious pamphlets were published in Boston, almost no French-language imprints were published in British colonial America. See Samuel J. Marino, "French-Language Printing in the United States, 1711-1825," in David Kaser, ed., *Books in America's Past*, 44-61.

5. Brant, *James Madison*, 2:289. For Madison's book list, see William T. Hutchinson et al., eds., *Papers of James Madison, Congressional Series*, 17 vols. (Chicago and Charlottesville, Va., 1962-77), 6:62-115. On the publication of the *Encyclopédie méthodique*, see George B. Watts, "The Encyclopédie Méthodique," *PMLA* 73 (Sept. 1958): 348-66. On Jefferson and the *Encyclopédie méthodique*, see Sidney

L. Jackson, "The *Encyclopédie Méthodique*: A Jefferson Addendum," *VMHB* (July 1965): 303-11.

6. For a list of the books purchased by Congress in 1800, see LOC, *The First Booklist of the Library of Congress* (Washington, D.C., 1981). For a comparison between Madison's book list and the books Congress acquired in 1800, see Tom Glynn and Craig C. Hagensick, "Books for the Use of the United States in Congress Assembled, 1783 and 1800," *Libraries & Culture* 37 (Spring 2002): 109-22. The book list that Jefferson began while rooming with Madison, the "1783 Catalog of Books," is held by the Massachusetts Historical Society, which has digitized the manuscript and made it available on its web site at the following address: www.masshist.org/thomasjeffersonpapers/ catalog1783.

    Madison's passion for French books continued unabated despite his rebuff from Congress. While Thomas Jefferson was in Paris, for example, Madison asked that Jefferson send him any books that were "either old & curious or new & useful." (James Madison to Thomas Jefferson, April 27, 1785, in Hutchinson et al., eds., *Papers of James Madison, Congressional Series*, 8:265-66.) Jefferson obliged with trunks full of more than 200 books, a telescope, and other equipment. (Ibid., 8:500-504; Thomas Jefferson to James Madison, Sept. 1, 1785, in *TJP*, 8:462-67.)

7. Thomas Jefferson to Samuel H. Smith, Sept. 21, 1814, in Ford, ed., *Works of Thomas Jefferson*, 11:427-28. Surprisingly, Jefferson's book collecting in Paris has escaped comprehensive treatment. Jefferson's diplomatic service in Paris is recounted in William H. Adams, *The Paris Years of Thomas Jefferson* (New Haven, Conn., and London, 1997), but Adams has almost nothing to say about Jefferson's book collecting or literary interests. Although William Peden acknowledged that Jefferson's Paris years "were probably the most important ones during his entire career as a book-collector," his examination of the topic was meager. See William H. Peden, "Thomas Jefferson: Book-Collector" (PhD diss., University of Virginia, 1942), 113, 114-19. Kevin J. Hayes covers the topic well, but also briefly in his *Road to Monticello* (chap. 20). On the number of books purchased by Jefferson in France, see Douglas L. Wilson, "Thomas Jefferson's Library and the French Connection," *Eighteenth-Century Studies* 26 (Summer 1993): 682. A brief discussion of the principal Parisian booksellers from whom Jefferson bought books is in Howard C. Rice, *Thomas Jefferson's Paris*

(Princeton, 1976), 77-79. Regarding Jefferson's French book orders after his return to Monticello, see, for example, Thomas Jefferson to M. Froullé, May 26, 1795, in *TJP*, 28:357-59. Jefferson advised James Monroe that Froullé was "one of the most conscientiously honest men I ever had dealings with." (Thomas Jefferson to James Monroe, May 26, 1795, *TJP*, 28:361.) In 1793 Froullé published the names of the French deputies of the Committee of Public Safety who condemned Louis XVI to death, an act of literary liberté for which Froullé was himself executed by order of the same body.

8. Samuel Ward, "William Short: The Picturesque Career of the First Man Appointed to Office By President Washington," *Tyler's Quarterly Historical and Genealogical Magazine* 18 (Jan. 1937): 132-38. For a biography of Short, see George G. Shackelford, *Jefferson's Adoptive Son: The Life of William Short, 1759-1848* (Lexington, Ky., 1993). Regarding Short's diplomatic career, see idem, "William Short: Diplomat in Revolutionary France, 1785-1793," *APS Proceedings* (Dec. 1958): 596-612. Neither work mentions Short's book buying. Short's correspondence with the duchesse de La Rochefoucauld has been published in Doina P. Harsanyi, ed., *Lettres de la duchesse de La Rochefoucauld á William Short* (Paris, 2001). For a partial catalogue of Short's library that he composed in France and amended after his return to America, see "William Short's Library List," Papers of William Short, 1759-1853, LOC. Though William Short was a Virginian, his many books were shipped from Paris to Philadelphia, and therefore do not technically qualify as a Virginia or Maryland library during his lifetime.

9. Harry Ammon, *James Monroe: The Quest for National Identity* (Charlottesville, Va., and London, 1990), 18. The exact number of Adams's French titles is 478, according to Elizabeth Prindle, manager of the John Adams Library Project, Boston Public Library, who kindly counted them at the author's request (e-mail to author, April 11, 2007). Curiously, as Professor Spurlin noted, no monograph has been written about Adams and his extensive collection of French authors. For a printed catalogue of Adams's library, see Lindsay Swift, ed. *Catalogue of the John Adams Library in the Public Library of the City of Boston* (Boston, 1917). (A new print catalogue is in progress.) The John Adams Library, which now holds 3,510 volumes, includes books from John Quincy Adams and others members of the Adams family. For a partial reconstruction of Monroe's library, including some 706

French-language books, see Gordon W. Jones, *The Library of James Monroe (1758-1731), 5th President (1816-1824) of the United States* (Fredericksburg, Va., 1967). (A manuscript version of this book was revised in 2007 by John N. Pearce, director of the James Monroe Museum and Memorial Library.) For the books sold by Jefferson to Monroe, see "List of Books Sold to James Monroe," [May 10, 1784], in *TJP*, 7:241.

10. Wolf and Hayes, *Library of Benjamin Franklin*, 31.

11. Hayes, *Library of William Byrd*, 88, 365-96; Spurlin, *French Enlightenment in America*, 102-103; Michael T. Parker, "'The Fittest Season for Reading': The Library of Charles Carroll of Carrollton" (MA thesis, University of Maryland, 1990), 15. For the story of the Carrolls in Ireland and Maryland through the Revolution, see Ronald Hoffman, *Princes of Ireland, Planters of Maryland: A Carroll Saga, 1500-1782* (Chapel Hill, N.C., and London, 2000).

12. Charles Carroll of Carrollton to Charles Carroll of Annapolis, Aug. 14, 1759, Charles Carroll Papers, 1731-1833 (MS 206), MHS. The 1758 list of French books owned by Charles Carroll of Annapolis has been published in Ronald Hoffman et al., eds., *Dear Papa, Dear Charley: The Peregrinations of a Revolutionary Aristocrat...* (Chapel Hill, N.C., and London, 2001), appendix II. The estimate of additional French-language books acquired by Charles Carroll of Carrollton is based upon books listed in an 1864 catalogue of the Carroll library that were published before 1783. See Parker, "The Fittest Season for Reading," 2-4.

13. A related problem in many instances is the identity of a specific title that the Baylors owned. For example, the reference to Herman Boerhaave on Baylor's book list of Enlightenment-era European authors mentions only "Botany &c." Boerhaave, a prolific scientific writer, wrote tracts on botany, chemistry, medicine, and other subjects, and it appears from this reference that Baylor owned an assemblage or collection of Dr. Boerhaave's works. The definitive modern edition of Voltaire's works is Theodore Besterman et al., eds., *The Complete Works of Voltaire/Oeuvres complètes de Voltaire*, 141 vols. to date (Geneva, Toronto, and Oxford, 1968—) (imprint varies; series now published by Voltaire Foundation, Oxford University).

14. George Washington to Benjamin Franklin, March 27, 1779, in Barbara B. Oberg et al., eds., *Papers of Benjamin Franklin*, 29:224; Inventory of George Mason Jr., Dec. 10, 1797, Fairfax Co., Va., Book H-1, 38-52. For a biography of George Mason IV, see Jeff Broadwater, *George Mason: Forgotten Founder* (Chapel Hill, N.C., 2006).

15. Inventory of Daniel Dulany, Esq., May 21, 1754, Testamentary Papers, Box 55, fol. 42, Maryland State Archives, Annapolis. Regarding George Mason V's European sojourn, see Pamela C. Copeland and Richard K. MacMaster, *The Five George Masons: Patriots and Planters of Virginia and Maryland* (Charlottesville, Va., 1976), 198-99, 212-15.

16. Despite its flaws, Tobias Smollett's translation of *Télémaque*, published posthumously in 1776, was the most popular version in Britain and America through century's end. For a critical edition of Smollett's translation, see Tobias Smollett, *The Adventures of Telemachus, Son of Ulysses*, ed. O. M. Brack Jr. (Athens, Ga., and London, 1997).

17. James H. Davis Jr., *Fénelon* (Boston, 1979), 109; Howard Mumford Jones, "The Importation of French Books in Philadelphia, 1750-1800," *Modern Philology* 32 (Nov. 1934): 160; Lucinda Lee Orr, *Journal of a Young Lady*, 44-45; *VG* (Hunter), May 24, 1751. On Jefferson and Fénelon, see Wilson, "Thomas Jefferson's Library and the French Connection," 674-75.

18. From his study of French books offered for sale in Philadelphia, Howard Mumford Jones concluded that "the weight of the interest is certainly in Voltaire's historical work." Jones, "Importation of French Books in Philadelphia," 165. Yet, in an important study of the relative frequency with which major British and European authors were cited by prominent colonial Americans in their speeches and writings, Voltaire ranked only thirty-second out of thirty-seven authors. See Donald S. Lutz, "The Relative Influence of European Writers on Late Eighteenth-Century American Political Thought," *American Political Science Review* 78 (March 1984): 189-97. On Voltaire's literary reception in early America, see Mary-Margaret H. Barr, *Voltaire in America, 1744-1800* (Baltimore, 1941) (*N.B.*: Barr does not discuss Voltaire's reputation in the colonial South; for a brief overview, see Spurlin, *French Enlightenment in America*, chap. 8). Regarding Voltaire's popularity in Britain, a study of 218 private libraries from the

period 1750-1800 found that 172 of them had a least one Voltaire title, and his histories—in both French and English—were by far the most common books in those libraries. See Ronald S. Crane, "The Diffusion of Voltaire's Writings in England, 1750-1800," *Modern Philology* 20 (Feb. 1923): 267. Regarding Molière, Racine, and Pierre Corneille in colonial America, see Spurlin, *French Enlightenment in America*, 60-61; Jones, "Importation of French Books in Philadelphia," 160-61.

19. For a modern translation of Bossuet's *Discours*, see Jacques-Bénigne Bossuet, *Discourse on Universal History*, ed. Orest Ranum (Chicago, 1976).

20. Henri Van Laun, *History of French Literature*, 3 vols. (London, 1876-83), 2:354. Regarding Voltaire and Massillon, see J. Patrick Lee, "Voltaire and Massillon: Affinities of the Heart," *French Review* 50 (Feb. 1977): 437-45. On Saurin and his works, see Alexandre R. Vinet, *Histoire de la prédication parmi les réformés de France au dix-septième siècle* (Paris, 1860), 597-714.

21. Holbrook Jackson, *The Anatomy of Bibliomania* (Urbana, Ill., and Chicago, 2001), 562; Ann Blair, "Reading Strategies for Coping with Information Overload, ca. 1550-1700," *Journal of the History of Ideas* (2003): 11. Robert Burton (1577-1640), librarian of Christ Church College, Oxford, and perhaps the best-read Briton of his generation, also decried a "vast Chaos and confusion of books." "[W]e are," he wrote, "oppressed with them, our eyes ache with reading, our fingers with turning." Robert Burton, *Anatomy of Melancholy*, 16th ed. (1621; London, 1838), 7. Baillet's *Jugemens* is not listed in Fithian's inventory of Carter's library, but has been identified by scholar and librarian John R. Barden, Richmond, Va., as having been almost certainly owned by Carter. Dr. Barden, through years of dogged and careful investigation, has identified more than a thousand books owned by Carter that do not appear on Fithian's list, including works by French authors such as Bayle, Boileau, Bossuet, La Rochefoucauld, Pascal, Rollin, and others. According to Fithian, Carter owned 458 books at his Williamsburg home, but no catalogue survives. Dr. Barden believes that the majority of Carter's foreign-language titles were located in Williamsburg (e-mail from John R. Barden to author, May 8, 2007).

22. A recent critical edition of Bruyère's book is Patrice Soler's *Jean de La*

Bruyère, Les Caractères (Paris, 1994). For a biography of Bruyère in English, see Edward C. Knox, *Jean de La Bruyère* (New York, 1973). For a modern English translation of La Rochefoucauld's *Maximes*, including a useful introduction, see Leonard Tancock, trans., *La Rochefoucauld: Maxims* (Baltimore, 1959) According to Dr. John Barden's list, Robert Carter of Nomini Hall owned a 1742 edition of La Rochefoucauld's *Maximes*.

23. Blaise Pascal, *Pensées and Other Writings*, ed. Anthony Levi, trans. Honor Levi (Oxford, 1995), vii. For a select bibliography of contemporary and modern editions of Pascal's *Pensées*, see Blaise Pascal, *Pensées*, ed. and trans., Roger Ariew (Indianapolis, Ind., 2005), xv.

24. Perrault, who ignited the battle in 1687 when he read his poem, *Le Siècle de Louis le Grand* (*The Century of Louis XIV*), before the Académie Française, premised his argument on the rejection of ancient conceptions of the universe among a growing number of early Enlightenment scientists. Homer, Virgil, and other classical literary figures, he suggested, should be relegated to the teleological dustbin like Aristotle. In 1711 Dacier published a revised edition of the *Iliad* with a polemical preface and extended notes that comprised her chief counterarguments in *la querelle*, followed by a similarly revised version of the *Odyssey* in 1716. For a biography of Madame Dacier in English, see Fern Farnham, *Madame Dacier: Scholar and Humanist* (Monterey, Calif., 1976). On the intellectual debate of the ancients versus the moderns (in English), see Douglas L. Patey, "Ancients and Moderns," in *The Cambridge History of Literary Criticism: The Eighteenth Century*, vol. 4, ed. Hugh B. Nisbet and Claude Rawson (Cambridge, Eng., 1997), 32-71; Joseph M. Levine, *The Battle of the Books: History and Literature in the Augustan Age* (Ithaca, N.Y., 1991). For French sources on the debate, see Marc Fumaroli, introductory essay in *La quarelle des Anciens et des Modernes, XVIIᵉ-XVIIIᵉ siècles*, ed. Marc Fumaroli and Anne-Marie Lecoq (Paris, 2001), 1-200; Hubert Gillot, *La querelle des Anciens et des Modernes* (Paris, 1914).

25. For a biography of Madame de Sévigné in English, see Frances Mossiker, *Madame De Sevigne: A Life and Letters* (New York, 1983). See also Michèle Longino Farrell, *Performing Motherhood: The Sévigné Correspondence* (Hanover, N.H., and London, 2001). Regarding court

life under Louis XIV's reign, the classic source remains Norbert Elias, *The Court Society*, trans. Edmund Jephcott (New York, 1983). For a study of the status of elite women in seventeenth-century France, see Carolyn C. Lougee, *La Paradis des femmes: Women, Salons, and Social Stratification Seventeenth-Century France* (Princeton, N.J., 1976).

26. John H. Baas, *Outlines of the History of Medicine and the Medical Profession*, trans. Henry E. Handerson (New York, 1889), 813; *VG* (Hunter), Aug. 1, 1755. Regarding Boerhaave's works in the libraries of Virginia doctors, see Wyndham B. Blanton, *Medicine in Eighteenth-Century Virginia* (Richmond, Va., 1931), chap. VI. For a biography of Boerhaave in English, see Gerrit A. Lindeboom, *Herman Boerhaave: The Man and His Work* (London, 1968).

27. For a list of Jefferson's astronomy books, see James Gilreath and Douglas L. Wilson, eds., *Thomas Jefferson's Library: A Catalog with the Entries in His Own Order* (Washington, D.C., 1989), 96-97. On Gassendi in Byrd's and Jefferson's libraries, see Hayes, *Library of William Byrd*, 548; Sowerby, *Library of Thomas Jefferson*, 5:165. Gassendi's *Astronomica* appears to have been more common in New England libraries in the seventeenth and eighteenth centuries than elsewhere in America. In 1682 Cotton Mather purchased an early edition of Gassendi's book from the Harvard College library, along with ninety-five other titles, mostly theological. See Colonial Society of Massachusetts, *Transactions*, 404, 414. On Gassendi's *Astronomica* in colonial America, see Mel Gorman, "Gassendi in America," *Isis* 55 (Dec. 1964): 409-17. For a modern English translation of Gassendi's book, see Joseph T. Clark, "The Institutio Astronomica (1647)" (PhD diss., Harvard University, 1964). For a biography of Gassendi in English, see Howard Jones, *Pierre Gassendi (1592-1655): An Intellectual Biography* (Nieuwkoop, The Netherlands, 1981).
    At Jefferson's insistence, the University of Virginia offered instruction in astronomy, but a domed observatory he planned there was not completed until after his death. On Jefferson's interest in astronomy, see Silvio A. Bedini, *Jefferson and Science* (Chapel Hill, N.C., 2002), chap. 3.
    James Logan, who owned a large collection of rare astronomy books, had more astronomy volumes than Jefferson due to Logan's obsession with collecting multiple copies of the same titles in order to possess the rarest or best editions of a particular work. John Page,

given his passion for astronomy, undoubtedly owned an impressive astronomy library, but sadly no list survives. Robert Beverley (1701-33) of Newlands in Spotsylvania Co., Va., owned nearly 300 books, including at least three titles by British astronomers John Pell (1611-85), John Keil (1671-1721), and William Leybourne (1626-1716). For Beverley's book list, see W. G. Stannard, "Major Robert Beverley and His Descendants," *VMHB* 3 (April 1896): 388-91.

28. Cornelis D. Andriesse, *Huygens: The Man Behind the Principle*, trans. Sally Miedema (Cambridge, Eng., 2005), 392.

29. Edwin Wolf II, *The Book Culture of a Colonial American City: Philadelphia Books, Bookmen, and Booksellers* (Oxford, 1988), 108. For a study of Boulainvilliers's views of the French monarchy, see Harold A. Ellis, *Boulainvilliers and the French Monarchy: Aristocratic Politics in Early Eighteenth-Century France* (Ithaca, N.Y., 1988). See also Renee Simon, *Henry de Boulainviller: Historien, politique, philosophe, astrologue (1658-1722)* (Paris, 1941). It should be noted that Vertot employed the term *revolution* to mean a substantial political change, not necessarily a violent overthrow of government. Thus, one should not interpret the broad enthusiasm in colonial America for Vertot's histories as indicative of a wide sentiment for armed insurrection against Britain before that feeling actually developed in the 1770s.

30. William Gribbin, "Rollin's Histories and American Republicanism," *WMQ*, 3rd ser., 29 (Oct. 1972): 616. For a brief but useful overview of Jansenism, see Monique Cottret, "Jansenism," in *Encyclopedia of the Enlightenment*, ed. Alan C. Kors et al., 4 vols. (Oxford, 2003), 2:278-84 (this work is an excellent source for many of the French and European Enlightenment figures mentioned in this chapter). See also Nigel Abercrombie, *The Origins of Jansenism* (Oxford, 1936).

31. Wood, *Creation of the American Republic*, 51; Gribbin, "Rollin's Histories," 619.

32. [Thompson Mason], Letter to the Editor, *Virginia Gazette* (Rind), May 4, 1769; Charles Lee to Robert Morris, Jan. 3, 1776, in *The Lee Papers: Collections of the New York Historical Society*, 4 vols. (New York, 1872-75), 1:233.

33. Stephen N. Nadler, *A Companion to Early Modern Philosophy* (Oxford, 2002), 258. For a modern English translation of Malebranche's *De la recherche de la vérité*, see Nicholas Malebranche, *The Search After Truth*, ed. and trans. Thomas M. Lennon and P. J. Olscamp (Cambridge, Eng., 1997). Regarding Bayle's influence on Locke, see John Marshall, *John Locke, Toleration and Early Enlightenment Culture* (Cambridge, Eng., 2006), 470-71. Despite a surge of Bayle scholarship in the last twenty-five years, the best overall biography of Bayle remains Élizabeth Labrousse's *Pierre Bayle*, 2 vols. (The Hague, 1963-64). For a useful overview of the man and his writings in English, see Martinus Nijhoff, *Bayle*, trans. Denys Potts (Oxford, 1983). For a selection of Bayle's most important philosophic writings in his *Dictionnaire historique*, see Pierre Bayle, *Historical and Critical Dictionary: Selections*, ed. and trans. Richard H. Popkin (Indianapolis, Ind., 1991).

34. Rice, *Thomas Jefferson's Paris*, 84. For a biography of Buffon, see Jacques Roger, *Buffon: A Life in Natural History*, trans. Sarah L. Bonnefoi (Ithaca, N.Y., and London, 1997).

35. The history of the theory of degeneracy is examined in splendid detail in Antonello Gerbi, *The Dispute of the New World: The History of a Polemic, 1750-1900*, trans. Jeremy Moyle (Pittsburgh, Pa., 1973).

36. Thomas Jefferson, *Notes on the State of Virginia*, ed. William Peden (Chapel Hill, N.C., and London, 1982), 64.

37. Jefferson, *Notes*, 47. For a detailed analysis of Jefferson's refutations of Buffon's thesis, see Ruth Henline, "A Study of *Notes on the State of Virginia* as an Evidence of Jefferson's Theories Against the French Naturalists," *VMHB* 55 (July 1947): 233-46. See also Charles A. Miller, *Jefferson and Nature: An Interpretation* (Baltimore and London, 1988), chaps. 2 and 3.

38. Jefferson, *Notes*, 268.

39. Thomas Jefferson to John Sullivan, Jan. 7, 1786, in *TJP*, 9:160; John Sullivan to Thomas Jefferson, April 16, 1787, April 26, 1787, ibid., 11:296-96, 320-21. Regarding the moose hunt, see Anna C. Jones, "Antlers for Jefferson," *New England Quarterly* 12 (June 1939): 333-

48.

40. Thomas Jefferson to John Sullivan, Oct. 5, 1787, in *TJP*, 12: 208; Thomas Jefferson to Comte de Buffon, Oct. 1, 1787, ibid., 12:202; "Notes of Mr. Jefferson's Conversations at Monticello, 1824," in Charles M. Wiltse and Harold D. Moser, eds., *Papers of Daniel Webster: Correspondence*, ser. 1, 7 vols. (Hanover, N.H., 1974-89), 1:370-78. On the persistence of degeneracy theory, see Gerbi, *Dispute of the New World*, passim; Dwight Boehm and Edward Schwartz, "Jefferson and the Theory of Degeneracy," *American Quarterly* 9 (Winter, 1957): 448-53.

Jefferson, who loved tall tales, delighted in recounting the story of a dinner at which Raynal was supposedly humiliated over his beliefs by none other than Benjamin Franklin. In a letter written more than three decades after the event, Jefferson claimed that Franklin told him about a dinner he hosted in Paris for Raynal prior to Jefferson's arrival there in August 1784. "During the dinner," Jefferson reported, Raynal "got on his favorite theory of the degeneracy of animals and even of man, in America, and urged it with his usual eloquence." Realizing that, to a man, the Americans around the table were noticeably taller than their French guests (particularly Raynal, who Jefferson described as a "mere shrimp"), Dr. Franklin taunted, "Come, M. L'Abbe, let us try the question by the fact before us. We are here one half Americans & one half French…. Let both parties rise and we will see on which side nature has degenerated." (Thomas Jefferson to Robert Walsh, Dec. 4, 1818, in Ford, *Works of Thomas Jefferson*, 12:110-11 n.)

Jefferson's source for the story was a letter from William Carmichael (ca. 1739-95), an American diplomat who attended Dr. Franklin's dinner. In 1787 Carmichael wrote Jefferson, thanking him for a copy of *Notes on Virginia* and complimenting him for having "victoriously combated" the theories of Buffon, De Pauw, and Raynal. In his letter, Carmichael went on to describe the dinner, at which "14 or 15 persons" were in attendance, including five Americans (considerably less than half the guests present, as Jefferson said). "At [the] Table," Carmichael wrote, "*some one of the Company* asked the Doctor [Franklin] what were his Sentiments on the remarks made by the Author of the Recherches sue L'Amerique [De Pauw]. The Venerable Doctor regarded the Company and then desired *the Gentleman who put the question* to remark and to Judge whether the human race had degenerated by being transplanted to another section of the Globe" (emphasis added). "In fact," Carmichael proudly recalled, "there was not one American present who could not have tost out of the Windows any one or perhaps two of the rest of the Company." (William Carmichael to Thomas Jefferson, Oct. 15, 1787, in *TJP*, 12: 240-41.) Given Carmichael's remarks about Buffon, Raynal, and De Pauw, he was clearly familiar with Raynal and the academic mischief he had caused, and if Raynal had indeed been present at such an occasion, Carmichael would surely have noticed him and mentioned that important fact to Jefferson. Instead, Carmichael simply referred to Dr. Franklin's inquisitor as "some one of the Company," as if his particular identity was unimportant to the story. Moreover, if Carmichael was really referring to Raynal in his letter but trying to mask his identity, he likely would have referred to him as "Mr R—" or similar opaque reference common in eighteenth-century letters. The only logical conclusion is that Jefferson embellished the story, placing Raynal at the center of the dinner and making him the butt of Dr. Franklin's humor.

41. Hiller B. Zobel, *The Boston Massacre* (New York, 1970), 289; Gary Wills, *Inventing America: Jefferson's Declaration of Independence* (New York, 1978), 152. For a modern edition of Beccaria's work, including useful commentary and annotations, see Cesare Beccaria, *On Crimes and Punishments, and Other Writings*, ed. Richard Bellamy, trans. Richard Davies (Cambridge, Eng., 1995). On Beccaria and penal reform, see Marcello Maestro, *Cesare Beccaria and the Origins of Penal Reform* (Philadelphia, 1973). Regarding Beccaria's influence on Jefferson, see Harold Hellenbrand, *The Unfinished Revolution: Education and Politics in the Thought of Thomas Jefferson* (Newark, N.J., 1990), 107-11; John Chester Miller, *The Wolf by the Ears: Thomas Jefferson and Slavery* (New York and London, 1977), 20-21; Marcello Maestro, "A Pioneer for the Abolition of Capital Punishment: Cesare Beccaria," *Journal of the History of Ideas* 34 (July-Sept., 1973): 463-68. See also Kathryn Preyer, "Crime, the Criminal Law and Reform in Post-Revolutionary Virginia," *Law and History Review* 1 (Spring 1983): 53-85.

Chapter 8

1. Jackson, *The Anatomy of Bibliomania*, 21; Nicholas A. Basbanes, *A Gentle Madness: Bibliophiles, Bibliomanes, and their Eternal Passion for Books* (New York, 1995), 9; Thomas Jefferson to Lucy Paradise, June

1, 1789, in *TJP*, 15:163. E. Millicent Sowerby, modern bibliographer of Jefferson's library, accepted his self-diagnosis of bibliomaniac as "probably correct." (E.M. Sowerby, "Thomas Jefferson and His Library," *Papers of the Bibliographical Society of America* 50 [1956]: 217.) However, as Jefferson biographer Dumas Malone has pointed out, for Jefferson "books were tools" and "storehouses of knowledge and wisdom" rather than mere collectible objects. (Malone, *The Sage of Monticello*, 170.) There is no generally accepted scholarly consensus on the definitions of *bibliophily* and *bibliomania* and the symptoms often overlap. For example, James Logan of Philadelphia, who moaned that "books are my disease," had no less than seven editions of Homer, three each of Aeschylus and Sophocles, six of Horace, and so on among his thousands of volumes. When Sir Isaac Newton's third edition of *Principia* was announced in 1726, Logan quickly ordered a copy even though he already owned the first and second editions. (Logan is said to have been the first American colonial to have owned the first edition of Newton's *Principia*.) See Frederick B. Tolles, *James Logan and the Culture of Provincial America* (Boston and Toronto, 1957, 191-92; Frederick E. Brasch, "James Logan, A Colonial Mathematical Scholar, and the First Copy of Newton's *Principia* to Arrive in the Colony," *APS Proceedings* 86 (Sept. 1942): 6. Yet Logan was more than a mere book addict; though mostly an autodidact he was perhaps the most erudite man of his generation in colonial America. He could read French, Spanish, Hebrew, Greek, and Latin with ease and wrote numerous learned papers and letters. On bibliophily and bibliomania in early modern France, see Jean Viardot, "Livres rares et pratiques bibliophiliques," in *Le Livre triumphant, 1660-1830*, ed. Henri-Jean Martin and Roger Chartier, vol. 2, *Histoire de l'édition française* (Paris, 1984), 447-67; idem, "Naissance de la bibliophile: Les Cabinets de livres rares," in *Les Bibliothequès sous l'Ancien Regimé, 1530-1789*, vol. 2, *Histoire des bibliothequès françaises* (Paris, 1988), 268-89. See also Neil Kenny, "Books in Space and Time: Bibliomania and Early Modern Histories of Learning and 'Literature' in France," *Modern Language Quarterly* 61 (June 2000): 253-86.

2. Guillaume-François Debure le Jeunne, *Bibliographie instructive: ou traité de la connaisance des livres rares*, 7 vols. (Paris, 1763-68) (Debure added a two-volume supplement in 1769 and a now nearly impossible-to-find volume on anonymous authors in 1782); Jean-Henri-Samuel Formey, *Conseils pour former une bibliothequè peu nombreuse mais choisie* (Berlin, 1746) (subsequent editions appeared

in Paris and Amsterdam). For a directory of some 932 booksellers in France in 1777-78, see Antoine Perrin, *Almanach de la Librairie* (Paris, 1778).

3.   Walker Maury to Thomas Jefferson, April 20, 1785, in *TJP*, 8:101; Thomas Jefferson to Walker Maury, Aug. 19, 1785, ibid., 8:411-12.

4.   Denis Diderot et al., eds., *Encyclopédie, ou dictionnaire raisonné des sciences, des arts et des métiers*, 35 vols., (Paris, 1751-80): 12:259. Because the French Royal Council, which licensed the publication of all books in France, had ordered that the *Encyclopédie* be suppressed, the last ten volumes of text, including volume 12, were published in 1765 under the false imprint of "A Neufchastel, Chez Samuel Faulche & Compagnie," a Swiss publisher. Regarding the *Encyclopédie*, see Philip Blom, *Enlightening the World: Encyclopédie, The Book That Changed the Course of History* (New York, 2004); Robert Darnton, *The Business of Enlightenment: A Publishing History of the Encyclopédie, 1775-1800* (Cambridge, Mass., 1979). In a fascinating shift of papal viewpoint, on September 14, 1998, Pope John Paul II issued an important encyclical letter, *Fides et Ratio* (*Faith and Reason*), in which he argued that faith *and* reason are indispensable to the human search for truth. "Faith and reason," he began, "are like two wings on which the human spirit rises to the contemplation of truth." Nicholas Wolterstorff, a Christian philosopher, believes that the papal letter is a bold and visionary rejection of prior Catholic dogma regarding faith and science. "How surprising and ironic," he exclaims, "that roughly two centuries after Voltaire and his cohorts mocked the church as the bastion of irrationality, the church, in the person of the pope, should be the one to put in a good word for reason, and for faith as reason's ally." Nicholas Wolterstorff, *Educating for Shalom: Essays on Christian Higher Education* (Grand Rapids, Mich., 2004), 294. On the history of science and Christianity since the sixteenth century, see John H. Brooke, *Science and Religion: Some Historical Perspectives* (Cambridge, Eng., 1991).

5.   Jones, "French Literature in New York City," 250; idem, "French Books in Philadelphia," 170. See also Spurlin, *French Enlightenment in America*, chap. 9. On July 5, 1782, after Jefferson had held fast to the Commonwealth's copy of the *Encyclopédie* for nearly two years, the Virginia Council passed a resolution asking him to return the encyclopedia "belonging to the public." (*TJP*, 6:258). For Charles

Carroll's set of the *Encyclopédie*, see Parker, "'The Fittest Season for Reading," 187. It is possible that Baylor declined to acquire a set of the *Encyclopédie* while he was in France for purely practical concerns—cost and bulk. The first four editions of the *Encyclopédie* were published in very expensive folio editions through 1778, when Baylor left France. Quarto editions were published in Geneva and Neuchâtel from 1777 to 1779, but Baylor may not have had ready access to them. See Darnton, *Business of the Enlightenment*, 33-37. Jefferson eventually bought an octavo edition of the *Encyclopédie* for himself. Ibid., 318-19.

Jefferson's reluctance to relinquish the Commonwealth's copy of the *Encyclopédie* may have occurred with other books he borrowed. While Jefferson was governor of Virginia, Baylor icily informed him: "Hoping that you have supplyed yourself with an American Atlas, in the space of six or eight months, you will please to deliver to General Weedon's care my Atlas." (John Baylor IV to Thomas Jefferson, Feb. 12, 1781, in William P. Palmer et al. eds., *Calendar of Virginia State Papers and Other Manuscripts...*, 11 vols. [Richmond, Va., 1875-93], 1:507.)

The root of Baylor's animosity toward Jefferson, which seems from the tone of this demand to be much deeper than mere annoyance over an unreturned book, is unknown. A likely explanation is Jefferson's radical politics as a Virginia legislator and later as governor of the Commonwealth. During a three-year period beginning in 1776, Jefferson introduced 126 bills in the Virginia House of Delegates, many of which were designed, as Jefferson later recalled with great pride, to erect a "system by which every fibre would be eradicated of ancient or future aristocracy and a foundation laid for a government truly republican." (Thomas Jefferson, "Autobiography," in Ford, ed., *Works of Jefferson*, 1:77.) As a member of Virginia's "ancient aristocracy," such an agenda could not have sat well with Baylor. One scholar has argued that Jefferson had a lifelong devotion to reforming the Virginia gentry. See Ronald L. Hatzenbuehler, *"I Tremble for My Country": Thomas Jefferson and the Virginia Gentry* (Gainesville, Fla., 2006); idem, "Growing Weary in Well-Doing: Thomas Jefferson's Life Among the Virginia Gentry," *VMHB* 101 (Jan. 1993): 5-36.

6.   Spurlin, *French Enlightenment*, ix; Scott McDermott, *Charles Carroll of Carrollton: Faithful Revolutionary* (New York, 2001), 218, 220; Charles Carroll of Carrollton to Charles Carroll of Homewood, July 17, 1801, [Charles Carroll] Correspondence, 1797-1828 (MS 203),

MHS.

7. Entry of Sept. 8, 1783, Journal of Nathanael Greene, in Richard K. Showman et al., eds., *The Papers of General Nathanael Greene*, 13 vols. (Chapel Hill, N.C., 1976-2005), 13:117.

8. Nathanael Greene to Samuel Ward Jr., Oct. 9, 1772, Sept. 26, 1771, in Showman, ed., *Papers of Nathanael Greene*, 1:47, 23.

9. James Cox, College Archivist, Gonville and Caius College, Cambridge University (e-mail to author, July 31, 2007); Venn, *Biographical History of Gonville and Caius College*, 2:89.

10. On Frere's academic accomplishments at Cambridge, see Venn, *Biographical History of Gonville and Caius College*, 2:75. Regarding his scientific findings, see John Frere, "Account of Flint Weapons Discovered at Hoxne in Suffolk," *Archaeologia* 12 (1800): 205-8; J. Reid Moir, "A Pioneer in Paleolithic Discovery," *Notes and Records of the Royal Society of London* 2 (April 1939): 28-31.

11. John Frere to John Baylor IV, June 3, 1800, July 17, 1800, BP.

Chapter 9

1. John J. McCusker and Russell R. Menard, *The Economy of British America, 1607-1789* (Chapel Hill, N.C., and London, 1985), 373. Regarding British depredations, see Elizabeth Cometti, "Depredations in Virginia During the Revolution," in *The Old Dominion: Essays for Thomas Perkins Abernathy*, ed. Darrett B. Rutman (Charlottesville, Va., 1964), 135-51. Though Thomas Jefferson estimated the number of slave defections to the British at 30,000, recent scholarship suggests the number was much smaller, perhaps as few as 6,000. See Cassandra Pybus, "Jefferson's Faulty Math: The Question of Slave Defections in the American Revolution," *WMQ*, 3rd ser., 62 (April 2005): 243-64. On Virginia's private indebtedness to British creditors, see Emory G. Evans, "Planter Indebtedness and the Coming of the Revolution in Virginia," *WMQ*, 3rd ser., 4 (Oct. 1962): 511-33.

2. Richard Hanson to John T. Ware, June 28, 1796, Dec. 13, 1800, in Charles F. Hobson, ed., *The Papers of John Marshall*, vol. 5, *Selected Law Cases, 1784-1800* (Chapel Hill, N.C., 1987), 391; Affidavit of Edmund Pendleton [Jr.], June 3, 1809, in *DR*. Baylor's legal fees regarding his debts are in "Account of the Estate of Col. John Baylor, John Baylor Jr., Executor," May 28, 1802, in *DR*. See also John Marshall to John Baylor, July 23, 1804, in Hobson, ed., *Papers of John Marshall*, vol. 6, *Correspondence, etc.*, 303. The U.S. Supreme Court case is *Ware v. Hylton*, 3 U.S. 199 (1796). The suit against Baylor is *Backhouse v. John Baylor, Administrator*, U.S. Circuit Court (1798), Ended Cases (1790-1861) (restored), LVA. Another major suit against Baylor in the 1790s was filed by Donald & Burton, a large London-based tobacco consignment firm with agents in Virginia. Baylor gave the firm a deed of trust covering 2,000 acres of land and eleven slaves to secure a £819 debt. Baylor defaulted and lost the land and slaves in foreclosure in 1795, but he and his heirs refused to vacate the property and contested the creditor's sale for a quarter century afterwards. See *Pollard v. Baylor's Devisees*, 14 Va. 223 (1809), overruled by *Pollard v. Baylor*, 20 Va. 433 (1819). On the collection of prewar British debts in Virginia in the 1790s, see Charles F. Hobson, "The Recovery of British Debts in the Federal Circuit Court in Virginia," *VMHB* 92 (April 1984): 176-200.

3. John Taylor to John Baylor V, July 25, 1820, BP. For Baylor's sale of

lumber, see, for example, *Virginia Gazette or the American Advertiser* (Richmond), Aug. 24, 1782, Sept. 21, 1782.

4. John Baylor IV to George Washington, April 25, 1785, in W. W. Abbot et al., eds., *Papers of George Washington, Confederation Series*, 2:518-19; Dr. Robert Wellford to John Baylor IV, Aug. 28, 1800, Misc. MS (Mss2 W4595a3), VHS.

5. Newton's conceptual renderings in Baylor's book are unsigned and no documentary evidence survives that links them to Newton. However, architectural historian Jeff Tilman has persuasively demonstrated that they were probably prepared by William Newton. See Jeffrey Thomas Tilman, "The Houses of Newmarket" (MA thesis, University of Virginia, 1993). (Other scholars, however, reject the notion that Newton composed the drawings, though Tilman's analysis is more thorough and convincing. See Charles E. Brownell et al., eds. *The Making of Virginia Architecture* [Richmond, Va., 1992], 224.) Newton, a cousin of Sir Isaac Newton, worked in the shadow of architect James Stuart, a fact that largely consigned Newton to undeserved obscurity. On Newton's work for Greenwich Hospital, see Lesley Lewis, "The Architects of the Chapel at Greenwich Hospital," *Art Bulletin* 29 (Dec. 1947): 260-67. For a brief biographical sketch of Newton, see Stephen, ed., *Dictionary of National Biography*, 40:405-6.

6. Thomas Tileston Waterman, *The Mansions of Virginia, 1706-1776*, (New York, 1945), 116, 422. Regarding Rosewell's history, see Claude O. Lanciano Jr., *Rosewell: Garland of Virginia* (Gloucester Co. Historical Committee, 1978). For a study of its architecture, see Bennie Brown Jr., "An Architectural Study of an Eighteenth-Century Plantation" (MA thesis, University of Georgia, 1973). According to the surviving records of the housing census conducted for the federal 1798 direct tax, the most valuable (though not necessarily the largest or most elegant) house in America was owned by merchant Elias Hasket Derby (1739-99) in Salem, Mass. Derby's three-story mansion had 8,757 square feet spread over 15 rooms and was valued at just over $30,000. See Lee Soltow, "Egalitarian America and its Inegalitarian Housing in the Federal Period," *Social Science History* 9 (Spring 1985): 199-213. The only know records of the 1798 housing tax in Virginia are for Berkeley Parish in Spotsylvania Co. (VHS).

7. Bernard Bailyn, *To Begin the World Anew: The Genius and Ambiguities of the American Founders* (New York, 2003), 12. Though the colonial American gentry were deeply vexed that the British elite generally refused to acknowledge their gentility, their response, particularly in the Chesapeake, was to try harder. See Michael J. Rozbicki, "The Curse of Provincialism: Negative Perceptions of Colonial American Plantation Gentry," *Journal of Southern History* 63 (Nov. 1997): 751 (in which the author concludes that the "main effect of this [British] disapproval on plantation elites lay in providing a powerful and sustained stimulus to overcome it by pursuing earnestly and unyieldingly the tenets of traditional landed ethos and lifestyle"). See also Jack P. Greene's essay, "Search for Identity: An Interpretation of the Meaning of Selected Patterns of Social Response in Eighteenth-Century America," in his *Imperatives, Behaviors, and Identities: Essays in Early American Cultural History* (Charlottesville, Va., and London, 1992), 143-73.

8. Edward C. Clark and Angeline Polites, eds., *The Virginia Journals of Benjamin Henry Latrobe*, 2 vols. (New Haven, Conn., and London, 1977), 2:127, 160-61, 164. For a discussion and analysis of the Virginia gentry whom Latrobe befriended, see Lee W. Formwalt, "An English Immigrant Views American Society: Benjamin Henry Latrobe's Virginia Years, 1796-1798," *VMHB* 85 (Oct. 1977): 387-410.

9. Commonplace Book of Ellen Bruce Baylor, 1752-1906, VHS.

10. Ibid.

11. Will of John Baylor IV, Oct. 30, 1807, in *DR*; *Virginia Herald* (Fredericksburg, Va.), Feb. 12, 1808 (death notice of John Baylor IV). On Baylor's death in debtor's prison and the loss of his personal property, see Answer of Thomas R. Rootes, February 26, 1810, in *DR*. Some debtors, such as "Light Horse" Harry Lee, were actually confined within a jail cell or block. Others, apparently including Baylor, were allowed to roam within "prison bounds," a defined perimeter around the county jail, usually an area of two to ten acres. If there was a tavern within the prison bounds, an imprisoned debtor could spend his time there, except during court proceedings related to his case. For examples of dimensions and locations of prison bounds within various Virginia counties, see Carl R. Lounsbury, *The Courthouses of Early Virginia: An Architectural History* (Charlottesville, Va., and London,

2005), 94, 227, 266, 349, 352.

12. Will of John Baylor IV, Oct. 30, 1807, in *DR*. Beginning in the 1790s, Baylor sought, apparently with little or no success, live-in tutors at Newmarket for his children. In 1799, for example, he advertised he would "give liberal encouragement to a good classical Tutor, for two boys only." (*Virginia Herald* [Fredericksburg, Va.], Sept. 24, 1799.)

13. Though the Baylor family's connections to British universities were finished, Col. John Baylor III's grandson, Robert Emmet Bledsoe Baylor (1793-1874), a Kentucky-born lawyer and judge, was a co-founder and principal benefactor of Baylor University, which was named for him. He later served as the university's first law professor.

Appendix

1. On Allestree's authorship of the *Whole Duty of Man*, see Paul Elmen, "Richard Allestree and The Whole Duty of Man," *The Library*, 5th ser., 6 (1951): 19-27.

2. This popular book was sold in Williamsburg. See, for example, *VG* (Hunter), Aug. 1, 1755. The 1735 edition is often confused with an enlarged 1778 edition (1 vol., quarto, London) published under the title *Sportsman's Dictionary; or, the Country Gentleman's Companion, for Town and Country...*.

3. This atlas was the subject of John Baylor IV's letter to Thomas Jefferson, Feb. 12, 1781, in William P. Palmer et al., eds., *Calendar of Virginia State Papers and Other Manuscripts...*, 11 vols. (Richmond, Va., 1875-93), 1:507.

4. For a bibliography and critical discussion of the various editions of Bayle's *Dictionnaire historique*, see Pierre Rétat, *Le Dictionnaire de Bayle et la lutte philosophique au XVIIIe siècle* (Paris, 1971). See also Thomas M. Lennon, *Reading Bayle* (Toronto and Buffalo, N.Y., 1999); Elisabeth Labrousse, *Pierre Bayle et l'instrument critique* (Paris, 1965).

5. For a bibliographic discussion of Beccaria's treatise, see Bellamy, ed., *On Crimes and Punishments*, xli-xlix.

6. Authorship of *Éloge de l'énfer* has also been attributed to Abbé Quesnel (fl. 1725-66). See James Mew, "The Christian Hell," *The Nineteenth Century: A Monthly Review* 30 (July-Dec. 1891): 723. The genre of satire employed in *Éloge de l'énfer*, in which the abhorrent or appalling is praised with mock eloquence, is known as a "paradoxical economium." (Henry Knight Miller, "The Paradoxical Economium: With Special Reference to Its Vogue in England, 1600-1800," *Modern Philology* 53 [Feb. 1956]: 145-78.)

7. The Bickham family were engravers most known for their *Universal Penman* , which was initially issued to subscribers in fifty-two parts (London, 1733-41). A complete edition, including 212 plates, was published in London in 1741. See P. H. Muir, "The Bickhams and Their *Universal Penman*," *The Library* 25 (1944): 162-83.

8. The best studies of Bossuet's writings are Jacques Le Brun, *La spiritualité de Bossuet* (Paris, 1972); Thérèse Goyet, *L'humanisme de Bossuet* (Paris, 1965). For a modern edition of some of Bossuet's works, see J. Standring, ed., *Bossuet: A Prose Anthology,* (London, 1962) (introduction and notes in English; selected Bossuet prose in French). See also Jacques-Bénigne Bossuet, *Selections from Meditations on the Gospel,* trans. Lucille Corinne Franchère (Chicago, 1962). For a biography of Bossuet in English, see Ernest E. Reynolds, *Bossuet* (New York, 1963). For a modern English translation of Bossuet's *Discours*, see Jacques-Bénigne Bossuet, *Discourse on Universal History*, trans. Elborg Forster, ed. Orest Ranum (Chicago and London, 1976).

9. This book, held by VHS, does not turn up in the primary sources on which this bibliography is based, but it is catalogued by VHS as having once belonged to the Baylor family. VHS holds five additional books catalogued with a Baylor family association, but each of those was published after the death of John Baylor IV.

10. On Buchanan and his works, see Bert Emsley, "James Buchanan and the Eighteenth Century Regulation of English Usage," *PMLA* 48 (Dec. 1933): 1154-66.

11. William Massey, *The Origin and Progress of Letters* (London, 1763), 42-43.

12. In 1759 Col. Baylor asked one of his British merchants to send him "2 large print plain common prayer books." John Baylor III to Flowerdewe and Norton, Jan. 18, 1759, BLB. For a bibliography of the *Book of Common Prayer*, see David N. Griffiths, *The Bibliography of the Book of Common Prayer, 1549-1999* (London and New Castle, Del., 2002).

13. On the importance of Cicero's writings among the Founders, see Lutz, "The Relative Influence of European Writers," 193; McDonald, "A Founding Father's Library," 4-15.

14. Corderius, the schoolmaster of John Calvin, published his *Colloquiorum scholasticorum* in 1564. On Cordier and his *Colloquies*, see Elizabeth K. Hudson, "The Colloquies of Maturin Cordier: Images of Calvinist School Life and Thought," *Sixteenth Century Journal* 9 (Autumn, 1978): 56-78; Foster Watson, "Maturinus Corderius: Schoolmaster at Paris, Bordeaux, and Geneva, in the Sixteenth Century," *School Review* 12 (Apr. 1904): 281-98.

15. On Coles's work and other English dictionaries, see DeWitt T. Starnes and Gertrude E. Noyes, *The English Dictionary from Cawdrey to Johnson 1604-1755* (Chapel Hill, N.C., 1946).

16. For a biography of Corneille and discussion of his works in English, see Robert J. Nelson, *Corneille: His Heroes and Their Worlds* (Philadelphia, 1963). For a collection of most of his plays in English, see Pierre Corneille, *The Chief Plays of Corneille*, trans. Lacy Lockert (Princeton, 1957). For a modern edition of Corneille's plays in French, see Pierre Corneille, *Oeuvres complètes*, ed. Georges Couton, 3 vols. (Paris, 1980-87).

17. For a biography of Thomas Corneille, see David A. Collins, *Thomas Corneille: Protean Dramatist* (The Hague, 1966).

18. John Montgomerie, the colonial governor of New York and New Jersey, owned an early edition of Dacier's translation of Terence's comedies. (Kevin J. Hayes, *The Library of John Montgomerie, Colonial Governor of New York and New Jersey* [Newark, N.J., and London, 2000], 168.)

19. For an insightful discussion of Mme. Deshoulières and her work, see John J. Conley, *The Suspicion of Virtue: Women Philosophers in Neoclassical France* (Ithaca, N.Y., and London, 2002), 45-74.

20. For a modern edition of Dryden's works, see Vinton A. Dearing et al., eds. *The Works of John Dryden*, 20 vols. to date (Berkeley, Calif. 1956—).

21. The best modern edition of *Télémaque* remains François de Salignac de la Mothe de Fénelon, *Les avantures de Télémaque*, ed. Albert Cahen, 2 vols. (Paris, 1927). For a modern edition of Fénelon's literary writings, see François de Salignac de la Mothe-Fénelon, ed. Jacques Le Brun, *Oeuvres I and II*, 2 vols. (Paris, 1983-97). Le Brun's two-volume work does not include most of Fénelon's ecclesiastical correspondence, which may be found in Jean Gosselin, ed., *Oeuvres complètes*, 10 vols. (Paris, Lille, and Bescançon, 1848-52).

22. The definitive modern edition of Gibbon's *History* is Edward Gibbon, *The Decline and Fall of the Roman Empire*, ed. David P. Womersley, 3 vols. (Harmondsworth, Eng., 1994). Although Gibbon did not hide his contempt for slavery in his work, some of the southern slave-holding gentry drew selectively from Gibbon's *Decline and Fall* in their intellectual rationalizations of slavery, noting, for example, that the Roman Empire was at its peak when slavery was a dominant element there. See Elizabeth Fox-Genovese and Eugene D. Genovese, *The Mind of the Master Class: History and Faith in the Southern Slaveholders' Worldview* (Cambridge, Eng., and New York, 2005), 267-69. Regarding the reception among the British literati of Gibbon's work, see H. R. Trevor-Roper, "Gibbon and the Publication of *The Decline and Fall of the Roman Empire*, 1776-1976," *Journal of Law and Economics* 19 (Oct. 1976): 489-505.

23. George Washington owned a copy of Gibson's *Treatise on the Diseases of Horses*. Donald Jackson and Dorothy Twohig, eds., *The Diaries of George Washington*, 6 vols. (Charlottesville, Va., and London, 1976-1979), 1:244.

24. According to his most recent biographer, Barclay "saved the Quaker movement from extinction by giving [George] Fox's preaching an intellectual form, capable of rational defense." D. Elton Trueblood,

Robert Barclay (New York, 1968), 20. In 1682, Barclay became the nonresident governor of East New Jersey. His *Apology* went through numerous editions throughout the eighteenth and nineteenth centuries, including several published in Philadelphia, and it remains in print today.

25. On the influence of Tacitus among the Founders, see Ronald Mellor, *Tacitus* (New York and London, 1993), 153. See also Pauline Maier, *From Resistance to Revolution: Colonial Radicals and the Development of American Opposition to Britain, 1765-1776* (New York, 1972), 42.

26. On Haywood and *The Female Spectator*, see Helene Koon, "Eliza Haywood and the *Female Spectator*," *Huntington Library Quarterly* 42 (1978): 43-55. For selections from *The Female Spectator*, see Eliza Haywood, *The Female Spectator: Being Selections from Mrs. Eliza Haywood's Periodical*, ed. Mary Priestly (London, 1929).

27. John Baylor IV's inventory indicates "27 volumes on horse racing." A full run of both Cheny's and Heber's series of racing calendars would have had forty-two volumes. It appears from Col. Baylor III's correspondence that in fact he ordered each issue, but apparently some volumes were lost. On Heber's insanity and death, see Jonathan Andrews and Andrew Scull, *Customers and Patrons of the Mad-Trade: The Management of Lunacy in Eighteenth-Century London* (Berkeley, Calif., and London, 2003), 173-74. For a select catalogue of British books regarding horse racing and breeding, see John B. Podeschi, *Books on the Horse and Horsemanship: Riding, Hunting, Breeding and Racing, 1400-1941* (London, 1981).

28. On Hume's *History*, see Victor G. Wexler, *David Hume and the* History of England (Philadelphia, 1979); Nicholas Phillipson, *Hume* (London, 1989). See also David F. Norton, *The Cambridge Companion to Hume* (Cambridge, Eng., 1993) (includes extensive bibliography).

29. For a bibliography of Huygens's works, see Herbert Jaumann, *Handbuch Gelehrtenkultur der Frühen Neuzeit, Band 1: Bio-bibliographisches Repertorium* (Berlin, 2004), 351-52.

30. To add to the bibliographic confusion, a later edition of Hyde's *History of the Rebellion and Civil Wars in England* was combined with his

Historical View of the Affairs of Ireland and published under the title *The History of the Rebellion and Civil Wars in England: To Which Is Added, An Historical View of the Affairs of Ireland.* This combined edition, first issued in 1819 (6 vols. in 3, Oxford) and in a revised edition in 1826 (8 vols., Oxford), was published too late to have been the one mentioned in Baylor's inventory. For a bibliography of most of the early editions of Hyde's works, see William T. Lowndes, *The Bibliographer's Manual of English Literature...*, 4 vols., rev. ed. (London, 1858), 2:467-69.

31. A likely candidate for this book was John Dryden's English translation, *The Satires of Decimus Junius Juvenalis*, first published in London in 1693, with nine more editions published by 1754.

32. For a modern edition (in French) of Lesage's *Gil Bas*, see Alain-René Lesage, *Histoire de Gil Blas de Santillane*, ed. Roger Laufer, 2 vols. (Paris, 1977).

33. For a bibliography of various editions of Livy's *History* published in the seventeenth and eighteenth centuries, see Joseph W. Moss, *A Manual of Classical Bibliography: Containing A Copious Detail of the Various Editions of the Greek and Roman Classics...*, 2 vols., 2nd ed. (London, 1837), 2:186-222.

34. Gilreath and Wilson, *Thomas Jefferson's Library*, chap. 3.

35. For a modern, critical edition of Malebranche's *De la recherche*, see Nicolas Malebranche, *The Search after Truth*, trans. Thomas M. Lennon and Paul J. Olscamp (Cambridge, Eng., 1997). For a bibliography of Malebranche's publications and of works about him, see Patricia Easton, Thomas M. Lennon, and Gregor Sebba, *Bibliographia Malebranchiana: A Critical Guide to the Malebranche Literature Into 1989* (Carbondale, Ill., 1992). There is no modern biography of Malebranche. The standard, albeit flawed, biography was written by the Jesuit, Yves Marie André (1675-1764), *La Vie du R.P. Malebranche* (Paris, 1886), which was not published until more than a century after André's death.

36. For a useful bibliographic discussion of Malpighi's published works, see Emanuel Swedenborg, *The Animal Kingdom Considered*

Anatomically, Physically, and Philosophically, 2 vols. (London, 1844): 2:604.

37. For a modern edition of Martyr's writings in English, see Alexander Roberts and James Donaldson, eds., *The Ante-Nicene Fathers: Translations of the Writings of the Fathers Down to A.D. 325*, rev. ed., 10 vols. (Grand Rapids, Mich., 1985). For a biography of Martyr, see Leslie W. Barnard, *Justin Martyr: His Life and Thought* (Cambridge, Eng., 1967).

38. The best of the many editions of Lady Montagu's letters remains Robert Halsband, ed., *The Complete Letters of Lady Mary Montagu*, 3 vols. (Oxford, 1965-76). For Lady Montagu's other writings, see Mary Wortley Montagu, *Essays and Poems* and *Simplicity: A Comedy*, ed. Robert Halsband and Isobel Grundy (Oxford, 1977). For a biography of Montagu, see Isobel Grundy, *Lady Mary Wortley Montagu: Comet of the Enlightenment* (Oxford, 1999).

39. Rev. Hugh James Rose, *A New General Biographical Dictionary*, 12 vols. (London, 1857), 10:220.

40. Regarding Sandys's translation of *Metamorphoses*, see Richard B. Davis, *George Sandys: Poet Adventurer* (London, 1955), chap. 8.

41. Regarding the inventory's designation of the author as "Parkins," American colonial estate appraisers, not generally known for their diligence regarding book inventories, typically made their lists from spine titles, which were often truncated or inaccurate. In addition, one of the three locals who appraised Col. Baylor's estate, upon examining the spine, may have called out "Perkins" to his colleague, who heard "Parkins" and jotted it down thus. The book list in Col. Baylor's estate inventory is replete with misspellings.

42. On Pichon, see John C. Webster *The Life of Thomas Pichon, "The Spy of Beausejour"* (Halifax, N.B., Can., 1937).

43. For a study of Raynal's life and important writings, see Gianluigi Goggi and Gilles Bancarel, *Raynal, de la polémique à l'histoire* (Oxford, 2000). As of this writing, the Voltaire Foundation at Oxford University, which published *Raynal, de la polémique à l'histoire*,

has announced its intention to publish a critical edition of Raynal's *Histoire de deux Indes*.

44. On the publication and reception of *Émile* in Britain, see James H. Warner, "Émile in Eighteenth-Century England," *PMLA* 59 (Sept. 1944): 773-91. For a modern English version of *Émile*, see Jean-Baptiste Rousseau, *Emile, or On Education*, ed. and trans. Allan Bloom (New York, 1979).

45. English editions of Saurin's sermons were popular in North America, including *Eleven Select Sermons of the Late Rev. James Saurin on Various Important Subjects* (Portsmouth, N.H., 1806), which also includes one of the few biographical summaries of Saurin in English. In the same year in which the New Hampshire edition was published, Nathan Bangs, a Methodist preacher from Connecticut then living in Canada, jotted in his journal: "I am now amusing myself in reading Mr James Saurin's Sermons which appear to be a masterly performance. His ingenuity was certain[l]y great, his ideas noble and sublime—but some of his sentiments are calvinistic." (March 1, 1806, Journal and Notebook of Nathan Banks, 1805-6, Drew University, Madison, N.J.) In addition to Saurin's *Sermons*, another contender for the Saurin title owned by Baylor is *Discours historiques, critiques, theologiqués, et moraux sur les événements les plus mémorables du Vieux et du Nouveau Testament*, 6 vols. (The Hague, 1728-39).

46. For a biography of Montesquieu, see Robert Shackleton, *Montesquieu; a Critical Biography* (Oxford, 1961). The Voltaire Foundation at Oxford University, in conjunction with the Société Montesquieu, has begun publication of *Oeuvres complètes de Montesquieu* (22 vols.), which will be the first critical edition of all of Montesquieu's works. On Montesquieu's influence in America, see Paul M. Spurlin, *Montesquieu in America, 1760-1801* (Baton Rouge, La., 1940). According to a decade-long analysis of how often the Founders referred to classical and foreign intellectual authorities, Montesquieu was the most frequently cited authority during the period 1760-1805, exceeding even Blackstone and Locke (who were respectively second and third). See Lutz, "Relative Influence of European Writers," 189-97.

47. On Shakespeare's literary reputation in colonial America, see Edwin

E. Willoughby, "The Reading of Shakespeare in Colonial America," *Papers of the Bibliographical Society of America* 30, pt. 2 (1936): 45-56.

48. Almost all copies of the fifth volume of the *Continuation*, which one scholar described as "very rare," were reportedly destroyed because of Smollett's allusion to George III's illness in 1765 (i.e., the king's first bout with the disease now known as *porphyria*, which eventually disabled him) greatly displeased the monarch, who wished to keep his malady a secret (Lewis M. Knapp, "The Publication of Smollett's *Complete History* ... and *Continuation*," *The Library*, 4th ser., 16 [1935]: 302-03.)

49. The title of another work by Stackhouse, *A Defence of the Christian Religion*... (London, 1733), matches the inventory description somewhat more closely, but *A Defence* was published in a single volume, while his *New History of the Holy Bible* was published in two volumes, which is the number indicated on Col. Baylor's inventory list.

50. On Stith and his progeny, see Christopher Johnston, "The Stith Family," *WMQ*, 1st ser., 21 (1913): 181-93).

51. For the publishing history of *Cato's Letters* in the eighteenth century, see John Trenchard and Thomas Gordon, *Cato's Letters: Or, Essays on Liberty, Civil and Religious, and Other Important Subjects*, ed. Ronald Hamowy, 4 vols. in 2 (Indianapolis, Ind., 1995), xi-xiii and "Introduction," xxxiii, xxxv.

52. Joseph Gwilt, *The Architecture of Marcus Vitruvius Pollio in Ten Books* (London, 1826), xxii-xxiii. A biographical sketch of Newton published in 1894 states that his translation "closely adheres to the original, and is on the whole a creditable performance." Stephen, ed., *Dictionary of National Biography*, 40:405. Although Newton's work was the first full-length English translation of *Vitruvius*, two important earlier works rendered many of Vitruvius' concepts into English. The first was *Elements of Architecture* (London, 1624), by diplomat and scholar Sir Henry Wotton (1568-1639), who was the English ambassador to Venice for many years and had first-hand access to countless sources and classical and neoclassical buildings

in Italy. Drawing largely upon Daniele Barbaro's Italian translation of *Vitruvius* (Venice, 1565), Palladio's *Quattro libri* (Venice, 1570), along with works by Alberti, Vignola, and others, Sir Wotton produced a 123-page critical essay on classical architecture. The second was a translation of Claude Perrault's abridgement of Vitruvius' work, *Les dix livres d'architecture de Vitruve* (Paris, 1673), which was "Englished" and published in London by Abel Swall under the title *An Abridgement of the Architecture of Vitruvius* (1692). An unpublished, idiosyncratic English translation (holograph, ca. 1770) of Vitruvius' Books I-V is held by the Chester Beatty Library, Dublin. See Christine Casey, "'De architectura': An Irish Eighteenth-Century Gloss," *Architectural History* 37 (1994): 80-95. For a modern, scholarly translation of *Vitruvius*, see Ingrid D. Rowland and Thomas Noble Howe, *Vitruvius. Ten Books on Architecture* (Cambridge, Eng., 1999).

53. Though John Baylor IV's booklist description suggests he owned a large set of Voltaire's works, only three volumes remained in his estate following the creditor's sale of the bulk of his library.

Index

165

Nelson, Hugh, 29

Nelson, William, 29

New and Complete System of Practical Husbandry, A (Mills), 87

New History of the Holy Bible (Stackhouse), 86–87, 163

New Kent County, 17

New London, Connecticut, 72

New London, Virginia, 34

New Pantheon, The (Boyse), 29

New System of Agriculture, A (Anon.), 27, 87, 138

New Testament, 84, 85. *See also* Bible

New Treatise on the Diseases of Horses, A (Gibson), 87, 149–150

New York City, 35–36, 88, 99, 123

Newmarket plantation, 1–12, 45, 56, 58, 80, 130. *See also* "Baylor's Folly

Newmarket race course, 1–3, 47

Newton, Isaac, 29, 30

Newton, William, xvii, 131, 246

Nicholas, Robert Carter, 29

Night Thoughts (Young), 94, 167

Noailles, Marquis de, 70

Noel, Garrat, 35–36

North, Lord (Frederick North), 68, 69, 72, 134

Northern Neck Proprietary, 6

Northumberland County, 35, 46, 86

Norton, Courtenay (Walker), 57

Norton, Frances. *See* Baylor, Frances (John IV's wife)

Norton, John. *See* John Norton & Sons

Norton, John Hatley, 57–58, 59

Norwich, 126

Notes on the State of Virginia (Jefferson), 116

Nugent, Thomas, 98

O

Odyssey (Dacier), 108

Odyssey (Pope), 82

Oeuvres complètes (Voltaire), 103, 166

Ohio Company, 8

On Crimes and Punishments (Beccaria), 118, 139

Oraisons funèbres (Bossuet), 106, 141

Oraisons funèbres (Mascaron), 107, 155

Orange County Court, 5

Orations of Demosthenes (Leland), 85

Orrey, Earl of, 93, 142

Ovid, 45, 81, 157

Oxford University, 46, 56, 209

P

Pacifique. See Thamas Koulikan

Page, John, 29–30, 81, 110, 132

Page, Lucy (Baylor), 132

Page, Mann I, 20, 28

Page, Mann II, 20, 52

Page, Mann III, 133

Paine, Thomas, 44

Pall Mall, 27

pamphlets, 39–44

Panckoucke, Charles-Joseph, 99

Paoli, Pennsylvania, 75

Paris, 61, 65–66, 97, 99, 100–102, 103–104, 109, 114, 117, 121–122

Parker, William, 51

Parliament, British, 10, 42, 43, 56,

Voltaire, 31, 90, 94, 97, 98, 100,
102, 103, 105, 106, 107,
113, 114, 118, 122, 166

W

Walker, Courtenay (Norton), 57
Walker, Frances Lucy. *See* Baylor,
Frances Lucy
Walker, Jacob, 4
Walker, Thomas, 8
Walker, William, 34
Walpole, Horace, 166
War of 1812, 23
Ward, Samuel Jr., 125
Ware v. Hylton (1796), 129, 171
Warsaw, Virginia, 46
Warville, J. P. Brissot de, 99
Washington, D.C., 13, 101
Washington, George, 8, 9, 15,
21–22, 27–28, 34, 37, 38,
46–47, 51, 55, 61, 66, 67,
85, 92, 93, 99, 101, 103–
104, 125, 130, 133
Washington, Lund, 67
Webster, Daniel, 118
Wellford, Robert, 130
Westminster Bridge, 61
Westover, 6, 132
Weymouth, Lord, 72
Wheeler, Joseph T., 25
Whigs, 88–90, 92
Whole Duty of Man (Allestree), 86
Wilberforce, William, 56, 81
William and Mary, College of, 2,
11, 30, 82, 84, 99, 100, 122
William III, 89
Williamsburg, 4, 15–16, 23, 31–32,
33, 42, 60, 61, 79, 88, 95,
105, 106, 110, 122
Wills, Gary, 118
Winchester, Virginia, 9

Wirt, William, 20, 174
Witherspoon, John, 99
Wolf, Edwin 2nd, 26, 102, 111–
112
Wood, Gordon S., 112
Wormeley, Ralph Jr., 44
Wright, Louis B., xiv-xv, xvi, 14
Wythe, George, xvii, 82, 85, 100

X

Xenophon, 82
Xenophon's Memoirs of Socrates
(Fielding), 82

Y

Yale College, 84, 97
Young, Edward, 93–94, 167